The Philosophy of Sri Rāmakṛṣṇa Paramahaṃsa

Searching Metaphysics in His Mysticism

Ms. Dyuti Jayendrakumar Yajnik

Originals
Delhi

ISBN 10: 81-8454-116-3
ISBN 13: 978-81-8454-116-8

Published by
Originals
A-6, Second Floor, Nimri Commercial Centre,
Ashok Vihar Phase-IV, Delhi 110052 (INDIA)
tel.: +91.11.27302453 fax.: +91.11.47061936
url: www.Lppindia.com e-mail: info@Lppindia.com

Printed at
D K Fine Art Press P. Ltd.
Delhi

PRINTED IN INDIA

Contents

Scheme of Pron

Consonants

Gutturals,	क	ख	ग	घ	ङ	अ
	ka	kha	ga	gha	ṅa	a
Palatals,	च	छ	ज	झ	ञ	उ
	ca	cha	ja	jha	ña	u
Cerebrals,	ट	ठ	ड	ढ	ण	ए
	ṭa	ṭha	ḍa	ḍha	ṇa	e
Dentals,	त	थ	द	ध	न	ळ
	ta	tha	da	dha	na	ḷ

Preface

Present research is aimed at deriving a systematic philosophy of Sri Rāmakṛṣṇa Paramahaṃsa. The whole research is divided into twelve chapters. In the first chapter of Introduction, the contemporary relevance of Rāmakṛṣṇa and his philosophy is discussed. A very brief sketch of Sri Rāmakṛṣṇa's life and the citations of great thinkers of the world which show the greatness and uniqueness of Sri Rāmakṛṣṇa as a mystic, are depicted. In this chapter the nature and history of Gospel is also described. The rationale for selecting the present topic of research and the method followed in it, is discussed in detail. The second chapter of the thesis discusses Rāmakṛṣṇa's views about Ultimate Reality as derived from his own mystical experiences. Therefore, as Ramakrishna was a mystic, the nature of mysticism is clarified here. The form and the formless aspects of Ultimate Reality as propounded by Sri Rāmakṛṣṇa are elaborated here. In the third chapter the concept of self and its salvation are discussed. Nature of self, Law of Karma and rebirth, and problem of good and evil according to Rāmakṛṣṇa are discussed. The forth chapter deals with cosmology of Ramakrishna. God's three types of activities of creation, preservation, and destruction, as discussed by Rāmakṛṣṇa, are explained here. In the fifth chapter on religion, place of knowledge, devotion and action in religious life is pointed out and Rāmakṛṣṇa's peculiar concept of Vijnani is discussed in detail. The sixth chapter discusses the concept of Guru and seventh chapter discusses the fundamental unity of all religions for which Ramakrishna is very famous. Rāmakṛṣṇa was basically a mystic and therefore he views on Sādhanā were practically very much directive and inspiring. So Rāmakṛṣṇa's suggestions and analysis of Sādhanā is elaborated in the eighth chapter. The nineth chapter highlights Rāmakṛṣṇa's views about the duties of house-holders and renunciates are depicted. The tenth chapter analyzes the social concern of Rāmakṛṣṇa in which his views about social problems like status of women, caste system and compassion for the poor and the deprived are discussed. The eleventh chapter analyzes Rāmakṛṣṇa's mystical behavior from psychological point-of-view, because of the prevalent controversy about the pathology of Rāmakṛṣṇa's behavior. Sudhir Kakar's defence of Rāmakṛṣṇa's behavior, against the alleged pathology is elaborated here. Critical views of J. Kripal regarding Rāmakṛṣṇa's seemingly pathological behaviour are highlighted and its detailed and logically sound criticism of Kripal's criticism of Rāmakṛṣṇa's behaviour given by Somnath Bhattacharya are also presented here. The twelfth chapter constitutes the conclusion of the thesis. It explains the philosophical position of Ramakrishna and it is shown here that with reference to Metaphysics, his philosophical position is Comprehensive Absolute Monism. With reference to Philosophy of Religion, his philosophical position is Panentheism.

It is not necessary for me to give a separate list of abbreviations, used in this. Because I have used only one abbreviation and it is 'GSR': 'The Gospel of Sri Rāmakṛṣṇa'.

I have followed in this work the APA Style Manual for putting references as found in 'MLA Handbook' (2004).This book provides a standard form of presentation of any research work. The method of putting references given in this book is widely accepted and used in recently published many books as well as academic materials on different websites. This is the reason why this MLA Handbook has entered into a number of editions, out of which, the sixth edition has been used here for indicating the references.

My feeling of gratitude towards my father, Dr. J. A. Yajnik, is totally inexpressible. Yet I try to express it, which is poor, dim, and imperfect copy of what I really feel. I am very much indebted to him for helping me in building my character and in making progress in my education. The very topic of present work, i.e., 'Philosophy of Sri Rāmakṛṣṇa Paramahaṃsa' is being selected by getting the inspiration from his own book 'The Philosophy of Sri Svaminarayana'. His help was constantly and untiringly available to me during the writing. Without his academic guidance, inspiration, and his moral support, the work would not have been presented in this form.

My gratitude is also due to my elder sister Dr. Achinta Yajnik for constantly remaining with me in all type of work and in all my requirements. As she is a Associate Professor in Psychology, though pre-occupied with number of commitments, she thoroughly examined my chapter on the psychology of Sri Rāmakṛṣṇa and gave very important suggestions.

I express my sincere sense of gratitude to my elder brother Prof. Gaurang Yajnik, who is Associate Professor in Economics, for his substantial help in all type of settings and transliteration followed here, in spite of his very much busy schedule.

I express my heartily gratitude to my father's friend revered Shri Dr.S.R.Bhatt for his kind help in publishing this book. I also express my heartily gratitude to a scholar Shri Radheshyam Shasriji for his ahetuki care and concern for the publication of this book. I will never forget the grace of both of these saintly, noble personalities.

Finally, I thank my family members, my teachers, and all other persons who have directly or indirectly helped me in completing my work.

Ahmedabad
16th April, 2012 Ms. Dyuti Jayendrakumar Yajnik

1
Introduction

1. Contemporary Relevance of Understanding The Philosophy of Rāmakṛṣṇa Paramahaṃsa

It is believed that there has not been a single culture and civilization without having one or the other form of religion as its basic constituent. Thus, on the one hand, religion constitutes the hard-core of culture, and on the other hand, we find that almost all quarrels and wars occur under the name of religion only. The global issue of terrorism is nothing but the outcome of the misapprehension of true religion. This shows that in contemporary age, mankind needs true religious understanding whereby he can practice his own religion thoroughly, and at the same time, he may develop truly universal attitude towards other religions too. Modern man, living in the age of anxiety, stress, and competition, can't afford to be an atheist and sacrifice the healing and supporting power of religion under the name of secularism, nor can he afford to become fanatic to survive with scientific temper in the 21st century of globalization. Thus the knowledge and respect for other religions together with the practice of the universally applicable tenets of one's own religion (upāsanā) are very relevant and inevitable in modern age for peaceful co-existence.

The well known writer on Rāmakṛṣṇa, Margaret Bedrosian described the situation of nineteenth century period, by quoting an American writer Ellison that, "The twentieth century American writer Ralph Ellison has stated: 'Those who know their culture and love it unchauvinistically are never lost when encountering the unfamiliar. Rāmakṛṣṇa extended this principle to include the knowledge of God, it was, in fact, the supreme mark of his universality. Having touched the base with depth of his own culture and religion, he paradoxically validated all the dharmas as well. In the process, he also reminded us that the true merit of a religion or way of action lies in our willingness to test and follow the path to the end, until it opens into the universal.

Thus living in the midst of the nineteenth century, a period in which colonialism was carving the world into antagonistic empires, when the modern consciousness was about to be fragmented as evolution, communism and relatively theory turned traditional views of our place in the cosmos topsy-turvy, leaving millions confused and rootless, this madman of Dakṣiṇeśvara jolts us with his sanity and rootedness. Studying his picture, whether in the yogic posture or standing with his hand raised to teach, one knows he was never lost or confused by the turmoil of theorizing. Neither was he perturbed by speculation regarding the non-essential, quibbles over abstractions that only raise barriers between people and block perception of the living Truth. Instead, be persistently peeled away layers of ignorance that kept the disciple separated from the Self. So masterful was he that even Narendra, a model of cosmopolitan brilliance, bowed before his teacher's skill." (Studies on Rāmakṛṣṇa, Rāmakṛṣṇa: The Universal Man, Margaret Bedrosian: 70)

Thus, in the modern era of nineteenth century, Rāmakṛṣṇa provided the spiritual leadership to the cognitively confused and rootless mentality to millions of people. To use Festinger's words, Rāmakṛṣṇa, through his logically consistent and coherent philosophy and through practice of spirituality, removed "Cognitive Dissonance" of people at large, generated by triumph of modernity.

2. Brief Biographical Details of Rāmakṛṣṇa (1836-1886)

Rāmakṛṣṇa's biography is written by several thinkers like Max Muller and Romain Rolland and number of devotees. The life of Rāmakṛṣṇa written by Swami Nikhilananda in the 'Introduction' of Kathāmṛta named as 'The Gospel of Śrī Rāmakṛṣṇa is a very detailed description of Rāmakṛṣṇa's life story. Therefore, here, we very briefly give the sketch of his life. The brief expression of Rāmakṛṣṇa's life is nicely presented at the flap of the cover of 'The Gospel of Śrī Rāmakṛṣṇa', translated by Swami Nikhilananda. It is presented here by the following passage:

"Born amidst the utter simplicity of a Bengali village, Śrī Rāmakṛṣṇa felt, from his very boyhood, a passionate yearning for the vision of God. At the age of sixteen he went to Calcutta, but was disgusted by the materialistic ideals of the people of the great metropolis. Refusing to direct his attention to secular studies, he became a priest in the Dakṣiṇeśvara temple, where God is worshipped as the Mother of the Universe. By dint of intense prayer and longing, and practically without the help of any teacher, he obtained the vision of God. He then desired to realize Him by following the paths laid down in the scriptures. There came to him, attracted by his irresistible spiritual power, people of all classes-men and women, young and old, educated and illiterate, agnostic and orthodox. All felt the radiation of his spirit and were uplifted in his presence. His love for men knew no barriers of race, colour or creed, and he gave without stint to all who sought his counsel and blessing. He specially trained a small band of young monastic disciples, who, at his bidding, took the vows of God-realization for themselves and of service to humanity. After their Master's passing they carried his message to distant countries, across lands and oceans."

In giving a brief life sketch of Rāmakṛṣṇa, we had not entered into the details of his encounter with his relations like his wife, śāradāmani Devī and brother, Rāmprasāda. We have eliminated here number of very interesting and inspiring incidents of his life. It goes without saying that all these eliminations are made with a view to maintain brevity in the presentation of his life sketch in this thesis.

3. Glimpses of Rāmakṛṣṇa's Sādhanā

Maintaining our concern about brevity, we give here the glimpses of different aspects of his unique sādhanā. These glimpses are presented in the following passages from a book, 'The Way to God As Taught by Śrī Rāmakṛṣṇa' by Swami Lokeswarananda:

"First he had a vision of Mother Kālī, seeing her as his Divine Mother. After that he practiced the discipline of Dāsya, viewing himself as Hanuman, the monkey who was Rāma's servant. The Master would sit on the limb of a tree and cry 'Rāma! Rāma!' and at last he had the vision of Rāma. Then he practiced the 'Tāntrika disciplines. Under the supervision of the Bhairavi Brahmani and attained perfection in all sixty-four branches of that discipline.

After that he underwent the discipline of madhur-bhāva, thinking of himself as a woman yearning for Śrī Kṛṣṇa. He spent six months dressing and behaving in all ways like a woman. All the signs of ecstatic samādhi found in our devotional scriptures appeared in his body, and he had the vision of Kṛṣṇa. He thus proved that the Madhurabhāva, which had fallen into disrepute, could also lead one to God.

Then he practiced the discipline of Vātsalya, regarding himself as a parent of God. A sādhu gave him an image of the child Rāma, called Rāmalalā, with which the Master carried out this discipline. He was like a mother, full of love for her little son. He felt that the child Rāma, God himself, was truly his son.

At last he saw Rāmalalā everywhere–not only in the image–thus achieving the heights of perfection in this discipline.

But this was not the end of his spiritual journey. He now practiced the disciplines of Advaita Vedānta. The monk Totapuri was his guru at this time. Totapuri after forty years of hard practice had experienced the ultimate goal of all spiritual disciplines–nirvikalpa Samādhi, Śrī Rāmakṛṣṇa reached this state in three days." (Swami Lokeswarananda, 1997: 340)

"Later, he practiced the disciplines of Islam, behaving and dressing exactly like a Muslim – repeating the namaz five times a day. He lived like this for three days, never entering the temple of Kālī. He completely forgot the Divine Mother without whom he thought he could do nothing and achieved God realization as a devout Muslim.

Next he had the vision of Jesus Christ. It happened like this: One day when he visited Jadu Mallick's garden house, his eyes fell on a picture of the child Jesus seated on the Virgin Mary's La As Śrī R. K. gazed intently at the picture, a ray of light suddenly emanated from it and entered his body. At once all his Hindu ways and mental impressions disappeared and he became a devotee of Christ. He saw in a vision Christian devotees praying to Jesus Christ in a Church. For three days, Śrī Rāmakṛṣṇa felt himself to be a devotee of Christ. Then, on the third day, while walking in the Pañcavaī at Dakṣiṇeśvara, a God man of fair complexion wearing an unusual garment, came walking towards him. It was Jesus Christ. He came near and entered into the Master, who then went into deep Samādhi.

Śrī Rāmakṛṣṇa's whole life was truly one vast centre for religious research. He took many different paths to God, and had many conceptions of Him - this was all part of his research. As a result of this research he could say with certainty, 'There are innumerable ways to God'." (Swami Lokeswarananda, 1997: 341)

There are so many other occasions which are very inspiring to the seekers. But here our task is to search Rāmakṛṣṇa's philosophy in general and metaphysics together with social concern and unity of religion in particular. In the light of this limitation we have not given here very interesting and inspiring events of the life of Rāmakṛṣṇa. However, we think it necessary to quote here from selected eminent persons and disciples in order to have some more glimpses of Rāmakṛṣṇa's personality.

4. What the selected eminent persons and disciples had said is as under:

(i) F. Max Muller

"The late Rāmakṛṣṇa Paramahaṃsa was a far more interesting specimen of a Sannyāsi. He seems to have been, not only a high-souled man, a real Mahatma, but a man of original thought....a life singularly uneventful in his relations with the outer world, though full of stirring events in the inner world of his mind" (Max Muller F., 1896: 2)

"The state of his religious exaltation...has been witnessed again and again by serious observers of exceptional psychic states. It is in its essence some thing like our talking in sleep, only that with a mind saturated with religious thoughts and with the highest sublime ideas of goodness and purity the result is what we find in the case of Rāmakṛṣṇa, no mere senseless hypnotic jabbering, but a spontaneous outburst of profound wisdom clothed in beautiful poetical language." (Max Muller F., 1896: 3)

(ii) Romain Rolland

"...the sovereign personality concentrating in himself the diversity of these elements and fashioning them into a royal harmony, is always the one who gives his name to the work, though it contains within itself the labour of generations. And with his victorious sign he marks a new era." (Rolland R., 1979: 11-14)

"He was no hero of action like Gandhi, no genius in art or thought like Goethe or Tagore. He was little Brahmin of Bengal, whose outer life was set in a limited frame without striking incident, outside the political and social activities of his time. But his inner life embraced the whole multiplicity of men and Gods." (Rolland R., 1979: 11-14)

(iii) Mahatma Gandhi

"His life enables us to see God face to face... Rāmakṛṣṇa was a living embodiment of godliness... In this age of skepticism Rāmakṛṣṇa presents an example of a bright and living faith which give solace to thousands of men and women who would otherwise have remained without spiritual light. Rāmakṛṣṇa's life was an object-lesson in Ahiṃsā. His love knew no limits, geographical or otherwise. May his divine love be an inspiration to all..." (Gandhi M. K., 1977: xi)

(iv) Rabindranath Tagore

"To the Paramahaṃsa Rāmakṛṣṇa Deva
Diverse courses of worship
From varied springs of fulfillment
Have mingled in your meditation.
The manifold revelation of the joy of the Infinite
Has given form to a shrine of unity in your life
Where from far and near arrive salutations
to which I join mine own." (Tagore R., 1936: 53)

(v) Arnold J. Toynbee

"...it is already becoming clear that a chapter which had a Western beginning will have to have an Indian ending if it is not to end in the self-destruction of the human race....The Emperor Ashoka's and the Mahatma Gandhi's principle of non-violence and Śrī Rāmakṛṣṇa's testimony to the harmony of religions, here we have the attitude and the spirit that can make it possible for the human race to grow together into a single family-and, in the Atomic Age, this is the only alternative to destroying ourselves." (Toynbee A. J., 1970: vii-ix)

(vi) Henry R. Zimmer

"These two realities bar each other,-the phenomenal tangible, and the supra-phenomenal intangible; they are as if two sides of the same and only coin. They preclude each other logically, but they are meant to be reconciled through life by each of us. That is Śrī Rāmakṛṣṇa's message on the lines of India's perennial wisdom." (Zimmer H. R. quoted in Swami Lokeswaranada, 1983: 12)

(vii) Joseph Campbell

"Śrī Rāmakṛṣṇa cut the hinges of the heavens and released the fountains of divine bliss." (Campbell J. 1941: 499)

(viii) George Williams

"Without the impulse of Rāmakṛṣṇa, the great treasures of the Indian philosophical speculation might not have become so available, in the present flexible and constructive form, to the Western world." (Williams G. 1956: 57)

(ix) Harlow Shapley

"The mind and heart of Śrī Rāmakṛṣṇa encompasses all who work and think on the problem of man's place in the scheme of things." (Shapley H., 1956: 18)

(x) E.C. Brown

"What a wonderful thing that a divine Incarnation should have attained to the highest realization of God as Divine Mother at a time when women all over the world were struggling for emancipation! Is it difficult to believe that the incarnation on earth of this great advocate of womanhood should have given their cause a powerful impetus." (Brown E. C., 1923:183)

(xi) Leo Tolstoy

"Alexander Shifman, Adviser to the Tolstoy State Museum, in his book, "Tolstoy and Indian" writes: 'During the last decade of Tolstoy's life Rāmakṛṣṇa Paramahaṃsa and his pupil Swami Vivekananda occupied his (Tolstoy's) thoughts..."

"On 13 Feb, 1903, Tolstoy read the journal "Theosophischer Wegweister" sent to him from Germany and in his copy underlined a number of Rāmakṛṣṇa's aphorisms. "There is much in common with my conception"- he noted in his diary. (Complete collection of Works of Tolstoy, Vol. 54, 155) (Tolstoy L., quoted in Shifman A., 1969: 28-31)

(xii) Śrī Aurobindo

Three messages received from Śrī Rāmakṛṣṇa Diary Entry of Dec. 5, 1912: (Record of Yoga) 18th October, the third & last message from Śrī Rāmakṛṣṇa was received...."Make complete sanyāsa of Karma. Make complete sanyāsa of thought. Make complete sanyāsa of feeling. This is my last utterance". [SA: A & R, April 1937: 11-12] (quoted from Swami Vivekananda and Śrī Rāmakṛṣṇa in Śrī Aurobindo's Writings: 8)

"Śrī Rāmakṛṣṇa came to begin and all the development of the previous two thousand years and more since Buddha appeared has been a preparation for the harmonization of spiritual teaching and experience by the Avatāra of Dakṣiṇeśvara." [Vol. I, PP 799-801] (Ibid: 14)

"Both (Śrī Caitanya and Śrī Rāmakṛṣṇa) exercised an extraordinary influence and did something supreme in their own sphere. Rāmakṛṣṇa (spoke) constantly from a swift and luminous spiritual intuition." [Vol. 22,: 94; Vol. 22,:87-88, Vol. 22: 407-423] (Ibid: 35)

"It is she (India) [Vol. 1, 66] who must send forth from herself the future religion of the entire world, the Eternal Religion which is to harmonize all religion, science and philosophies and make mankind one soul. In the sphere of morality, likewise, it is her mission to purge barbarism (Mlechchhahood) out of humanity and to Arynise the world. In order to do this she must first re-Aryanise herself. It was to initiate this great work, the greatest and most wonderful work ever given to a race that Bhagavāna Rāmakṛṣṇa came and Vivekananda preached." [Vol. 1, PP 66-67] (Ibid: 13)

"An illiterate, poor and obscure Bengali peasant, one who to the end of his life used a patois full of the most rustic forms and expressions, ignorant of Sanskrit, of any language but his own provincial dialect, ignorant of philosophy and science, ignorant of the world, yet realized in himself all the spiritual wisdom of the ages, shed in his brief sayings a light so full, so deep on the most difficult profundities of our inner being, the most abstruse questions of metaphysics that the most strenuous thinkers and the most learned Pundits were impressed by his superiority." (Ibid: 36)

"This is the Vakalam (Delegation of Authority), of which Rāmakṛṣṇa always spoke." [Vol. 2, P 431-432] (Ibid: 41)

(xiii) Pratap Chandra Mozoomdar

"The Hindu saint is a man much under forty. He is a Brahmin by caste, he is well-formed naturally, but the dreadful austerities through which his character has developed have permanently disordered his system, inflicted a debility, paleness, and shrunkenness upon his form and features that excite the deepest compassion. Yet, in the midst of this emaciation, his face retains fullness, a child-like tenderness, a profound visible humbleness, an unspeakable sweetness of expression and smile that I have seen in no other face that I can remember." (Mozoomdar quoted in Swami Lokeswaranada, 1983: 21)

(xiv) Jadunath Sarkar

"His life has brought solace to many a heart afflicted with sorrow and had shown that the Kingdom of Heaven can be brought to this earth." (Sarkar J., 1936: 136-37)

(xv) Jawaharlal Nehru

Śrī Rāmakṛṣṇa Paramahaṃsa obviously was completely outside the run of average humanity. He appears to be in the tradition of the great ṛṣis of India, who have come from time to time to draw our attention to the higher things of life and of the spirit..."

"One of the effects of Śrī Rāmakṛṣṇa's life was the peculiar way in which he influenced other people who come in contact with him. Men often scoffed from a distance at this man of no learning, and yet when they came to him, very soon they bowed their heads before this man of God and ceased to scoff and 'remained to pray'." (Nehru J., 1960: 2-4)

(xvi) Subhash Chandra Bose

"The effectiveness of Rāmakṛṣṇa's appeal lay, however, in the fact that he had practiced what he preached and that...he had reached the acme of spiritual progress." (Bose S. C., 1965: 34)

(xvii) S. Rādhākṛṣṇan

"Under the inspiration of this great teacher there has been a powerful revival of social compassion. ... He has helped to raise from the dust the fallen standard of Hinduism, not in words merely, but in works also." (Rādhākṛṣṇan S., 1970: xxxvi)

(xviii) William Digby

"During the last century the finest fruit of British intellectual eminence was, probably, to be found in Robert Browning and John Ruskin. Yet they are mere gropers in the dark compared with the uncultured and illiterate Rāmakṛṣṇa of Bengal, who knowing naught of what we term 'learning', spoke as not other man of his age spoke, and revealed God to weary mortals." (Digby W., 1901: 99)

(xix) R.C. Majumdar

"He gave a moral sanction, a philosophical basis and a new spiritual significance to the neo-Hinduism which laid the foundation of Hindu nationalism on a secure foundation." (Majumdar R. C., 1962: 299)

(xx) Swami Lokeswarananda

Swami Lokeswarananda says, "Swami Virajananda, the sixth president of the Rāmakṛṣṇa Order, referred to Śrī Rāmakṛṣṇa in a hymn as 'the illiterate-yet-all-knowing-perceiver of the essence of the scriptures'. Of course the Master was not completely illiterate, but in the common meaning of the term he was, as he was unschooled. Still we find in the Gospel what vast knowledge of the scriptures he had. He could clearly explain abstruse passages. Moreover, the essence of all the scriptures can be found in his words collected in the Gospel. Where did he get such knowledge? Through his direct spiritual realization. Knowing that (the Divine Reality, Brahman), you have knowledge of everything – and he knew that. So though he was almost illiterate, he was 'All-knowing'." (Swami Lokeswarananda, 1997: 112)

(xxi) Margaret Bedrosian

"...like the Buddha and Christ, Rāmakṛṣṇa asserted an impact that extends beyond India. Rising from the soil of his native ground, his teachings have become a tree under which all humanity can rest and be nurtured. A 'universal' man in every sense, endowed with a faultless sense of the transcendent dimension in every human act, Rāmakṛṣṇa achieved his God-realization through the impetus of a singularly creative C-, sensibility. This creativity was reflected in every facet of his life, encompassing his willingness to plunge into *Samādhi* in its various forms, to express the Self in each thought and action, to harmonize the dualities of life witl1 1he aesthetic grace of a born artist." (Bedrosian M., 1988: 61)

5. A Very Brief Introduction to 'The Gospel of Śrī Rāmakṛṣṇa' (March 1882 to April 1886)

Swami Lokeshwaranada's book "The Way to God- As Taught by Śrī Rāmakṛṣṇa" is most authentic and classical book on Rāmakṛṣṇa's teachings based on detailed study of 'The Gospel of Śrī Rāmakṛṣṇa'. Considering the importance of Swami Lokeshwaranada's work, we have carefully selected few passages introducing The Gospel of Śrī Rāmakṛṣṇa from his book, without interfering with it by putting any comment in-between. He says,

"After the Bengali edition of the Gospel had been published on five volumes, Swami Nikhilananda translated it into English and published it in 1942 in New York. The forward, written by the renowned author Aldous Huxley, describes the Gospel as 'a book unique...in the literature of hagiography'. Huxley remarked that this was the first time that the words of an Incarnation of God, or any great soul, had been recorded with such meticulous detail. Romain Rolland also recognized the uniqueness of the conversations in the Gospel. He said: "Their exactitude is almost stenographic'." "Indian scholars had much earlier recognized the great significance of the Gospel. Nagendranath Ghosh, a highly reputed scholar, wrote in the 29th May, 1902 'Indian Nation', "They take us straight to the truth, and not through any metaphysical maze." Another intellectual, Nagendranath Gupta, also wrote about the Gospel. "His spoken words are available to all almost just as he uttered them'." "Swamiji (Swami Vivekananda) came to much the same conclusion, suggesting that M. was more faithful in reporting his master's words than was Plato who placed his own ideas in the mouth of his great teacher, Socrates. It is difficult to find the real Socrates. In contrast, Swamiji told M., 'you are entirely hidden'."

"Of course M. could not tell everything about the Master. One reason for this is that M. did not see Śrī Rāmakṛṣṇa everyday, and was therefore unable to hear all that he said. There is also another reason: when Śrī Rāmakṛṣṇa spoke to his future monastic disciples, he would speak of renunciation. He would not speak of this to others because their path was different. He used to say that all cannot digest the same food. He told his monastic disciples many things which M. could not know. Both Swami Premananda and Swami Shivananda have remarked that many of Śrī Rāmakṛṣṇa's teachings are not found in the Gospel."

"No one should assume from this that we are in any sense minimizing the importance of the Gospel. Swami Vijñānananda once told M., 'After inquiring, I have discovered that 80% or more of our monks have embraced the life of renunciation by reading the Gospel; and through contact with you'."

"The Gospel explains deep spiritual truths in a simple and appealing manner. By the light of his own spiritual experience, Śrī Rāmakṛṣṇa was able to make what is difficult to understand clearly and easily comprehensible."

"It should also be noted that everything Śrī Rāmakṛṣṇa says can be found in the śāstras; the Hindu scriptures. Every one of the Master's teachings has its basis in the Upanishads, the Bhagavad-Gītā, Śrīmad Bhāgavatamam or the Caitanya Charitamrut, the most important Hindu scriptures. Many of the stories from Hindu mythology are also included in the Gospel. The Gospel is like a jar which contains the essence of all scriptures." (Swami Lokeshwaranada, 1997: 11-15)

"The principle reason for the Gospel's popularity is Śrī Rāmakṛṣṇa's liberal message. The master did not teach any narrow religious doctrine, and he did not give undue prominence to any particular religious sect. Śrī Rāmakṛṣṇa emphasized the fact that all religious are true. 'Yata Mat Tata Path' – 'As many religions, so many paths to God' is one of his most fundamental teachings. Men and women of every religion are charmed by the Gospel because they find in it the essence of their own religion. (Swami Lokeshwaranada, 1997: 14)

6. Long-felt Need for Research on the Philosophy of Rāmakṛṣṇa

The book, Śrī Rāmakṛṣṇa's Thoughts on Man, World and God by Swami Tapasyanandaji, is a set of essays originally published as editorials in the Vedānta kesarī in 1939. Swami Tapasyanandaji was a vice president of the Rāmakṛṣṇa Order and the editor of the Vedānta kesarī from May 1931 to April 1939. This book was printed in 1993 in which the publisher 'The President, Śrī Rāmakṛṣṇa Math, Mylapore, Chennai in the 'Publisher note' said, "There is an urgent need today to make an in-depth study of Śrī Rāmakṛṣṇa's ideas, to discover his philosophy, and to present it in a systematic format. We hope this book will be helpful to those who wish to take up this challenging task." The researcher humbly took up the challenging task to derive a philosophy of Śrī Rāmakṛṣṇa with special reference to his Gospel and tried to make an in-depth study for systematic presentation of different aspects of Rāmakṛṣṇa's philosophy. As Aldus Huxley has said in the Foreword of 'The Gospel of Śrī Rāmakṛṣṇa' about the writing that "the casual and unstudied utterances of a great religious teacher" (GSR: v-vi), it was needed to present the utterances of Rāmakṛṣṇa in a systematic form. Therefore, here, this attempt has been made to systematize Rāmakṛṣṇa's utterances which in their own are logically very consistent and coherent.

The Gospel of Śrī Rāmakṛṣṇa originally known as The Kathāmṛta of Rāmakṛṣṇa is very much comparable to The Vacanāmṛta of Śrī Svaminārāyaṇa. (1781-1830) An internationally renowned Christian preacher and very intimate friend of the great German scholar of mysticism, Rudolf Otto, Bhai M. C. Parekh had introduces The Vacanāmṛta of Śrī Svaminārāyaṇa in the following words, "The book of the books, however, of this Sampradāya is the one that is known as Vacanāmṛta i.e. the Nectar of Discourses, a book which has already attained the position, and which may well take its place among the religious classics of the world. It contains the essence of the Doctrine of the Movement. It is not, however, devoted to philosophical or theological exposition as such, and whatever little there is of this is subordinated entirely to the religious and spiritual teaching which was the primary and sole aim of the master. Because of this, it has a distinct note of authority born of profound personal experience, and both language and thought have so matched one another as to make a beautiful and harmonious whole...It is devoted to the teaching of pure doctrine in such an easy, simple and attractive manner that even the simplest would not find the book difficult to understand, not the wisest too simple." (Parekh M. C., 1936: 261)

In the above passage it is said about The Vacanāmṛta that "the simplest would not find the book difficult to understand, not the wisest too simple". Dr. J.A. Yajnik give the reason for this character of The Vacanāmṛta by saying that, "The reason why the wisest does not find the book simple consists in the fact that most of the important topics of Metaphysics, Epistemology, Religion, Ethics are included among the various questions raised in The Vacanāmṛta. In spite of the scattered character of the discussions in The Vacanāmṛta, the clarity and consistency of Śrī Svaminārāyaṇa's vision pervades the whole collection. This, however, cannot be revealed unless a careful analysis is made. Thus, a painstaking and profound study of The Vacanāmṛta is absolutely necessary for the clear understanding of the epistemological, metaphysical, religious, and ethical principles of Śrī Svaminārāyaṇa." (Yajnik J. A., 1972: 9)

It is worth noting here that what Bhai M.C. Parekh and Dr. J. A. Yajnik said about The Vacanāmṛta of Śrī Svaminārāyaṇa, exactly applies to The Kathāmṛta of Rāmakṛṣṇa (The Gospel of Śrī Rāmakṛṣṇa). Dr. J.A. Yajnik's book "The Philosophy of Śrī Svaminārāyaṇa", published by L.D. Institute of Indology, Ahmedabad, in 1972, is based on analytical and in-depth study of The Vacanāmṛta. This book inspired me to make analytical and in-depth study of The Kathāmṛta (The Gospel of Śrī Rāmakṛṣṇa) in order to workout 'The philosophy of Śrī Rāmakṛṣṇa. Therefore, for my Ph.D. thesis, I selected the subject: "The Philosophy of Śrī Rāmakṛṣṇa Paramahaṃsa with Special Reference to His Gospel"

2
God as the Ultimate Reality

1. Mysticism and Philosophy

Swami Tapasyanandaji says, "He (Rāmakṛṣṇa) is no philosopher in the academic sense of the term. God is for him not an intellectual postulate, but a living presence, more real than the common objects we experience in everyday life. Hence it is not by syllogisms, but by testimony of his life that he demonstrates the existence and nature of God." (Swami Tapasyananda, 1993: 82)

As Rāmakṛṣṇa was a mystic, he had mystical experience of Ultimate Reality. In his conversations, he expressed his views on the Ultimate Reality. However, before analyzing his views, the concept of mystical experience and the concept of mystic as prevalent in philosophical discourses need to be clarified.

Walter Terence Stace in his book "The Teaching of The Mystics" (1960) gave description of the concept of mysticism and the central characteristic of mystical experience. He says that there are certain misconceptions about the concept of mysticism, which are as under:

(i) "The word mysticism" is popularly used in a variety of loose and inaccurate ways. Sometimes anything is called "mystical" which is misty, foggy, vague, or sloppy. There is nothing misty, foggy, vague, or sloppy about mysticism.

(ii) A second absurd association is to suppose that mysticism is sort of mystery mongering. There is, of course, an etymological connection between "mysticism" and "mystery." But mysticism is not any sort of hocus-pocus such as we commonly associate with claims to be the elucidation of sensational mysteries.

(iii) Mysticism is not the same as what is commonly called the "occult."

(iv) Nor does it include what are commonly called Para psychological phenomena such as telepathy, telekinesis, clairvoyance, precognition. These are not mystical phenomena. It is perhaps true that mystics may sometimes claim to possess such special powers, but even when they do so they are well aware that such powers are not part of, and are to be clearly distinguished from, their mystical experience.

(v) Finally, it is most important to realize that visions and voices are not mystical phenomena, though here again it seems to be the case that the sort of persons who are mystics may often be the sort of persons who see visions and hear voices.

After indicating the above mentioned misconceptions of mystical experience and mystic, W.T.Stace has clarified that what mystics say is that a genuine mystical experience is non-sensuous. It is formless, shapeless, colorless, odorless and soundless. But a vision is a piece of visual imagery having color and shape. A voice is an auditory image. Visions and voices are sensuous experiences. (Stace W. T., 1960: 10-12)

Thus W.T.Stace gave clear description of what should not be considered as a mystical. It, thus, becomes clear that the mystical phenomena are not experienced at the level of senses or mind but at the supreme level of consciousness. These experiences are very much different from the psychological state of awareness. After defining mystical phenomena negatively, i.e. through the Indian philosophical method of 'Neti, Neti', (Not this, Not this) Stace also defines positively the meaning of mystical phenomena. He describes the central, positive characteristics of mysticism as under:

"The most important, the central characteristic in which all fully developed mystical experiences agree, and which in the last analysis is definitive of them and serves to mark them off from other kinds of experiences, is that they involve the apprehension of an ultimate non-sensuous unity in all things, a oneness or a One to which neither the senses nor the reason can penetrate. In other words, it entirely transcends our sensory-intellectual consciousness."

Thus, the basic thesis Stace advances in his book 'Mysticism and Philosophy' is that mysticism is an area of experience that is neither objective nor subjective, and one that is beyond the laws of logic.

Logic is the set of rules which governs relationships between multiplicities of things. When that multiplicity disappears in the undifferentiated unity of the mystical experience, so does logic. And therefore the logical distinction between subjective and objective also becomes irrelevant. Thus, though, mystical experience is direct, but not like direct sensual perception. Further Stace explains that,

"It should be carefully noted that only fully developed mystical experiences are necessarily apprehensive of the One. Many experiences have been recorded which lack this central feature but yet possess other mystical characteristics. These are borderline cases, which may be said to shade off from the central core of cases. They have to the central core the relation which some philosophers like to call "family resemblance." (Stace W. T., 1960: 14-15)

2. Four characteristics of Mystical Experience

Besides W.T.Stace, the great American psychologist, William James also provided a description of the mystical experience in his famous collection of lectures published in 1902 as "The Varieties of Religious Experience." In Lectures 16 and 17 he gave the following four marks of mystical experience:

(i) **Ineffability** - The handiest of the marks by which I classify a state of mind as mystical is negative. The subject of it immediately says that it defies expression that no adequate report of its contents can be given in words.

(ii) **Noetic Quality** - Although so similar to states of feeling, mystical states seem to those who experience them to be also states of knowledge. They are states of insight into depths of truth unplumbed by the discursive intellect. They are illuminations, revelations, full of significance and importance, all inarticulate though they remain; and as a rule they carry with them a curious sense of authority for aftertime.

(iii) **Transiency** - Mystical states cannot be sustained for long.

(iv) Passivity - Although the oncoming of mystical states may be facilitated by preliminary voluntary operations, as by fixing the attention, or going through certain bodily performances, or in other ways which manuals of mysticism prescribe; yet when the characteristic sort of consciousness once has set in, the mystic feels as if his own will were in abeyance, and indeed sometimes as if he were grasped and held by a superior power." (William J.,: Lectures 16 and 17)

3. Rāmakṛṣṇa on Ineffability and Noetic Qualities of Mystical Experience

Though Rāmakṛṣṇa himself was a mystic having the mystical experiences with above stated characteristics, he also has expressed his views on the nature of the mystical experience of Ultimate Reality.

In various places Rāmakṛṣṇa expresses his views regarding the ineffability of mystical experience. He says, "What Brahman is cannot be described. All things in the world – the Vedas, the Purāṇas, the Tantra, the six systems of Philosophy – have been defiled, like food that has been touched by the tongue, for they have been read or uttered by the tongue. Only one thing has not been defiled in this way and that is Brahman. No one has ever been able to say what Brahman is." (GSR: 102) And further he says, "God cannot be realized through scholarship. He is beyond the scriptures – the Vedas, Purāṇas and Tantras." ((GSR: 882)

He further says that the mystical experience or the experience of the Ultimate Reality has been so pure that it is not 'polluted' by tongue-senses or mind or even intellect. According to him it is pure experience of the Whole, without the tint of any other physical or mental elements. He expresses, "What Brahman is cannot be described in words. Everything has been polluted...no one has been able to describe Brahman. It is therefore unpolluted." (GSR: 343)

He gives the informal reference of the Indian scriptural dictum– Yato vacho nivartante, aprapya manasa saha (From which the speech returns together with the mind unable to get). He says, "It is also said in the Vedas that Brahman is beyond mind and words....The nature of Brahman cannot be described. About It one remains silent." (GSR:

227) And "What Brahman is cannot be described speech stops there." (GSR: 835) It is the characteristics of the speeches of Rāmakṛṣṇa that a simple, illiterate and ignorant man also apprehend what he is trying to say. For this, he repeatedly uses the parables and examples. To explain the ineffability of the mystical experience his example of salt doll is very famous. He says, "Brahman is beyond mind and speech. A salt doll entered the ocean to measure its depth; but it did not return to tell others how deep the ocean was. It melted in the ocean itself." (GSR: 358) Thus Rāmakṛṣṇa says, "What Brahman is cannot be described. Even he who knows It cannot talk about it. (GSR: 268)

The mystical experience is of the nature that it can not be expressed through words. Still, almost all mystics have tried to explain the nature of the mystical experience as well as tried to narrate the nature of the Ultimate Reality. To understand this, the conversation of Rāmakṛṣṇa with Narendra is useful. Once Narendra (Swami Vivekananda) says, "God is beyond words or thought." Rāmakṛṣṇa says, "No, that is not true. He can be known by the pure buddhi, which is same as the pure self." (GSR: 733) We can compare this idea of Pure Intellect with that of Kant's idea of 'Pure Intellect' which can have the clear conviction of ethical truths. But there is a difference between the two. Through Kant's idea of 'Pure Intellect', one can reach at the highest level of ethics. While through the idea of 'Pure Intellect' of Rāmakṛṣṇa one can have the mystical experience, which is beyond ethics. That is, beyond good and evil.

Thus, the apprehension of Reality in pure intellect is possible and even if it is poor, deem and imperfect, it can be expressed through language. Though Rāmakṛṣṇa has not tried to prove the existence of God, he has tried to describe the nature of God in rational terms. Rāmakṛṣṇa cannot, therefore, consistently admit any antagonism between mysticism and logic. Dr. Rādhākṛṣṇan has remarked, "The function of reasoning is not so much proof as the determination of an indeterminate object." (Rādhākṛṣṇan S., 1951: 331) Rāmakṛṣṇa has accepted this viewpoint as far as his treatment of the problem of God is concerned. He has not tried to prove God, but he has definitely tried to describe the nature of God revealed in his intuitive experience. (Yajnik J.A., 1972: 47)

4. Ultimate Reality Having Form and Being Formless

Rāmakṛṣṇa tries to explain the nature of Ultimate Reality by telling that It has the form as well as It is formless. Having the form and being formless may appears logically contradictory, but this contradiction is not relevant here, because, as explained earlier, the mystical experience of the nature of the Ultimate Reality is beyond logic.

Rāmakṛṣṇa further says that though it can be conceived by the pure intellect and its expression is possible, but the expression of it can not be possible totally. The whole can not be expressed. He gave the illustration of an ant and sugar. He says, "Men often think they have understood Brahman fully. Once, an ant went to a hill of sugar. One grain filled its stomach. Taking another grain in its mouth it started homeward. On its way it thought, 'Next time I shall carry home the whole hill.' That is the way shallow minds think. They don't know that Brahman is beyond one's words and thought. However, great a man may be, how much can he know of Brahman? Shukadeva and sages like him may have been big ants, but even they could carry at the utmost eight or ten grains of sugar!" (GSR: 102)

Rāmakṛṣṇa proclaimed that the Ultimate Reality is infinite and the whole. Therefore, It is with form as well as without form. Rāmakṛṣṇa says, "...it seems to me that both the formless Deity and God with form are real...God with form is as real as God without form." (GSR: 90,217)

He says that form and formlessness both qualities of Reality are necessary for different people. Because, the Reality is so pure that there can not be occur any change by different forms assumed by It. So, he explains, "The Reality is one and the same. The difference is only in name. He who is Brahman is verily Atman and again, He is the Bhagavāna. He is Brahman to the followers of the path of knowledge, Parāmatman to the yogis and Bhagavāna to the lovers of God." (GSR: 134) A devotee worships the form of God and a jñānī meditates on the formless Ultimate Reality. He gives an illustration of water and ice in this way: "Satcidānanda is like an endless expanse of water. The water of the great ocean in cold regions freezes into blocks of ice. Similarly through the cooling influence of divine love, Satchidanand assumes forms for the sake of the bhaktas. The ṛṣis had the vision of the super sensuous Spirit-form and talked with it. But devotes acquire a 'love-body', and with its help they see the spirit-form of the Absolute. (GSR: 217) "The heat of the sun of knowledge melts the ice–like form of the Personal God. On attaining the Knowledge of Brahman and communing with It in nirvikalpa Samādhi, one realizes Brahman, the Infinite, without form or shape and beyond mind and words. (GSR: 218)

As It is Omnipotent, It can do anything. It can remain formless and also can assume a form whenever needed. Rāmakṛṣṇa says, "God with form & without form – both true. The form of God is not the image of clay but the image of spirit." (GSR: 80) According to Rāmakṛṣṇa the Ultimate Reality is Whole, which does not exclude anything. He says, "How can you eliminate from the Reality the universe and its living beings? If you do that, It will lack Its full weight." (GSR: 343)

5. Rāmakṛṣṇa and Western Philosophers' Position on The Omnipotence of God

J. S. Mill has tried to prove that God can not be said to be omnipotent, because He is required to work under limitations. (Mill J. S. 1855: 176-177) This is not acceptable to Rāmakṛṣṇa, because he does not admit anything which can exist independently, and in spite of God. Thus, Rāmakṛṣṇa would not accept God's helplessness in any sense. Rāmakṛṣṇa asserts that God possesses all powers (ṣadaiśvarya yukta) and hence, His sovereignty is absolutely unlimited.

This, however, does not mean that God can do things that are intrinsically contradictory. As Augustine has shown, it is impossible for God to die. McTaggart has argued that God is not omnipotent, because He cannot put aside the laws of identity, contradiction, and such other necessities of thought and action. (McTaggart J. M. E., 1906: 202) Against such argumentations Pringle Pattison has aptly remarked that "To affirm omnipotence in such a sense is unnecessary. (Pringle-Pattison A. S., 1917: 404) Thus, Rāmakṛṣṇa would say that inability to perform absurdities does not have any bearing on the positive concept of God's omnipotence. God is omnipotent because He is capable of working out any possibility which is consistent with His nature as God.

6. God as Omnipotent

Not only this, Rāmakṛṣṇa asserts that as the Reality is everything, It is infinite. So no one can limit It in either way. To show the limitlessness of the Reality he says, "God has form and He is formless too. Further He is beyond both form and formlessness. No one can limit Him." (GSR: 192) The Reality is Omnipotent, this is shown by Rāmakṛṣṇa that, "God is both with and without form. And He may have many more aspects. It is possible for Him to be everything." (GSR: 291) His own revelation in his own words is thus: "I accept all, Brahman and also Māyā, the universe and its living beings. If I accepted less, I should not get the full weight. Brahman is qualified by the universe and its living beings...He alone has become the twenty-four cosmic principles...The Nitya and the Līlā belong to the same Reality. Therefore I accept everything, the Relative as well as the absolute. I don't explain away the world as māyā. Was I to do that I should get short weight." (GSR: 652) While explaining the Infinite nature of the Ultimate Reality, Rāmakṛṣṇa resembles Arjuna's consciousness of realizing the cosmic vastness (Vishvarupa Darśana) of Lord Kṛṣṇa, as Rāmakṛṣṇa describes his own revelation: "It has been revealed to me that there exists an ocean of consciousness without limit. From It come all things of the relative plane, and in It they merge again. Millions of Brahmandas rise in that Chidakasa and merge in It again. All this has been revealed to me; I don't know much about what your books say." (GSR: 653) Thus Rāmakṛṣṇa has not read any scriptures in the academic way, though his revelations are very similar to the scriptural ideas of revelation.

7. God as Omnipresent

To express the Omnipresence of Reality, Rāmakṛṣṇa says that everything is in the Reality. "The macrocosm and microcosm rest in the Mother's Womb." And "Whatever is in the microcosm is also in the macrocosm." (GSR: 106,389) The Reality is all-pervading substance. As he says, "God exists everywhere as All-pervading Consciousness." (GSR: 567) Explaining the all-pervasive character of God, Rāmakṛṣṇa has emphatically stated that "God is not only inside us; He is both inside and outside." (GSR: 521), "God is both Inside and Outside. It is He who dwells inside us. Therefore, the Vedas says, 'Tattvamasi'– That thou art'. God is also outside us. He appears manifold through māyā; but in reality He alone exists. Therefore, before describing the various names and forms of God, one should say, 'Om Tat Sat'." (GSR: 587)

With regard to the attribute of omnipresence, it should be noted that for Rāmakṛṣṇa God is not omnipresent in the pantheistic sense. That is, God is not omnipresent, in the sense that He is everything or just totality of all things, and nothing more. Thus, though he believes in the all-pervading Reality, Rāmakṛṣṇa is not the believer of Pantheism. Because, unlike Pantheism Rāmakṛṣṇa also accepts separately the form of Reality. He does not limit the realm of God only to the Universe but also accepts It as beyond the universe too. He says, "The same Rāma who was the son of King Dasharatha has created this world. Again, as Spirit, He pervades all beings. He is very near us; He is both within and without." (GSR: 162) Thus in spite of accepting all-pervading Reality, Rāmakṛṣṇa is not pantheist.

Again, Rāmakṛṣṇa believes that all-pervading Brahman is manifested differently at different places. He explains, "I have realized that Brahman and Śakti are identical...Brahman dwells in all beings as the Bibhu, the All pervasive consciousness, though It's manifestation is greater in some places than in others." (GSR: 550) Further he explains the same truth in another way: "God is everywhere. But then you must remember that there are different manifestations of His Power in different beings. At some places there is a manifestation of His avidyāśakti, at others a manifestation of His vidyāśakti. Through different instruments God's Power is manifest in different degrees, greater and smaller. Therefore all men are not equal." (GSR: 733) Thus, according to Rāmakṛṣṇa though the Ultimate Reality pervades the whole universe, there are qualitative and quantitative differences in Its manifestations.

8. Rāmakṛṣṇa and Ishavasya Upaniṣada

Though Rāmakṛṣṇa has not studied the scriptures, still his philosophical wisdom is almost the same as experienced by the ṛṣi of Ishavasya Upaniṣada in the verse-9, "Andhahantama pravishnti ye avidyam upasate, tato bhuya iva te tamaha, ya u vidyayam rataha." There the ṛṣi has said that those who are engaged in only this-worldly affairs enter into darkness. But those who are engaged in other-worldly aims enter into still greater darkness. Rāmakṛṣṇa has also said that in ignorance as well as in knowledge, one is aware of the dualism and therefore, one goes in the darkness. In fact, one and the only One, God is real. So he says, "Brahman is beyond vidyā and avidyā, knowledge and ignorance. It is beyond māyā, the illusion of duality." God is beyond both knowledge and ignorance." (GSR: 101,899)

9. Rāmakṛṣṇa and Sāṅkhya Philosophy

Similar to this, to explain the concept of Ultimate Reality Rāmakṛṣṇa uses the concepts of Puruṣa and Prakṛti which looks like the concepts of Puruṣa and Prakṛti of Sāṅkhya philosophy. But here also, he basically differs from the Sāṅkhya tradition. He has his own concept of those. According to him the Reality is the one and the only one. According to him, Brahman and Its Primal Energy, both are the two aspects of the same Reality. The same Reality assumes different forms and performs different functions. He says, "Nothing exists except the one. That one is the supreme Brahman...That which is Brahman is also the Primal Energy...Brahman and the Primal Energy at first appears to be two. But after attaining the knowledge of Brahman one does not see the two. Then there is no differentiations, it is One, without a second." (GSR: 242)

In Sāṅkhya philosophy the Puruṣa is inactive and Prakṛti is ever active. While, in Rāmakṛṣṇa's thoughts, there is no two, but only One, the Ultimate Reality. He accepts the active and passive aspects of the Ultimate Reality. He expresses it in this way: "When the Reality appears as Creator, Preserver and Destroyer, we call It Śakti; when It is inactive, we call It Brahman. But really It is one and the same thing indivisible." (GSR: 567) Through using the philosophical terms of Sāṅkhya tradition, he explains, "He who is Brahman is the Adyasakti, the Primordial Energy. When inactive He is called Brahman, the Puruṣa; He is called Śakti, or Prakṛti, when engaged in creation, preservation and destruction. There are the two aspects of Reality: Puruṣa and Prakṛti. He who is the Puruṣa is also Prakṛti. Both are the embodiment of Bliss." (GSR: 321) Thus it is seen that the concept of Puruṣa and Prakṛti are different from Sāṅkhya philosophy in Rāmakṛṣṇa's thinking. In Sāṅkhya the puruṣa indicates the self while in Rāmakṛṣṇa, Puruṣa is one aspect of the Ultimate Reality. In the same way, in Sāṅkhya, the prakṛti is inert, while in Rāmakṛṣṇa, prakṛti also is the one aspect of the Ultimate Reality. And that itself becomes the world. As Rāmakṛṣṇa says, "The Chitsakti, Mahmāyā has become the twenty-four cosmic principles." (GSR: 291) And "It is the Primordial Power that has become the world and all living beings." (GSR: 343)

"It is a case of involution and evolution." (GSR: 320) Rāmakṛṣṇa explained the nature of God as the metaphysical ground of the universe. Though the universe exists in and through God, it is not true to say, form the point of view of Rāmakṛṣṇa, that it has been brought into existence 'ex nihilo' at a particular time. Like Sāṅkhya philosophy, Rāmakṛṣṇa accepts Satkāryavāda and emphasizes the ultimate identity of cause and effect. It follows from this that there is no absolute beginning of anything. What is called creation is really evolution, actualization of the potential. Thus, according to Rāmakṛṣṇa, the universe is not created but evolved from Mahāmāyā. Thus, Rāmakṛṣṇa believes in the theory of Satkāryavāda. The theory of Satkāryavāda in Sāṅkhya, the evolution is possible through the existence of Prakṛti, which is different from Puruṣa. While in Rāmakṛṣṇa, the Puruṣa (Brahman) and Prakṛti (It's Śakti) are identical. To explain the process of evolution, Rāmakṛṣṇa says, "All elements finally merge in akash. Again, at the time of creation, akash evolves into mahat and mahat into ahamkara. In this way the whole world-system is evolved. It is the process of involution and evolution." (GSR: 395)

10. One Cannot Exist Without The Other

Thus, Rāmakṛṣṇa has wide apprehension of the Reality which is everything and nothing other than that exists. He accepts that Brahman and Prakṛti or Śakti are identical. He says, "I call Brahman when It is inactive and Śakti when It creates, preserves and destroys." (GSR: 283) In other words he explains in this way: "Brahman and Śakti are identical. If you accept the one, you must accept the other... Thus one cannot think of Brahman without Śakti or of Śakti without Brahman. One cannot think of the Absolute without the Relative, or of the relative without the Absolute. Using the symbol of Rādhā-Kṛṣṇa duo, he explains the same philosophy in different way. It is thus follows: "Śrī Kṛṣṇa is the Puruṣa; Śrīmati is His Śakti, the Primal

Power. The two are Puruṣa and Prakṛti. What is the meaning of the Yugala Murti, the conjoined images of Rādhā and Kṛṣṇa? It is that Puruṣa and Prakṛti are not different; there is no difference between them. Puruṣa cannot exist without Prakṛti and Prakṛti cannot exist without Puruṣa. If you mention the one, the other is understood." (GSR: 667) In the same way he says, "Śrī Kṛṣṇa is the Puruṣa and Rādhā the Prakṛti, the citśakti, the Adyaśakti. Rādhā is the Prakṛti, the embodiment of the three gunas: Sattva, Rajas and Tamas are in her...The Brahman of Vedānta and the Citśakti are identical like water and its wetness." (GSR: 608)

11. Nitya and Līlā

Rāmakṛṣṇa says, "I accept both, the Nitya and the Līlā. Doesn't God exist if one looks around with open eyes? After realizing Him, one knows that He is both the absolute and the universe. It is He who is the Indivisible Satcidānanda. Again, it is He who has become the universe and its living beings." (GSR: 480,490,779) Thus, the concept of Nitya and Līlā are very important in Rāmakṛṣṇa's philosophy. He calles the inactive Brahman as 'Nitya and active aspect as 'Līlā'. According to Rāmakṛṣṇa, the Nitya is that which has eternal existence. But Līlā is not illusion, it is real, but it has transitory existence. That is why he says that Līlā will not be there when the ego vanishes and the realization occurs. He says, "So long as He keeps the 'I' in us, He reveals to us that it is He who, as the Primal Energy creates, preserves and destroys the universe." (GSR: 242) Because it is transitory, it may vanish but both are real in the sense that both belong to the same Ultimate Reality. Rāmakṛṣṇa says, "Both the Līlā and the Nitya belong to the same Reality. In one form It is the Absolute and in another, the Līlā. Even though the Līlā is destroyed, the Nitya always exists... in one form He is the Absolute and in another He is the Relative." (GSR: 801)

12. Brahman as Eternal Time (Kala)

Rāmakṛṣṇa explains the Ultimate Reality using the concept of eternal Time, Kala. Kala is another name of the Ultimate Reality. He says, "It is to know that God is the only Reality and that all else is unreal. That which is the Real is also called Brahman. It has another name: Kala, Time...That which sports with Kala is called Kālī. She is the Primal Energy. Kala and Kālī, Brahman and Śakti, are indivisible." (GSR: 585)

13. Rāmakṛṣṇa and Rāmānujācārya

Thus, according to Rāmakṛṣṇa, "Kālī is none other than Brahman. That, which is called Brahman, is really Kālī. She is the Primal Energy. When that Energy remains inactive, I call It Brahman, and when It creates, preserves or destroys, I call It Śakti or Kālī. What you call Brahman I call Kālī...Brahman and Kālī are not different (GSR: 733) So, "The Līlā belongs to Him to whom the Nitya belongs, and the Nitya belongs to Him to whom the Līlā belongs." (GSR: 778) The philosophical position of Rāmānujācārya is Qualified Monism. This philosophical position is accepted by Rāmakṛṣṇa that he has clearly stated this and also mentioned the name of Rāmānujācārya. Rāmakṛṣṇa mentions the name of Rāmānuja and explain his own theory in this way: "I clearly see that God is everything; He Himself has become all. I see that whatever is, is God. He is everything; It is the theory of Rāmānuja. According to this theory, Brahman, or the Absolute, is qualified by the universe and its living beings. These three–Brahman, the world and living beings–together constitute One." (GSR: 733)

In his own words Rāmakṛṣṇa accepts Rāmānujācārya's views that Brahman, universe and living beings together constitute One and as Brahman or the Absolute in this way, really related to the world and livings beings. There is an essence in which it can be said that Absolute is qualified by the world and living beings. However, He would fundamentally disagree with Rāmānujācārya regarding the matter (acit) and souls (cit) as constituting the body of Brahman or the Absolute. And, this is evident by the fact that while describing Rāmānujācārya's theory, he does not refer to śarīra-śarīrī relation at all.

Rāmakṛṣṇa has shown his agreement with Rāmānujācārya's theory. This basic agreement between Rāmānujācārya and Rāmakṛṣṇa is about importance given to bhakti or devotion, According to Rāmānujācārya, pure jñāna, or immediate intuitive knowledge of God is the direct cause of liberation. And which dawns only by God's grace. This pure or real knowledge is identified by Rāmāujācārya with the highest bhakti or devotion which is obtained by prapatti or self-surrender and constant remembrance of God as the only object of devotion.

The type of devotion to God is described by Rāmānujācārya is well comparable to what Rāmakṛṣṇa has called prema-bhakti, in which both knowledge and devotion are combined or become one. Thus, prema-bhakti which indicated the highest stage or the realization of the identity between knowledge and devotion.

Besides the above mentioned point of similarity between Rāmakṛṣṇa and Rāmānujācārya the following points concerning their philosophical agreement are worth noting:

(1) Both accept the Sāṅkhya order of evolution of cosmic principles from prakṛti and for both the twenty fifth, puruṣa is not one of the many puruṣas but, only one Puruṣa, God or Brahman.

(2) Both, unlike Sāṅkhya regard guṇas not as constitutive elements of prakṛti, but as its attributes or qualities.

(3) According to Sāṅkhya three guṇas are always remain together. There quantity may differ in different objects, but all the three are always there in all evolutes of prakṛti. But, both, Rāmānujācārya and Rāmakṛṣṇa believe that each of the three guṇas can work independently and separately from the other two guṇas.

(4) According to both, Rāmānujācārya and Rāmakṛṣṇa, the cosmic process of creation, preservation and destruction of the world is beginningless.

(5) Both believe in plurality of self. According to them, each bound soul is associated with particular body and identified oneself with it, on account of ignorance. During the state of preservation of the world, each bound soul reaps the fruits of his freely performed action. According to both, the purpose of creation of the world is the enable the soul to get liberation by practicing bhakti yoga, conceived as inclusive of jñāna yoga and disinterested karma yoga. All selves who remain attached to the world, will have to return again in the womb of prakṛti at the time of destruction of the world.

(6) Both, Rāmānujācārya and Rāmakṛṣṇa accept satkaryavada and regard the creation of the world as actualization of what was potentially present in the womb of prakṛti.

(7) Both, Rāmānujācārya and Rāmakṛṣṇa believe that from the point of view of Brahman or God, His three-fold activities of creation, preservation and destruction of the world is His līlā. (sport)

(8) Both, Rāmānujācārya and Rāmakṛṣṇa are against māyāvāda of Śaṅkarācārya, because, according to them, rightly conceived Absolute Monism is exclusive of māyāvāda as propounded by Śaṅkarācārya.

Thus, we see that there are number of metaphysically important points of agreement between Rāmānujācārya and Rāmakṛṣṇa. Rāmakṛṣṇa fully agrees with Śaṅkarācārya in maintaining that for jñānī, liberation is being completely merged in Brahman. One can therefore be, justified in observing that Rāmakṛṣṇa's Absolute Monism is very much like Rāmānujācārya's Monism and yet, unlike Rāmānujācārya, believes and argues for Śaṅkarācārya's concept of liberation and regards it as metaphysically most important point in Śaṅkarācārya's Absolute Monism.

14. Forms of The Ultimate Reality

According to Rāmakṛṣṇa, the highest form of realization is the realization of personal as well as the impersonal form of the Ultimate Reality. But, He says, "...the mind cannot be fixed, all of a sudden, on the formless aspect of God. It is wise to think of God with form during the primary stage...These images are the embodiments of consciousness." (GSR: 127) He asserts, "God with form and the formless God are both equally true...One cannot keep one's mind on the formless God a long time. That is why God assumes form for His devotees." (GSR: 459)

The Reality is Omnipotent. Hence, It can assume any form. "Nothing is impossible for God...Everything is possible for Him." (GSR: 124) So the Reality can assume different forms. God's purpose of assuming different forms is to take care of the difference in the psychology of different people. As he says, "God Himself has provided different forms of worship He who is the Lord of the Universe has arranged all these forms to suit different men on different stages of knowledge." (GSR: 81) This views of Rāmakṛṣṇa is similar to what has been said in the Viṣṇusahasranāma. It is said in Viṣṇusahasranāma that "Rucinām vaicitryāt ṛju kuila nānāpatha juṣām." It means that there are different paths of devotion for the people of different temperament.

The above mentioned purpose of God's assuming different forms is to be understood in only with reference to human expectation. With reference to God's own being, assuming different forms is His sweet Will. In Rāmakṛṣṇa's words, "It is His sweet will...The Divine Mother is full of bliss. Creation, preservation and destruction are the waves of Her sportive pleasure." (GSR: 818)

With reference to the above stated purposes of God's assuming different forms, Rāmakṛṣṇa's advice to the seeker is not to indulge into this kind of thinking. He should think, "Why should we try to know the reason for Brahman's acting this way or that?" (GSR: 496)

15. Rāmakṛṣṇa and McTaggart

Rāmakṛṣṇa's idea of God's assuming different forms with reference to human expectation can be fruitfully compared with McTaggart's views expressed by him in his Personal Idealism.

Mctaggart has rightly maintained that the fundamental aspirations of mankind should not be overlooked by philosophy. In order to indicate the fact that his philosophy recognizes the importance of individual selves or persons, he has called his philosophy 'Personal Idealism'. But like most of the Hegelian philosophers, Mctaggart suffered from the dread of anthropomorphism. He has, therefore, maintained, "The Absolute, although not personal, is nevertheless spiritual, and cannot, therefore be out of harmony with the most fundamental desires of our own spirits." (Mctaggart J. M. E., 1901: 90) According to Mctaggart, to be personal is to be self-conscious; and therefore, the Absolute which is just a 'society of selves' cannot be regarded as a person, any more that a college consisting of different persons can be regarded as a person.

Rāmakṛṣṇa would say to Mctaggart that the Absolute, if only an impersonal totality, there is no point in conceiving It as spiritual. Because whatever the character of an impersonal reality may be, It can never be regarded as responding to "the most fundamental desires of out own spirits." Mctaggart has admitted that our fundamental desires are desires which a personal spirit can have. But in spite of himself, he has failed to see that if the universe is not "out of harmony" with these desires, then It must reveal a teleological order which is solely determined by an ultimate spiritual self-conscious will. This means that the Ultimate Reality should not only be spiritual, but must also be personal.

The basic point to be noted is that to assume a form is only one aspect of the Ultimate Reality. It can remain formless also. According to Rāmakṛṣṇa there are different stats of consciousness of which the highest state, called by his 'Vijñānī' can realize both aspects of Reality. He says, "That which is realized intuitively as Brahman, through the eliminating process of 'Not this, not this', is then found to have become the universe and all its living beings. The Vijñānī sees that the Reality which is nirguṇa, without attributes, is also Saguṇa, with attributes...The Vijñānī sees that Brahman is immovable and action less, like mount Sumeru. This universe consists of the three gunas–Sattva, rajas and tamas. They are in Brahman. But Brahman is unattached...The Vijñānī further sees that what is Brahman is the Bhagavāna, the Personal God. He who is beyond the three gunas is the Bhagavāna, with His six supernatural powers. Living beings, the universe, mind, intelligence, love, renunciation, knowledge–all these are the manifestations of His power...God is endowed with the six supernatural powers." (GSR: 103-104,271,400,417,548,818)

16. The Images of God

With reference to God's assuming different forms, it is necessary to point out that according to Rāmakṛṣṇa, the images are the visible forms of God. This has been explained by Rāmakṛṣṇa in the following report of his conversation:

"Referring to the image, one of the parties remarked: "I heard it was made by the sculptor Nabin." The master answered: "Yes, I know. But to me she is the Embodiment of Spirit." (GSR: 487)

Both the aspects of Ultimate Reality-with form and without form-are achieved in the culmination of the sādhanā by Vijñānī. Rāmakṛṣṇa asserts, "One must believe in the Divine Presence in the image." (GSR: 275)

17. God is Unattached

Rāmakṛṣṇa unambiguously teaches that while the existence and functioning of all-that-there-is in the universe depend upon God, God Himself is completely independent. "God has revealed to me that only the Paramātman, whom the Vedas describe as the Pure Soul, is as immutable as Mount Sumeru, Unattached and beyond pain and pleasure." (GSR: 398) Thus, we find that Rāmakṛṣṇa would agree with Madhvācārya in so far as he has taught the metaphysical dependence of other realities upon God, and argued for the absolute independence of God Himself.

18. Incarnation of Ultimate Reality

(i) Divine form of Incarnation

Rāmakṛṣṇa asserts the reality of the form of incarnation. Rāmakṛṣṇa would, therefore, fully agree with Aurobindo who said: "The word 'Avatāra' means a descent; it is a coming down of the Divine below the line which divides the divine from the human world or states." (Śrī Aurobindo, 1950: 140)

Dr. Rādhākṛṣṇa has interpreted the concept of avatāra as "the explanation of human nature to the level of Godhead." He has, therefore, observed that "when any finite individual develops spiritual qualities and shows large insight and charity, he sits in judgment on the world and starts a spiritual and social upheaval and we say that God is born." (S. Rādhākṛṣṇan S., 1948: 38) Such an interpretation would not at all be acceptable to Rāmakṛṣṇa for the simple reason that, in the words of Dr. R. D. Ranade, "The expression Avatāra connotes descent more than ascent, the prefix 'Ava' meaning 'down'. Avatāra, therefore, literally ought to mean descent of spirit into matter instead of ascent of matter into spirit." (Ranade R. D., 1959: 174)

Rāmakṛṣṇa believes that this theory of incarnation as divine descent would be acceptable to a true devotee. As he has said, "One who constantly thinks of God can know His real nature; he alone knows that God reveals Himself to seekers in various forms and aspects." (GSR: 150)

Rāmakṛṣṇa accepts the reality of formless God as well as God with form. He disagrees with the thinkers who believe that Incarnation of God is not possible. He says, "I accept God with form when I am in the company of people who believe in that ideal, and I also agree with those who believe in the formless God." Together with this agreement, Rāmakṛṣṇa expresses his disagreement with the jñānī, who believe in the formless God and do not accept divine incarnations. As he has said, "Divine Incarnations without number appear and disappear on the tree of the absolute Brahman." (GSR: 128)

While explaining the incarnation as one of the many divine forms, Rāmakṛṣṇa has said, "Various divine forms are seen to rise out of the Great Akash of consciousness. The incarnation of God is one of these forms. The Primal Energy sports, as it were, through the activities of Divine Incarnation." (GSR: 180) And "With the help of Adyasakti God sports as an Incarnation. God through His Śakti, incarnates Himself as man. Then alone does become possible for the Incarnation to carry on His work. Every thing is due to the Śakti of the Divine Mother." (GSR: 460) Thus, Rāmakṛṣṇa believes in incarnation as divine descent assuming numerous forms.

(ii) Rāmakṛṣṇa's Understanding of Incarnation in The Sanātana Dharma

According to Rāmakṛṣṇa, as the Sanātana Dharma of India accepts various paths of realizing God, the theory of incarnation can be accepted as the important theory by it. In the words of Rāmakṛṣṇa, "The Eternal Religion, the religion of the ṛṣis, has been in existence from time out of mind and will exist eternally. There exist in this Sanātana Dharma, all forms of worship-worship of God with form and worship of the Impersonal Deity as well. It contains all paths – the path of knowledge, the path of devotion and so on." (GSR: 406)

(iii) Incarnations Follow The Natural Laws

Rāmakṛṣṇa says that when the Brahman assumes the body, It Itself follows the authority of Māyā. That means He will surrender to the natural order of Primal Energy. He says, "Everyone is under the authority of the Divine Mother, Mahāmāyā, the Primal Energy. Even the Incarnations of God accept the help of māyā to fulfill their mission on earth. Therefore they worship the Primal Energy." (GSR: 226) In this way the Reality plays with and obeys Its own rules. Rāmakṛṣṇa classifies the categories of human beings. When The Incarnation of

God assumes the human body, it is also put under one category. That category is called Iśvarakoṭi. Iśvarakoṭi come on earth to save the people from the sufferings and to help the men to achieve salvation. They can move from absolute plain to relative plain and vice-versa. Rāmakṛṣṇa says, "None but Isvarakotis can return to the plane of relative consciousness after attaining Samādhi...when God Himself is born as a man, as an Incarnation, holding in His hand the key to other's liberation, then for the welfare of humanity the incarnation returns from Samādhi to consciousness of the world." (GSR: 237)

Rāmakṛṣṇa asserts that in all manifestations of God, the manifestation of God in men is highest. He says, "...there is a greater manifestation of God in man. You may say, 'How is it possible for God to be incarnated as a man who suffers from hunger, thirst and the other traits of an embodied being and perhaps also from disease and grief?' The reply is, 'Even Brahman weeps, entrapped in the share of the five elements'." (GSR: 415) Because the human body of Incarnation is surrendered to Māyā. Here it is specifically noted that Māyā and He (The Incarnation) is identical. So it is His will to obey the function of Māyā. Other humans are slave of the will of Māyā while incarnations, though bounded by māyā, are masters of it. Rāmakṛṣṇa gives the illustration of the incarnation of Rāma and says, "There is one kind of manifestation of Rāma in the Incarnation of God and another in men. Even the Incarnations are conscious of the body. Embodiment is due to māyā. Rāma wept for Sītā. But the Incarnation of God puts a bandage over His eyes by His own will." (GSR: 243)

As the incarnation is appeared as the object of māyā and affected by māyā, it is difficult to recognize him with finite intellect. Few with pure intellect can recognize Him. Rāmakṛṣṇa says, "Can one ever understand the work of God? He is so near; still it is not possible for us to know him...God has covered all with His māyā. He doesn't let us know anything. Māyā is 'woman & gold'. He who puts māyā aside to see God, can see Him." (GSR: 260) Only "the bhakta sees that He who is God has also become māyā." (GSR: 243)

(iv) The Concept of Vibhūti

If there is a divine quality or any good in man, it is of God's only. This truth proclaimed by Bhagavad Gītā as the idea of Vibhūti, is also accepted by Rāmakṛṣṇa. He says, "It is God alone who has become all this. But in certain places for instance, in a holy man–there is a greater manifestation than in others." (GSR: 181) Further he says, "As the all-pervading spirit He exists in all beings, even in the ant. But the manifestations of His power are different in different beings." (GSR: 104) Rāmakṛṣṇa explains the different manifestations among different objects as well as among different men. He says, "After realizing God, one knows definitely that it is He who has become everything. In some objects He is manifested more clearly, and in others less clearly... But His greater manifestation is in man. Again, among men, God manifests Himself more clearly in those devotees who are Sattvika, in those who have no desire whatever to enjoy 'woman and gold'." (GSR: 320)

According to Rāmakṛṣṇa one can be regarded as a vibhūti, if he has great proficiency in any art or he is highly honest or having any such outstanding quality. He says, "There is a special manifestation of God's power in a man who has any outstanding gift, (such as proficiency in music)." (GSR: 111)

The person with child like purity of heart and simplicity without the tint of hypocrisy is regarded by Rāmakṛṣṇa as vibhūti. In his words, "It is God alone who has become everything. But in man He manifests Himself that most God is directly present in the man who has the pure heart of a child and who laughs and cries and dances and signs in divine ecstasy." (GSR: 208)

The person who are sātvika and free form worldly desires, also belongs to the class of vibhūti. Clarifying this he has said, God's "manifestation is everywhere, at some places it is apparent and at other places it is hidden. In some objects He is manifested more clearly, and in others less clearly...But His greater manifestation is in man. Again, among men, God manifests Himself more clearly in those devotees who are Sātvika, in those who have no desire whatever to enjoy 'woman and gold'." (GSR: 320,342,803,822)

According to Rāmakṛṣṇa a vibhūti can be and should be accepted as the incarnation of God or the manifestation of God's quality. Quoting Rāmakṛṣṇa, Lokeswaranand says that there are some external characteristics through which one can understand one as an incarnation. "Śrī Rāmakṛṣṇa says, 'If you see a man endowed with ecstatic love, overflowing with prema, mad after God, intoxicated with His love, then know for certain that God has incarnated Himself through that man. (GSR– 726)" (Swami Lokeswaranand, 1997" 367)

(v) Birth of Incarnations

With regard to the birth of the Avatāra, Rāmakṛṣṇa believes that the Avatāra is not always born in the way in which an ordinary human being is born. It is said in the Gītā that pure hearted soul take birth in the pious family. "śucināṃ Śrīmatāṃ gehe yogabhraṣobhijāyate." (Śrīmad Bhagvad Gītā) According to Rāmakṛṣṇa this applies to the incarnations of God too. He says, "Don't you see that God incarnates Himself only in a family where innocence exists? (GSR: 448) And there also He behaves like a kind and soft hearted person. Quoting Rāmakṛṣṇa Lokeswaranand says, "God becomes tender for the sake of His devotees. He appears before them, setting aside His powers. (GSR–282)" (Swami Lokeswaranand, 1997: 359)

The plausibility of the belief in such supernaturalism of divine birth as propounded by Rāmakṛṣṇa, has also been shown by Aurobindo in the following words, "the divine birth is that of the conscious Godhead in our humanity and essentially the opposite of the ordinary birth even though the same means are used, because it is not the birth into the ignorance, but the birth of knowledge, not a physical phenomenon, but a soul-birth. It is the soul's coming into birth as the self-existent Being controlling consciously its becoming and not lost to self-knowledge in the cloud of ignorance." (Śrī Aurobindo, 1950: 140)

(vi) Number of Incarnation

With reference to the question of the number of incarnation, Rāmakṛṣṇa has said, "Some say that there are ten Divine Incarnations, some twenty-four, while others say that there are innumerable Incarnations. If you see anywhere a special manifestation of God's Power, you may know that God has incarnated Himself there." (GSR: 851) Thus, Rāmakṛṣṇa is against fixing any particular number of incarnation and emphasizes the innumerability of incarnation. Because he believes that wherever there is divine manifestation, there is an incarnation of God.

(vii) Purpose of Incarnation

Rāmakṛṣṇa explains the purpose of incarnation in this way, "The Incarnation of God is a part of the līlā of Śakti.

(1) The purpose of the Divine Incarnation is to teach man ecstatic love for God...God incarnates Himself as man. There is a great accumulation of divinity in an Incarnation." (GSR: 283) Because of the longing of devotee, God assumes a human body. In the words of Rāmakṛṣṇa, "God plays in the world as man for the sake of His devotees. They can love God only if they see Him in a human forms; only then can they show their affection for Him as their Brother, Sister, Father, Mother or Child. It is just for this love of the devotees that God contracts Himself into a human form and descends on earth to play His līlā." (GSR: 382)

Again, according to Rāmakṛṣṇa to develop love for God is the ultimate goal of human life. And this is best satisfied through the incarnation of God in the human form. As he says, "God incarnates Himself on earth in a human body. He is, no doubt, present everywhere and in all beings, but man's longing is not satisfied unless he sees God in a human form. Man's need is not satisfied without the Divine Incarnation." (GSR: 883) This incarnation obviously needed by a bhakta. So looking to the purpose, Rāmakṛṣṇa says, "God incarnates Himself for the bhakta and not for jñānī." (GSR: 638) "That is why God incarnates Himself as man and teaches people the path of devotion. He exhorts people to cultivate self-surrender to God." (GSR: 355,359,638,725)

Explaining the importance of incarnation as one of his different forms, Rāmakṛṣṇa has said, There are different ways God perform His function. As that Reality Itself is Infinite, Its ways of functions are also infinite. "God has different forms, and He sports in different ways. He sports as Isvara, deva, man and the universe. In every age He descends to earth in human form, as an incarnation, to teach people love and devotion...One can taste devotion and love of God only through His incarnations. Infinite are the ways of God's play, but what I need is love and devotion." (GSR: 257)

(2) Another purpose is just play. "God is born as man for the purpose of sporting as man." (GSR: 405) For Rāmakṛṣṇa, Līlā is as true as

Nitya is. The Nitya and the Līlā are the two aspects of the same Reality. "The Absolute plays in many ways: as Isvara, as the God as man and as the universe...The incarnation is the play of the absolute as men." (GSR: 359) In men, it is greater manifestation, but It is everywhere. So he says, "It is God Himself who sports in the world as both vidyā and avidyā. Therefore I salute both." (GSR: 528)

(3) Still another purpose of Incarnation is to free human beings form bondage. He says, "He who relieves us of sin is Hari. He relieves us of our three afflictions in the world." (GSR: 528) Again he says, "He who liberates others is an Incarnation of God. The scriptures speak of ten, of twenty four, and also of innumerable Incarnations." (GSR: 850)

Rāmakṛṣṇa says, "According to some people, Shukadeva tasted only a drop of that ocean of Brahman–consciousness...He is like those who retain their bodies even after attaining Brahmajñāna, in order to teach others. Divine Incarnations belong to this class. (GSR: 354) So the realized ones and incarnations retain their body to do well to others. He says, "Some retain bhakti even after realizing Brahman, in order to teach humanity. The incarnation of God is one of these...The ego of Incarnation returns them when they come down from the plane of Samādhi, but then it is 'the ego of knowledge' (Shankarācārya) or the 'ego of Devotion'." (GSR: 700) Further, "He assumes different forms and reveals Himself in different ways for the sake of His devotees." (GSR: 858)

(4) There is also another dimension Rāmakṛṣṇa points out regarding the purpose of Incarnation. He says, "Do you know why God incarnates Himself as a man? It is because through a human body one can hear His words. He sports through it. He tastes divine bliss through a human body. But through His other devotees God manifests only a small part of Himself." (GSR: 782)

(viii) Apprehension of Incarnation

Rāmakṛṣṇa says that it is possible for a Vijñānī to realize the Whole of Reality which include God without attributes as well as God with attributes and God without form as well as God with form, i.e. incarnation. He says, "Ordinary people do not recognize the advent of an Incarnation of God. He comes in secret. Only a few of His intimate disciples can recognize Him." (GSR: 189)

Rāmakṛṣṇa shows the following reasons why all men can not recognize the Incarnation.

(ix) Incarnations follow the Natural Laws

He says, "Not all, by any means, can recognize an Incarnation of God. Assuming a human body, the Incarnation fall a victim to disease, grief, hunger, thirst and all such things, like ordinary mortals. Rāma wept for Sītā. Brahman weeps, entrapped in the share of the five elements." (GSR: 359) Further he says, "It is very difficult to understand that God can be a finite human being, and as the same time the all-pervading soul of the universe. The Absolute and the Relative are His two aspects. How can we say emphatically with our small intelligence that God cannot assume a human form? Can we ever understand all these ideas with our little intellect?" (GSR: 864)

(x) There is no Analogy of Incarnation

Further, as It is One and the only One, it is difficult to apprehend It by analogy too. Rāmakṛṣṇa says, "However great and infinite God may be, His Essence can and does manifest itself through man by His mere will. God's Incarnation as a man cannot be explained by analogy. One must feel it for oneself and realize it by direct perception." (GSR: 725)

19. Complete Apprehension is Impossible

Thus, he claims, "All can not recognize an incarnation." (GSR: 640) Rāmakṛṣṇa says that we are finite and the infinite Reality can never be conceived by our mind. But he says that it is not needed also to know the whole. He says, "What need is there of your knowing the infinite qualities of God? You may discriminate for millions of years about God's attributes and still you will not know them." (GSR: 463) And further he says, "Who can comprehend everything about God? It is not given to man to know any aspect of God, great or small. And what need is there to know everything about God? It is enough if we only realize Him. And we see God Himself if we but see His Incarnation." (GSR: 725-726) And this part of It is not beyond our reach. As he says, "He is, no doubt, unknowable by this ordinary mind, but He can indeed be known by to pure mind." (GSR: 726) He defines the pure mind in this way, "He can be known by the pure buddhi, which is same as the pure self. The seers of old directly perceived the pure self through their pure buddhi." (GSR: 733)

20. Rāmakṛṣṇa and Madhvācārya and Anselm

The most central point to be noted about the nature of the Ultimate Reality or God is His Infinitude. As we have seen, the attributes of existence, knowledge, and bliss, possessed by Him are not limited anyway. Similarly, the limitations of space, time and causality are not applicable to God, because he is omnipresent and eternally self-existing being. Again, God in Rāmakṛṣṇa is beyond the limitation of change and mutability because, as we saw, Rāmakṛṣṇa has emphasized the imperishability and eternal perfectness of God. According to Madhvācārya, the limitations of finite existence are: (1) ignorance, (2) dependence, (3) liability to misery, (4) material embodiment, and (5) equality with, or inferiority to others. (Sharma B. N. K., 1962: 235-236) As God is (1) omniscient, (2) self-existent, (3) essentially blissful, (4) immaterial and (5) one without a second, it is evidently clear that He is beyond all the limitations of finitude.

Rāmakṛṣṇa would fully agree with Anselm who has said that God is infinite because He is "something than which a greater can not be conceived." He would not, however, stop at just this. Rāmakṛṣṇa has made the concept of God's infinitude more meaningful by saying that God is infinite, because He cannot be fully conceived. This is, according to Rāmakṛṣṇa, the reason why scriptures describe God with the negative method of 'Neti, Neti'. Thus, we find that according to Rāmakṛṣṇa, this negative method is employed not for the denial of the reality of the finite, but for the denial of the finitude of the infinite.

21. Realization of Ultimate Reality

(i) Bhakta and Jñānī

For Bhakta and for Jñānī, the realization of the same Ultimate Reality is different in nature. Both are true. Rāmakṛṣṇa says, "No one can say with finality that God is only 'this' and nothing else. He is formless and again He has forms. For the Bhakta He assumes forms. But He is formless for the Jñānī that is for him who looks on the world as a mere dream. The Bhakta feels that he is one entity and the world another. Therefore God reveals Himself to him as a person. But the Jñānī—the Vedāntist, for instant always reasons, applying the process of 'Not this, not this'. Through this discrimination he realizes, by his inner perception, that the ego and the universe are both illusory, like a dream. Then the Jñānī realizes Brahman in his own consciousness. He cannot describe what Brahman is." (GSR: 141) But "A devotee thinks of God as he sees Him. In reality there is no confusion about God. God explains all this to the devotee if the devotee only realizes Him somehow." (GSR: 149)

Describing the state of jñānī, he says, "The forms and aspects of God disappear when one discriminates in accordance with the Vedānta Philosophy. The ultimate conclusion of such discrimination is that Brahman alone is real and this world of names and forms illusory. It is possible for a man to see the forms of God, or to think of Him as a Person, only so long as he is conscious that he is a devotee. From the standpoint of discrimination this 'ego of a devotee' keeps him a little away from God." (GSR: 150) He says, "After attaining Perfect Knowledge one realizes that they (God & Śakti) are not different. They are the same." (GSR: 635)

(ii) Both realizations jointly possible

Rāmakṛṣṇa admits that the realization of both the aspects of Reality is the true realization. But it is not easy for everyone to conceive that whole. Formless aspect of Reality is suitable to meditate for some people and with form is suitable to another kind of people. Ultimately every one will reach up to the same highest level of consciousness. Neither of the two is inferior. The images of God are themselves consciousness.

Accepting the possibility of both, "Rāmakṛṣṇa instructed the devotee about meditation on the Personal God and on the Impersonal Reality." (GSR: 258)

Rāmakṛṣṇa says that if a devotee is sincere then he will certainly realize Reality with Its both aspects. There sincerity and devotion are needed, not just scholarship He says, "God cannot be realized through scholarship He is beyond the scriptures – the Vedas, Purāṇas and Tantras." (GSR: 882) He says, "He is the Ruler of the soul within...whether you follow the ideal of the Personal God or that of the Impersonal Truth, you will realize God alone, provided you are restless for Him." (GSR: 867) He says, "If the devotee but once feels this attachment and ecstatic love for God, this mature devotion and longing, then he sees God in both His aspects, with form and without form." (GSR: 173) And "One can see both aspects of God - God with form and without form. One can see God with form, the embodiment of Spirit. Again, God can be directly perceived in a man with a tangible form. Seeing an Incarnation of God is the same as seeing God Himself. God is born on earth as man in every age." (GSR: 186) Not only that "The Paramahaṃsa realizes that all these-good and bad, virtue and vice, real and unreal–are only the glories of God's māyā." (GSR: 250) He asserts, "If you accept the Nitya, you must also accept the Līlā. It is the process of negation and affirmation. You realize the...Nitya by negating the Līlā. Then you affirm the Līlā, seeing in it the manifestation of the Nitya. One attains this state after realizing Reality in both aspects: Personal and Impersonal. The Personal is embodiment of Chit, consciousness; and the Impersonal is the Indivisible Satcidānanda." (GSR: 477)

He accepts the value of formless Reality but equally he put emphasis on the form of Reality. He says. "Caitanya, consciousness is awakened after Advaita-jñāna, the knowledge of the non-dual Brahman. Then one perceives that God alone exists in all beings as consciousness. After this realization, comes Ananda, Bliss. Advaita, Caitanya and Nityananda...Let me ask you not to disbelieve in the forms of God. Have faith in God's forms...In order to bring people spiritual knowledge, an Incarnation of God lives in the world in the company of devotees, cherṣing an attitude of love for God." (GSR: 272) Describing the process to achieve both he says. "As long as a man associates himself with upādhis, so long he sees the manifold... but on attaining perfect knowledge he sees only one consciousness everywhere. The same perfect knowledge again, makes him realize that the one consciousness has become the universe and its living beings and the twenty four cosmic principles. But the manifestations of Divine Power are different in different beings. It is He, undoubtedly who has become everything; but in some cases there is a greater manifestation than in others." (GSR: 319) "Then he sees that God, māyā, living beings and the universe form one whole. God includes the universe and its living beings." (GSR: 328)

Rāmakṛṣṇa synthesizes all types of realization and asserts that the Reality is the One. "One should not harbour malice toward any person or any opinion. The believers in the formless God and the worshippers of God with form are all, without exception, going toward God alone. The jñānī, the yogi, the bhakta are seeking Him alone. The follower of the path of knowledge calls Him 'Brahman'. The Yogi calls Him 'Atman' or 'Paramātman'. The bhakta calls Him 'Bhagavāna'. Further, it is said that there is the Eternal Lord and His Eternal Servant." (GSR: 374)

Rāmakṛṣṇa differentiate the types of realization and says, "That God exists may be known by looking at the universe. But it is one thing to hear of God, another thing to see God and still another thing to talk to God." (GSR: 368)

He says, "As you go nearer to God, you see less and less of his upādhis, His attributes. A devotee at first may see the Deity as the ten-armed Divine. Mother; when he goes nearer he sees Her possessed of six arms, still nearer, he sees the Deity as the two-armed Gopāla. The nearer he comes, to the Deity, the fewer attributes he sees. At last when he comes into the presence of the Deity, he sees only light without any attributes." (GSR: 853) And says, "But after realizing God one finds that He alone has become māyā, the universe and all living beings." (GSR: 836)

3
The Concept of Self and its Salvation

1. Nature

Unlike Christian and other theologians and like major Indian traditions, Rāmakṛṣṇa believes that the self is not a created thing. It is a subtle spiritual substance existing form eternity. As the self is never created, it is never going to be destroyed. He points out, "The body was born and it will die. But for the soul, there is no death." (GSR: 319) Thus, the self is not annihilated with the annihilation of the body. Without studying any scriptures, he proclaimed the Indian scriptural truth, 'Ajo nitya śāśvatoyam purāṇo..' Thus Rāmakṛṣṇa clearly believes in the immortality of soul.

2. Self in the body is separate from it

Rāmakṛṣṇa has showed that how can one understand the different nature of soul form body. The soul is neither body nor intellect. He says, "Is this 'I' the flesh, the bones, the blood or the marrow? Is it the mind or the buddhi? Analyzing thus, you realize at last that you are none of these." (GSR: 180) In spite of this separateness of body, it should maintain as a good instrument for self-realization. Hence, he advices, "As long as there is the body, one should take care of it. But I find that the body is quite separate from the self. When a man rids himself entirely of his love for 'woman and gold', then he clearly perceives that the body is one thing and the self another." (GSR: 870) explaining further the instrumental value of body and its separateness from soul, he has said, "Every now and then I think that the body is a mere pillow-case. The only real substance is the Indivisible Satcidānanda." (GSR: 847)

3. William James on Immortality of Self and Rāmakṛṣṇa

In his lectures on Immortality, William James has argued that if the self is immortal, the question of the accommodation of all the selves would be very difficult to solve. As he has put it, "the very heavens themselves and the cosmic times and spaces would stand aghast...at the notion of preserving eternity such an ever-swelling plethora and glut it." (Yajnik J.A., 1972: 107) With reference to this, Rāmakṛṣṇa would say that as the self is eternal, and not created with the birth of the psycho-physical organism, there is no question of the increase in the number of selves. Again, it is utterly wrong to think of a spiritual entity in terms of the problem of physical accommodation and population.

4. Knowledge of The Self

Rāmakṛṣṇa says that one can not know the self by science. If one relies on science for the knowledge of self, then the nature of self or man will remain a vast question. As has been pointed out by well-known Christian theologian named, Tillich. It is because the source of knowledge in science is basically sense perception. While, the knowledge of self is immediately known to the self-realized person. Rāmakṛṣṇa has rightly observed that, "The ṛṣis directly realized the self. One can not know the truth about God (or self) through Science. Science gives us information only about things perceived by the senses...One can not explain the vision of God to others." (GSR: 429)

5. Beginningless Association of Self With Body

Rāmakṛṣṇa says, "The Jīva at first remains in a state of ignorance. He is not conscious of God, but of the multiplicity." (GSR: 404) This multiplicity includes identification of body with self. Thus, according to Rāmakṛṣṇa the jīva or empirical self is having a beginningless association with body, with which it identifies through ignorance. "To think of the body as the Atman is Ajñāna, ignorance." (GSR: 582) Thus, in the philosophy of Rāmakṛṣṇa, there is no question of the first fall of Man. The problem of Ascent of Man, however, finds a prominent place in it. Rāmakṛṣṇa believes that the ultimate aim of human life is self-realization. At this stage of self-realization, it will be clear that the self is not body, but an eternally emancipated, most effulgent spiritual reality, whose essential nature is being, consciousness and bliss. As it is said that it never dies, so it is sat (being), then it is also citta or consciousness. Rāmakṛṣṇa defines citta in this way, "what is the Citta? It is 'I-Consciousness'." (GSR: 583) Again, it is also blissful. "Jīva is nothing but the embodiment of Satcidānanda." (GSR: 169) Hence, the possibility for each one of the jīes to dissociate itself with the upādhis, and realize its true metaphysical nature by following a temporal process of spiritual sādhanā.

Again, as the metaphysical nature of the self remains to be realized, Rāmakṛṣṇa is not required to face the unanswerable question: how is it that the knower, the ever enlightened, has become ignorant of his own nature? The problem with Rāmakṛṣṇa is only that of enabling the ignorant to actualize its enlightenment which it potentially possesses.

6. The Metaphysical Dependence of the Self upon God

Rāmakṛṣṇa points out that "There are two entities: Jīvātmā, the individual soul and Paramātma, the Supreme Soul. Through prayer all individual soul can be united with the supreme soul." (GSR: 205) Although the self can unite with the supreme soul and although the self is an eternally existing entity, it is by no means independent. The dependence of the self upon God has been explained by Rāmakṛṣṇa in the following various ways:

(i) As the devotee or a sādhaka wants to realize God, its dependence on God becomes very clear. Explaining this, Rāmakṛṣṇa says, "It is quiet different when God Himself, gratified by the aspirant's devotion, says to him, 'you are the same as myself'... It is not good for ordinary people to say, 'I am He'. The waves belong to the water. Does the water belong to the waves?" (GSR: 248)

(ii) Again, it is seen in his conversation, wherein he shows the dependence of self upon God by man's feeling of a 'devotee or of a 'servant'. He says, "When a man merges himself in God, he can no longer retain wicked or sinful tendencies...he keeps only the 'knowledge ego', the 'devotee ego', the 'servant ego' and the 'good ego' His 'wicked ego' disappears." (GSR: 252)

(iii) Still another point to be noted regarding the dependence of self upon God is that the true thinking, according to Rāmakṛṣṇa is, to think that God is the Doer. Thus self is incapable of doing anything without the power of God. He says, "Give up the ego that makes you feel, 'I am the doer. I am teaching people'...Give up 'wicked ego'... One does not develop the 'divine ego' as long as one retains the 'wicked ego'." (GSR: 405) The recognition of God as a Doer would be clearly understood if one regards oneself as a machine and God as the Operator. This feeling that I am the machine and God is the operator is the deep feeling of Rāmakṛṣṇa. This shows his conviction of the dependence of self upon God. "When the heart becomes pure through the practice of spiritual discipline, there one rightly feels that God alone is the Doer. He alone has become mind, self and intelligence. We are only His instruments." (GSR: 311)

(iv) The dependence of the self upon God is specified by Rāmakṛṣṇa through showing God as the Creator of man's mental states. Rāmakṛṣṇa says, "God is both within and without. From within He creates the various states of mind. After passing through the six centers, the jīva goes beyond the realm of māyā and becomes united with the Supreme Soul. This is the vision of God." (GSR: 243)

(v) Rāmakṛṣṇa has emphasizes the dependence of the self upon God even in the emancipated state. In the words of Rāmakṛṣṇa, "Even after the attainment of knowledge this 'I-consciousness' comes up, (therefore, one should think) O lord I am the servant; Thou art the Master. I am the child; Thou art the Mother...The relation of master and servant is the proper one. Since this 'I' must remain, let the rascal be God's servant." (GSR: 105) In other words he expressed this way, "Try to find out what this 'I' is. Is this 'I' the bones or flesh or blood or intestines? Seeking the 'I', you discover 'Thou'. In other words, nothing exists inside you but the power of God. There is no 'I' but only 'He'." (GSR: 819)

Although Rāmakṛṣṇa accepts the dependence of self, he also accepts the feeling of equality of self with God in the highest level of devotion. In the intensity of devotion, sometimes a devotee feels his loved to be equal to him. "Sometimes God becomes the magnet and the devotee the needle, and sometimes the devotee becomes the magnet and God the needle. The devotee attracts God to him. God is the Beloved of His devotee and is under his control." (GSR: 355)

7. States of Consciousness

Rāmakṛṣṇa has explained the states of consciousness of self with reference to, (1) different stages of consciousness (conscious, semi-conscious and inmost state), (2) three types of body (Gross body, subtle body and causal body) and (3) the theory of five sheaths. (Pañcakoṣa) as under:

(i) "Through the individual soul one can reach the supreme soul." (GSR: 404) In the journey from individual soul (jīva) to the supreme soul (śīva), mind passes through different state of consciousness. There are three states of consciousness-conscious, semi-conscious and the inmost state as put by Rāmakṛṣṇa. These states of consciousness are different from that of three states of consciousness accepted in psychology. In psychology, all states are just the states of mind, while in Rāmakṛṣṇa there is a journey from empirical self (jīva) to the transcendental self (śīva). Again, in psychology, in the sates of mind, there is no hierarchy between them, while in Rāmakṛṣṇa all the three states are in hierarchy and the culmination or the highest state is the state of liberation where the very mind is merged in the soul.

(ii) In all the three states, mind dwells either in gross or subtle body, or in causal body or goes beyond. He explains these different states of consciousness and the position of mind on different types of body, through the example of Śrī Caitanya Mahāprabhu. "Caitanya experienced three states of mind. First, the conscious state, when his mind dwelt on the gross and the subtle. Second, the semi-conscious state, when his mind entered the causal body and was absorb in the bliss of divine intoxication. Third, the inmost state, when his mind was merged in the Great Cause." (GSR: 330)

(iii) Again using the example of Śrī Caitanya Mahāprabhu, Rāmakṛṣṇa describes the states of consciousness upto Samādhi, in the terms of five sheaths described in the Taitarīya upaniṣad, Brahmānanda valli, Anuvāk-1 to 5. Rāmakṛṣṇa explains the process of gradual upliftment of the self. "Man, looking outward, sees the gross; at that time his mind dwells in the annamayakoṣa, the gross body. Next is the subtle body. Functioning through the subtle body, the mind dwells in the manomayakoṣa and the vijñānamayakoṣa. Next is the causal body. Functioning through the causal body the mind enjoys bliss; it dwells in the ānandamayakoṣa. This corresponds to the semi-conscious state experienced by Caitanya. Last of all, the mind loses itself in the Great Cause. It disappears. It merges in the great cause." (GSR: 330,604)

8. The Highest State of Consciousness

The mahākāraṇa, the Great Cause, is beyond the five sheaths. When Caitanya's mind merged in that, he would go into Samādhi. This is called Nirvikalpa or Jaḍa Samādhi." (GSR: 330) He clearly defines the nature of all the four states of consciousness, the gross body, subtle body, causal body and Cause of causes, thereby clarifies the real nature of self. "That which is Pure Atman is the Great Cause, the cause of the cause. The Gross, the subtle, the causal and the Great Cause. The five elements are gross. Mind, buddhi and ego are subtle. Prakṛti, the Primal Energy is the cause of all these. Brahman, Pure Atman, is the Cause of the cause...This Pure Atman alone is our real nature. What is jñāna? It is to know one's own self and keep the mind in It. It is to know the Pure Atman." (GSR: 582) This classification is explained differently at another place. "The body consisting of the five gross elements is called the gross body. The subtle body is made up of the mind, the ego, the discriminating faculty, and the mind-stuff. There is also a causal body, by means of which one enjoys the Bliss of God and holds communion with Him. The Tantra calls it the Bhāgavatami Tanu, the Divine Body." (GSR: 902)

The highest state of consciousness is also described by Rāmakṛṣṇa when he says, "Pure mind, pure buddhi and pure atman are one and the same thing." (GSR: 697)

9. Self is Beyond attributes

Rāmakṛṣṇa says, "what you call 'I' is really nothing but Atman. Reason it out. Are you the body or the flesh or something else? At the end you will know that you are none of these. You are free from attributes." (GSR: 208)The satcidānanda is beyond all the attributes of māyā. It is not known through senses or mind. "One can neither comprehend nor touch the Atman. It is without qualities or attributes." (GSR: 180) "That which is Pure Atman is unattached, Māyā or avidyā, is in It. In māyā there are three gunas: sattva, rajas and tamas. These three gunas also exists in the Pure Atman. But Atman Itself is unattached...and one cannot see It." But when man forgets his real nature, he becomes the slave of māyā and gets the attributes of sattva, rajas and tamas. They steal away from self its real nature. Simultaneously, one of them, the sattva, is helping in nature. It helps a person to achieve the destination. But as the real self is beyond attributes, the sattva will all disappear at the time of realization." (GSR: 582) "Under the spell of God's māyā man forgets his true nature. He forgets that he is heir to the infinite glories of his Father. This divine māyā made up of three gunas. And all three are robbers; for they rob man of all his treasures and make him forget his true nature. The three gunas are sattva, rajas and tamas. Of these sattva alone points the way to God. But even sattva cannot take a man to God." (GSR: 218)

(i) Traits of people having prominence of Sattva, Rajas and Tamas

The soul having forgotten its real nature, it is under the spell of māyā. All the three attributes are there in the man, who is under the control of māyā. But one or the other attribute is prominent in a particular man. Rāmakṛṣṇa has described the characteristics of people having the prominence of the one or the other attribute. It is narrated here through different quotations from Gospel. "The characteristics of sattva, rajas and tamas are very different. Egotism, sleep, gluttony, lust, anger and the like, are the traits of people with tamas. Men with rajas entangle themselves in many activities... But a man endowed with sattva is quiet and peaceful." (GSR: 630) "That is the characteristic of rajas. It stimulates the desire to 'Lecture' and to show off one's scholarship But Sattva makes one introspective. It makes one hide one's virtues." (GSR: 413)

Further he says, "Do you know a worldly person endowed with Sattva is like? Perhaps his house is in a dilapidated condition here and there. He doesn't care to repair it. The worship hall may be strewn with pigeon droppings and the courtyard covered with moss, but he pays no attention to these things. The furniture of the house may be old; he doesn't think of polishing it and making it look neat. He doesn't care for dress at all; anything is good enough for him. But the man himself is very gentle, quiet, kind and humble; he doesn't injure anyone...Again, among the worldly (persons) there are people with the traits of rajas. Such a man has a watch and chain, and two or three rings on his fingers. The furniture of his house is all spick and span. One the walls hand portraits of the queen, the Prince of Wales, and other prominent people; the building is white washed and spotlessly clean. His wardrobe is filled with a large assortment of clothes; even the servants have their livery and all that...The traits of a worldly man endowed with tamas are sleep, lust, anger, egotism and the like." (GSR: 146)

(ii) Utility of Even Tamas in Sādhanā

Though the self is beyond attributes, the sattva can help man to reach the destination. In the same way, tams can also be utilized for the cause. "If you can give a spiritual turn to your tamas, you can realize God with its help. Force your demand on God. He is by no means a stranger to you. He is indeed your very own...Again, you see, the quality of tamas can be used for the welfare of others." (GSR: 147) Rāmakṛṣṇa's thinking is positive, wide and all-inclusive. So, he advices to take positive advantage of tamas too. In another context also he shows his attitude of taking everything as positive. As everything is created by God, everything can be made meaning. As he has said that, "In His māyā there exists avidyā as well as vidyā. Darkness is needed too. It reveals all the more the glory of light. There is no doubt that anger, lust and greed are evil. Why, then, has God created them? In order to create saints. A man becomes a Saint by conquering the senses." (GSR: 97) In this way he also takes tams as the means to achieve the state of the real self which is beyond attributes (Guṇātīta). Still other characteristics of a guṇātīta person he narrated. "In some people spiritual consciousness has already been awakened but they have special mark. They do not enjoy hearing or talking about anything but God." (GSR: 205)

10. The plurality of the selves

Rāmakrihshna has maintained the doctrine of the plurality of the selves both at the empirical level and at the transcendental level.

(i) Empirical Level

Explaining the plurality of self at the empirical level, he has said, "All men look alike, to be sure, but they have different natures. Some have an excess of Sattva, others an excess of rajas and still others an excess of tamas." (GSR: 141) God dwells in all beings but "The manifestation of Divine Power are different in different beings." (GSR: 152) Further he says, "As the All-pervading Spirit He exists in all beings, even in the ant. But the manifestations of His Power are different in different beings; otherwise, how can one person put ten to flight, while another can't face even one?" (GSR: 104) and "God has given to some greater power than to others. In one man you see it as the light of a lamp, in another, as the light of a torch." (GSR: 249)

(ii) Transcendental Level

The above mentioned plurality of the selves is maintained even in the state of liberation. The state of liberation is called the state of a vijñānī by Rāmakṛṣṇa. In that state the liberated one has one to one relation with the God. This is possible only when the plurality of selves is accepted. Vijñānī talks with God. Rāmakṛṣṇa explains this metaphorically. "The man who knows that God exits is called a jñānī. A jñānī is like one who knows beyond a doubt that a log of wood contains firs. But a vijñānī is he who lights the log, cooks over the fire and is nourished by the food." (GSR: 476) As well as "The vijñānī sees that the Reality which is nirguṇa, without attributes, is also saguṇa, with attributes." (GSR: 103) And "The vijñānī accepts both God with form and the formless, both the personal God and the impersonal." (GSR: 802) Not only that, Rāmakṛṣṇa explains the relation of liberated soul with God in another way. "The vijñānī always sees God." (GSR: 477) Further he says, "The vijñānī enjoys the bliss of God in a richer way." (GSR: 478) Describing this state of vijñānī, Rāmakṛṣṇa believes that vijñānī talks with God, sees God, and the talk or sight can be possible only with one of many vijñānī. This state of vijñānī is the goal of every human being. This shows that in this state also there remains the independence of all selves. Thus, it is seen that at the transcendental level also Rāmakṛṣṇa believes in the plurality of selves.

11. Types of Men

Rāmakṛṣṇa explains the types of man through five different dimensions, which are: (1) Four classes of man, (2) Four group of seekers, (3) Two classes of Yogi, (4) Three levels of devotees, and (5) Two classes of selves. Before narrating the classifications precisely in his own words, it is desirable to present it through the following table:

(1) Four classes of man

(i) Bound
(ii) Seeker
(iii) Liberated
(iv) Ever free

(2) Four group of seekers

(i) Pravartaka
(ii) Sādhaka
(iii) Siddha
(iv) Siddha of Siddhas

(3) Two classes of Yogi

(i) Bahudaka
(ii) kuciṭaka

(4) Three levels of devotees

(i) Inferior
(ii) Mediocre
(iii) Superior

(5) Two classes of selves

(i) Jīvakoi
(ii) Iśvarakoṭi

(1) Four classes of Man

Man may be divided into four classes: those bound by the fetters of the world, the seekers after liberation, the liberated and the ever-free.

(i) Those in bondage are sunk in worldliness and forgetful of God. Not even by mistake do they think of God.

Non-awareness of the self

Among all, he describes the characteristics of bound people. 630-31 "There are still another classes and kinds of people. For instance, there are those who are internally free, those who have attained liberation, those who struggle for liberation and those entangled in the world. So many varieties of men?...the souls that are entangled, involved in worldliness, never come to their sense. They lie in the net but are not even conscious that they are entangled...The entangled souls repeat those very actions that make them suffer so much...The entangled creatures, attached to worldliness, talked only of worldly things in the hour of death." (GSR: 630-631)

"The spiritual wisdom of worldly people is seen only on rare occasions...Worldly people cannot the name of God, but there is no zeal behind it...Worldly people have no grit. If they succeed in an undertaking, it is all right, but if they don't succeed, it scarcely bothers them at all." (GSR: 1942: 208)

Lust and Greed

"The bound souls are tied to the world by the fetters of 'woman and gold'. The bound souls never think of God. If they get any leisure they indulge in idle gossip and foolish talk and they engage in fruitless work. If you ask one of them the reason, he answers 'oh, I cannot keep still, so I am making a hedge'." (GSR: 87)

"They are indeed bound souls who constantly dwell with 'woman and gold' and do not think of God even for a moment." (GSR: 206)

Pig-satisfaction

"A bound creature is immersed in worldliness, in 'woman and gold', having gone deep into the mire of degradation. But, still he believes he is quiet happy and secure. The liberated and the seeker after liberation, look on the world as a deep well. They do not enjoy it. Therefore, after the attainment of knowledge, the realization of God, some give up their bodies. But such a thing is rate indeed.

"A bound soul may have realized that there is no substance to the world that the world is like a hog plum, only stone and skin – but still he cannot give it up and turn his mind to God...There is another characteristic of the bound soul. If you remove him from his worldly surroundings to a spiritual environment, he will pine away." (GSR: 165)

Misery and agony

The bound creatures, entangled in worldliness, will not come to their senses at all. They suffer misery and agony, they face so many dangers, and yet they will not wake u A man of worldly nature suffers so much sorrow and affliction, but he forgets it all in a few days and beings his old life ever again." (GSR: 165)

(ii) The seekers after liberation want to free themselves from attachment to the world. Some of them succeed and others do not.

"All men may look alike from the outside, but some of them have fillings of 'condensed milk'...The desire to know God, ecstatic love of Him, and such other spiritual qualities are the 'condensed milk'." (GSR: 232)

(iii) The liberated souls such as Sādhus and Mahatmas, are not entangled in the world, in 'woman and gold' Crust and greed. Their minds are free from worldliness. Besides they always meditate on the Lotus Feet of God.

"The Paramahaṃsa is like a five-year old child. He sees everything filled with consciousness." (GSR: 490)

"He cannot distinguish between a stranger and a relative. He is not particular about worldly relationship...He doesn't keep any track of his whereabouts. He sees everything as Brahman. He is indifferent to his own movements. Sometimes, the Paramahaṃsa behaves like a madman." (GSR: 491)

"A Paramahaṃsa is always conscious that God alone is real and all else illusory." (GSR: 699)

"But a Paramahaṃsa is beyond the three gunas. Though they exist in him, yet they are practically non-existent. Like a child, he is not under the control of any of the gunas...The Paramahaṃsa realizes that all these – good and bad, virtue and vice, real and unreal – are only the glories of God's māyā. But these are very deep thoughts. One realizing this cannot keep an organization together or anything like that." (GSR: 250)

"He who has surrendered his body, mind and innermost self to God is surely a holy man." (GSR: 327)

"There are two classes of Paramahaṃsas, one affirming the formless Reality and the other affirming God with form. But those Paramahaṃsas who believe in God with form keep the love of God even after attaining knowledge of Brahman, so that they may teach spiritual truths to others...these perfected souls describe to others the various spiritual disciplines by which they have realized God. They do this only to teach others and to help them in spiritual life." (GSR: 500)

"There are two types of Paramahaṃsas : the jñānī and the premī. The jñānī is self-control; he feels that it is enough to have knowledge for his own self. The premī, like Shukdeva, after attaining his own realization, teaches men." (GSR: 679)

(iv) Among the ever free we may count sages like Narada. They live in the world for the good of others, to teach men spiritual truth.

"There is a class of devotees, the Nityasiddhas, the ever-perfect; from their very birth they seek God. They do not enjoy anything of the world...Those who are born as the companions of an Incarnation of God are eternally perfect." (GSR: 563)

"Narendra and the people of this type belong to the class of the ever free. They are never entangled in the world. When they grow a little older, they feel the awakening of inner consciousness and go directly towards God. They come to the world only to teach others." (GSR: 88)

"Those who are eternally free do not have to enter worldly life. Their desire for enjoyment has been satisfied with their very birth." (GSR: 386)

"Suka and other Sages stood on the shore of this Ocean of Brahman and saw and touched the water. According to one school of thought they never plunged into it. Those who do, cannot come back to the world again." (GSR: 102)

"Free souls are not under the control of 'woman and gold'...Then there is the class of the ever-perfect. They are born in each life with their spiritual consciousness already awakened." (GSR: 206)

"None but the Isvarkotis can return to the plane of relative consciousness after attaining Samādhi. Some ordinary men attain Samādhi through spiritual discipline, but they do not come back." (GSR: 237)

"Then there are devotees who are beyond the three gunas. They are eternally devoted to God, like Narada." (GSR: 481)

"Some souls realize God without practicing any spiritual discipline. They are called nityasiddha, eternally perfect. Those who have realized God through austerity, japa; and the like are called sādhanā siddha, perfect through spiritual discipline. Again, there are those called kṛpāsiddha, perfect through divine grace. There is also a class of devotees, the hathatsiddha, that is to say, those who have suddenly attained God-vision. There is still another class of devotee, the svapnasiddha, who have had the vision of God in a dream." (GSR: 483)

(2) Four groups of seekers

"According to Vaiṣṇavas the aspirant and seers of God may be divided into different groups: There are the Pravartaka, the Sādhaka, the Siddha and the Siddha of the Siddhas.

(i) He who just has set foot on the pạth may be called Pravartaka.

(ii) He may be called Sādhaka who has for some time been practicing spiritual disciplines, such as worship, japa, meditation and the chanting of God's name and glories.

(iii) He may be called Siddha who known from his inner experience that God exists.

(iv) There is another type, known as the Siddha of the Siddhas, the supremely perfect.

A Siddha has undoubtedly attained God, but the 'supremely perfect' has known God very intimately." (GSR: 114)

(3) Two classes of Yogis

"There are two classes of yogis: the Bahudakas and the kuciṭakas. The Bahudakas roam about visiting various holy places and have not yet found peace of mind. But the Kutichakas, having visited all the sacred place, have quieted their minds. Feeling serene and peaceful, they settle down in one place and no longer move about. In that one place they are happy, they don't feel the need of going to any sacred place. If one of them ever visits a place of pilgrimage, it is only for the purpose of new inspiration." (GSR: 128)

(4) Three levels of devotees

"If a man really has that knowledge, then he is indeed liberated though living in a body...there are different levels among the devotees of God: superior, mediocre and inferior...The inferior devotee says, 'God exists, but He is very far off, up there in heaven'. The mediocre devotee says, 'God exists in all beings as life and consciousness'. The superior devotee says: 'It is God Himself who has become every thing, whatever I see is only a form of God. It is He alone who has become māyā, the universe and all living beings. Nothing exists but God.

A man who has seen God sometimes behaves like a madman. He laughs, weeps, dances and sings. Sometimes he behaves like a child, a child five years old-guileless, generous, without vanity, unattached to anything, not under the control of any of the gunas, always blissful. Sometimes he behaves like a ghoul: he doesn't differentiate between things pure and things impure; he sees no difference...between things clean and the things unclean. And sometimes he is like an inert thing, staring vacantly, he cannot do any work; he cannot strive for anything." (GSR: 265)

"There are three kinds of devotees: superior, mediocre and inferior. The inferior devotee says,-'God is out there'. According to him God is different from His creation. The mediocre devotee says, 'God is the Aṃtaryāmī, the Inner Guide. God dwells in everyone's heart'. The mediocre devotee sees God in the heart. But the superior devotee sees that God alone has become everything He alone has become the twenty four cosmic principles. He finds that everything, above and below, is filled with God." (GSR: 396,909)

"There are three kinds of sādhus: good, mediocre and bad. The good sādhu makes no effort to get his food the dandies, among others, belong to the mediocre and bad classes. To get food the mediocre sādhu will knock at the door of a house and say, 'Namo nārāyaṇa'. The bad sādhu starts a quarrel if he doesn't get his alms...The good sādhu behaves like a python. He sits in one place and the food comes to him." (GSR: 656)

(5) Two classes of selves

"There are two classes of devotees (selves): Jīvakoṭis or ordinary men and Iśvarakoṭi's, or Divine Messengers." (GSR: 707)

"There is a great difference between the Iśvarakoṭi and an ordinary man. An Iśvarakoṭi cannot commit sin." (GSR: 951)

"The Incarnation of God belongs to the class of the Iśvarakoṭis. They roam about in the open spaces. They never imprisoned in the world, never entangled by it. Their ego is not the 'thick ego' of worldly people...though they have a human body, they are always united with God... (they can go to Samādhi and can come back from there)... though established in Samādhi, they can again descend to the worldly plane." (GSR: 760)

"There is a vast difference between the jīva and Iśvara. Through worship and austerity, a jīva can at the most attain Samādhi; but he can not come down from that state. On the other hand, an Incarnation of God can come down from Samādhi." (GSR: 767)

"The iśvarakoṭis – Divine. Incarnations for instance can liberate themselves whenever they want to; but the Jīvakoṭis cannot. Jīvakoṭis are imprisoned by 'woman and gold'." (GSR: 777)

"An Incarnation of God or one born with some of the characteristics of an Incarnation is called an Iśvarakoṭi. An ordinary man is called a jīva or Jīvakoṭi. By dint of Sādhanā a Jīvakoṭi can realize God; but after Samādhi, he cannot come back to the plane of relative consciousness...The Iśvarakoṭi...he can climb and come down." (GSR: 749)

12. Rāmakṛṣṇa on the Kuṇḍalini Yoga

Rāmakṛṣṇa has tried to explain the spiritual development of man through the Kuṇḍalini yoga's concept of six centers and the three principle nerves. Its narration in his own words is as under:

"The Vedas speak of seven planes where the mind dwells. When the mind is immersed in worldliness it dwells in the three lower planes – at the navel, the organ of generation and the organ of evacuation. In that state the mind loses all its higher visions–it broods only on 'woman and gold'. The forth plane of the kind is at the heart. When the mind dwells there, one has first glimpse of spiritual consciousness. One sees light all around. Such a man, perceiving the divine light, becomes speechless with wonder" (GSR: 150)

"There is much similarity between the seven 'planes' described in the Vedānta and the six 'centres' of Yoga. The first three planes of the Vedas may be compared to the first three Yogic centers, namely Mulādhāra, Svādhiṣhāna and Maṇipura. With ordinary people the mind dwells in these three planes, at the organs of evacuation and generation, and at the navel. When mind ascends to the fourth plane, the centre designated in Yoga as Anāhata, it sees the individual soul as a flame. Besides, it sees light... When the mind rises to the fifth plane, the aspirant wants to hear only about God. This is the Viśuddha centre of Yoga. The sixth plane and the centre known by the yogi as ājñā are one and the same. When the mind rises there, the aspirant sees God. But still there is a barrier between God and the devotee... After passing the six centres the aspirant arrives at the seventh plane. Reaching it, the mind merges in Brahman. The individual soul and the Supreme Soul become one. The aspirant goes into Samādhi. His consciousness of the body disappears. He loses the knowledge of the outer world. He does not see the manifold any more. His reasoning comes to a stop. (GSR: 245)

"Īḍā, Piṅgalā and Suṣumnā are the three principle nerves. All the lotuses are located in the Suṣumnā. They are formed of consciousness. The Kuṇḍalini lies in the lotus of the Mulādhāra. That lotus has fourteen petals. The Primordial Energy resides in all bodies as the Kuṇḍalini...The Kuṇḍalini is speedily awakened if one follows the path of bhakti. God cannot be seen unless She is awakened. Sing earnestly and secretly in solitude: Waken, O Mother! O Kuṇḍalini, whose nature is Bliss Eternal!" (GSR: 362-363)

13. God and The Problem of Evil

While describing the metaphysical attributes of Ultimate Reality, we have seen that It is Omnipotent in the fullest sense of the term. Again, as he has no history, he enters into it and takes up the responsibility of the moral governorship simply through grace and benevolence. We are, thus, brought to the consideration of the question: if God is both benevolent and omnipotent, how is it that He allows the presence of evil in the world?

Rāmakṛṣṇa has not solved the problem of evil by declaring the unreality of evil. The fact of evil is admitted by him. Someone asked, Why God created wicked people? Rāmakṛṣṇa answered, "His will, His play. In His māyā there exists avidyā as well as vidyā. Darkness is needed too. It reveals all the more the glory of light. There is no doubt that anger, lust and greed are evil. Why, then, has God created them? In order to create saints. A man becomes a Saint by conquering the senses." (GSR: 97)

(i) Law of Karma and Freedom of Will

Rāmakṛṣṇa believes in the law of karma as the law of God. This law is based on the acceptance of both, the freedom of will of the individual and his responsibility to bare its fruits. Those who freely perform good actions get pleasure or happiness as the fruit or result of their actions. Those who perform bad actions get sufferings as the fruit or result of their actions. Rāmakṛṣṇa has expressed in very briefly this law by saying, "Sin begets its own result. This is God's law." (GSR: 97) "An action can not fail to produce its result...if you commit a sin, you must bear its fruits." (GSR: 369)

Again, Rāmakṛṣṇa has elaborately explained in the following passage the law of karma and the suffering that results from freely performed bad actions:

"No doubt a man experiences a little of the effect; but much of it is cancelled by the power of God's name. a man was born blind of an eye. This was his punishment for a certain misdeed he had committed in his past birth, and the punishment was to remain him for six more births. He, however, took a bath in the Ganges, which gives one, liberation. This meritorious action could not cure his blindness, but it saved him from his future births." (GSR: 951) The reality of evil, however, does not put any limitation upon God's benevolence or omnipotence because the presence of evil in the world, according to Rāmakṛṣṇa is neither because of not in spite of God.

(ii) Good and Evil

According to Rāmakṛṣṇa, "Good and evil apply to jīva, the individual soul, as do righteousness and unrighteousness but Brahman is not at all affected by them." (GSR: 101) He accepts the individual freedom of will in all human actions. He has said that "The thing is that everyone must reap the result of his past Karma." (GSR: 275) The material cause of the diversities and difficulties of the environment in which the self is put is the free actions of the self. God is only operative cause of these. Thus, the existence of evil is not due to God, but owes its origination to the freedom of moral actions of the finite self. Evil is, thus, to use Śrī Aurobindo's words, "a by-product of the world movement." According to Rāmakṛṣṇa it has significance also.

Rāmakṛṣṇa accepts both – Vidyāśakti and Avidyāśakti of God. But God respect the freedom of will of soul. "People act according to their inherent tendencies." (GSR: 459) Thus, it is not true that evil is because of God. "There is no doubt that virtue and vice exist in the world. But God himself is unattached to them... the very nature of God's creation is that good and evil, righteousness and unrighteousness, will always exist in the world." (GSR: 246) In other words he says, "It is God alone who has planted in man's mind what the 'Englishman' calls free will. People who have not realized God would become engaged in more and more sinful actions if God had not planted in them the notion of free will. Sin would have increased if God had not made the sinner feel that he alone was responsible for his sin. (GSR: 379)

It, however, does not follow that evil is there in spite of God, because even when soul chooses to work for the actualization of evil, its activities need to be supported by God. Ultimately it is God's will that works. But God fulfills the need of soul. It is His greatness that even though He possesses unlimited sovereign powers, He not only tolerates, but also sustains even those activities which can not be approved by Him. Such greatness can be shown by Incarnations or Iśvarakoṭi. He would, therefore, agree with Campbell Frazer's remark: "To say that if God is perfect, free agent can not produce volitions that they ought not to do is not to vindicate divine perfection but to destroy it."(Frazer A. C., 1894-96: 320)

Rāmakṛṣṇa has conceived the relation between God and evil in such a way that it satisfies the needs of both the ethical transcendence and the metaphysical immanence of God. We have seen that from the point of view of ethics, God of Rāmakṛṣṇa completely transcends evil.

But from the point of view of metaphysics, just like any other thing of the universe, evil also requires God as its 'causa immanens'.

(iii) Law of Karma and Grace of God

Rāmakṛṣṇa says, "He (a bound soul) can free himself from attachment to 'woman and gold' if, by the grace of God, he cultivates a spirit of strong renunciation." (GSR: 165) Thus, the grace of God can reduced the effect of action, if one performs sound discipline. According to Rāmakṛṣṇa, the will of God is rooted in righteousness by which He dispenses justice, in accordance with the moral worthiness of the free doer. This, however, does not mean that God is vindictive. God of Rāmakṛṣṇa is essentially redeemer. As God is redeemer, He does not always follow the law of retribution which requires as exact mathematical recompense for each one of the actions of the self. Such a law is an endless seesaw, and leaves no scope for the hope of release. Therefore, Rāmakṛṣṇa has said that "If a man has faith in God, then even if he has committed the most heinous sins–such as killing a cow, a Brahmin, or a women–he will certainly be saved through his faith. Let him only say to God, 'O Lord? Will not repeat such an action', and need not be afraid of anything." (GSR: 87)

Not only that, God gives the assurance for positive growth of jīva. "It is as if the Divine Mother said to the human mind in confidence, with a sign from Her eye, 'go and enjoy the world'. How can one blame the mind? The mind can disentangle itself from worldliness if, through Her grace, She makes it turn toward Herself. Only then does it become devoted to the lotus fee of the Divine Mother." (GSR: 137) Thus, one who receives the grace of God is not only release form the burden of all the past actions, but also attains positive happiness.

(iv) Karma and Kṛpā

This view does not involve any kind of dualism between karma and kṛpā, because Rāmakṛṣṇa has emphasized their harmonious interplay. God in Rāmakṛṣṇa's views, essentially merciful and actively responsive, His redemptive grace is readily available. This, however, does not mean that the grace of God is arbitrarily granted. Rāmakṛṣṇa clearly says that "God doesn't take entire responsibility for a devotee unless the devotee is completely intoxicated with ecstatic love for Him." And in that state, a person will feel, "I am the machine and God is the operator, I act as He makes me act, I speak as He makes me speak." (GSR: 176)

Thus, we find that Rāmakṛṣṇa has interpreted law of karma and grace as interdependent. In Judaism which is an ethical and monotheistic religion, the law predominates, and there is no place for God's grace. In the devotionalism of Vallabha, which is the sect of Vaiṣṇavism, the law is subordinate to the principle of God's grace. But in Rāmakṛṣṇa both grace and law find their legitimate place. And therefore, here the provision Is made for both, the stability of moral order and the guarantee of attaining salvation.

(v) Nicol Macnicol's criticism

In his thesis for the Doctor of Letters, Macnicol has maintained that the most obvious and commanding feature of every Indian religion is the acceptance of the doctrine of karma, which as a system of legalism "inevitably and invariably crushes out hope from the soul." (Macnicol N., 1915: 230)

Again Macnicol has remarked that "The God of its Theism (Indian Theism) never triumphs completely over this rival and had to be content with divided empire." Further he has said, "Never, we may say, never in the whole course of Indian theistic development this antimony fully resolved. Never, never is the attempt resolutely maid to re-think the karma doctrine so as to personalize it, and give it a content more fully ethical and so more reconcilable with Theism."

We may say that above mentioned criticism of Indian Theism by Macnicol expresses either Macnicol's prejudice against Indian religions or his ignorance about it. In Major Indian religions (Hinduism, Jainism and Buddhism) the law of karma is not propounded as a 'rigid system of legalism.' Hinduism regards prayer to God as a very important religious karma resulting in obtaining God's grace, which would make the devotee free from suffering as a result of one's free karma. This makes it clear that the law of karma is not the rival of God. The law of karma is God's law and without violating His own law He can be graceful to in answering to a devotee's prayer. This action of God shows that God is the supreme ruler of the world and He rules the world as a very kind and loving Moral Governor of the world.

What we have said above, the importance of prayer as a free action of a devotee and getting God's grace as a result is true not only for Hinduism but also for Jainism and Buddhism. Though theoretically these two religions are atheist, they don't believe in God at all and very much emphasis the law of karma. In spite of their theoretical atheism, the practitioners of these two religions do pray for forgivenness and getting grace of Tirthaṅkara like Mahavir and Gautam Buddha. This historical facts about Jainism and Buddhism clearly proves that there can be any religion without God, because, to lead a religious like is to lead a God-centric life.

It is very necessary to make it clear that all that has been said above about Macnicol's misunderstanding of Indian Theism, represents Rāmakṛṣṇa's point of view. For Rāmakṛṣṇa, God is the only omnipotent ruler of the world and His redemptive grace is infinite.

Niclo Macnicol had very rightly observed that "The power of Theism can only be revealed where these bonds are broken and where the idea is revealed of a God whose will, which is supreme, is love and righteousness." We have seen above that the theism advocated by Rāmakṛṣṇa very much posseses the power of theism expected by Macnicol. Hence, if Macnicol had known this power of Indian theism, then, he would not have made the above mentioned criticism of Indian theism.

(vi) Past Actions and Rebirth

According to Rāmakṛṣṇa, each one of the innumerable selves is having a beginningless association with the body constitutes of the prārabdha karma. On asking a question: 'Why doesn't one get rid of the World?' he answered, "It is due to the samskaras, inborn tendencies. Repeated births in this world of māyā make one believe that māyā is real...how powerful inborn tendencies are!" (GSR: 585) In accordance with these karmas, the self is placed by God into an environment which enables it to experience the fruits of its actions.

Rāmakṛṣṇa has said that "The thing is that everyone must reap the result of his past Karma. One must admit the influence of tendencies inherited from past births and the result of the Prārabdha Karma." (GSR: 275) Again, he accepts the continuity of spiritual progress even after death. "One cannot be guileless without a great deal of spiritual discipline in previous births. A hypocritical and calculating mind can never attain God." (GSR: 448) And "One must have done something, some form of tapasyā, either in this life or in another." (GSR: 542) Not only that, the idea of Yogabhraṣa from Gītā is also narrated by him. "To love God one must be born with good tendencies...If a man slips from the path of yoga, then he is reborn in a prosperous family and starts again his spiritual practice for the realization of God." (GSR: 533)

The enjoyment of worldly objects is not, however, the only aim of creation. Another aim of creation is to enable the self to endeavor for its release. Rāmakṛṣṇa remarks, "As long as you do not feel that God is the Master, you must come back to the world, you must be born again and again. There will be no rebirth when you can truly say, 'O God, Thou art the Master'." (GSR: 308) As well as "As long as a man remains ignorant, so long will he be born. But after attaining knowledge, he will not have to come back to this earth or to any other plane of existence...if a man is boiled in the fire of knowledge, he will not be used to for new creation, He is liberated." (GSR: 416)

The possibility of these endeavors presupposes the freedom of the self to go against its own empirical nature, which, being a part of its environment, is determined by its past actions. A man gradually attains the liberation. It may appear as a sudden achievement, but it is not the case. It is achieved after many births. "The truth is that a man succeeds to a great extent because of tendencies inherited from his previous births. People think he has attained the goal all of a sudden...In his last birth a man is endowed with sattva. His mind is directed to God. He longs for God. He withdraws his mind from worldly things." (GSR: 605)

Rāmakṛṣṇa says, "Some acquire raga-bhakti directly. It is innate in them. They have it from their very childhood." (GSR: 172) Here also it is accepted that the characteristics of previous birth are forwarded to next birth. Rāmakṛṣṇa pointed out that, "The truth is that one must reap the result of the Prārabdha Karma. The body remains as long as the result of past actions does not completely wear away." (GSR: 276)

The principle of karma has thus, to use Dr. Rādhākṛṣṇan's words, "two aspects, a retrospective and a prospective, continuity with the past and creative freedom of the self." Rāmakṛṣṇa has not only accepted both these aspects, but also emphasized the power of the self to use its freedom.

Giving an argument for the doctrine of rebirth, Rāmakṛṣṇa has said, "Many people have spoken about reincarnation, therefore I cannot disbelieve it." (GSR: 153)

(vii) Rebirth only upto the attainment of liberation

He considers the world as a stage to perform one's actions and thereby to end the possibility of rebirth. Explaining this Rāmakṛṣṇa has said, "When a man dies after attaining knowledge, he doesn't have to go to another plane of existence; he isn't born again. But as long as he has not attained knowledge, as long as he has not realized God, he must come back to the life of this earth; he can never escape it. For such a person there is a hereafter. A man is liberated after attaining knowledge, after realizing God. For him there is no further coming back to earth." (GSR: 668) When man is born, the world as a platform for attaining liberation is ready, and the means to achieve is to eliminate the ego. "A man achieves neither knowledge nor liberation as long as he has egotism. He comes again and again to the world." (GSR: 633)

It is said in the Indian scriptures that after the sādhanā in many births, one gets liberation. (Aneka janma saṃsiddhaḥ tato yāti parāṃ gatim..) This statement is well accepted by Rāmakṛṣṇa. "There is such a thing as inborn tendencies. When a man has performed many good actions in his previous births, in the final birth he becomes guileless." (GSR: 783)

14. Rāmakṛṣṇa on Voluntary Death

The yogis and saints sometimes, after realization, voluntarily leave the body before the natural death of the body. Rāmakṛṣṇa thinks it as a different from suicide. "Suicide is a heinous sin, undoubtedly. A man who kills himself must return again and again to this world and suffer its agony. But I don't call it suicide if a person leaves his body after having the vision of God. There is no harm in giving up one's body that way after attaining knowledge some people give up their bodies." (GSR: 164)

15. Importance of Present Thinking For Liberation

Another important point to be noted is that, Rāmakṛṣṇa believes that man takes rebirth according to his last thought at the time of death. It is true that whatever one thinks at that time, accordingly his next birth will be. But the important thing what Rāmakṛṣṇa says is that whatever you think presently, so will be your thought at the last moment. Therefore, it is true, "ante yā mati sā gati." But 'ante mati'-thought at the last moment will be the thought what one thinks now and here. "According to Gītā you will become in the next life what you think of in the hour of death…That is why day and night a man should practice worship, Japa, meditation and other spiritual exercise. Only then, by virtue of practice, will he be able to think of God in hour of death. If one dies thus, thinking of God, one will acquire God's nature…'As long as a man does not realize God, he will return to the world'." (GSR: 583,820,841) Thus, it is very important to continuously remembering God in order to make the present thinking continue till the time of death.

16. Concept of Liberation

(i) The Goal of Life is to Cultivate Love For God

Hoffding has observed that "every religious standpoint gathers up into its conception of God the highest known values." (Hoffding H., 1906: 61) For Rāmakṛṣṇa, this observation completely holds good. For, he believes that the only goal of human life is to cultivate love for God. Because he believes that the highest value from religious point of view is instance love for God. Regarding love of God as bhakti, he has written, "The aim of human life is to attain bhakti." (GSR: 161) Rāmakṛṣṇa asserts this to the extent that God will not let you go until to attain to liberation.

We have seen that the Ultimate Reality of Rāmakṛṣṇa is not only formless substance, but also an embodied substratum, possessing all auspicious qualities. To achieve the realization of God is the highest value. "The vision of God is the only goal of human life." (GSR: 331) Thus Rāmakṛṣṇa has described the Ultimate Reality not only as the metaphysical ground, but also as the highest goal of the endeavours of the finite self. This can be achieved through the non-attachment for worldly phenomena and through positive afford to cultivate love for God. This can be attained by prayers and the company of holy men. Rāmakṛṣṇa says, "Good company begets yearning for God. It begets love of God." (GSR: 96)

(ii) Overcoming of All Worldly Desires

Rāmakṛṣṇa believes that "No salvation is possible for a man as long as he has desire, as long as he hankers for worldly things. Therefore, fulfill all your desires regarding food, clothes and sex." (GSR: 534) It is his belief that the desire which becomes hindrance to the spiritual path, and which is legitimate, should be fulfill in order to come out of it. Because, hankering for the desire obstructs man from his progress. But the important thing here to be noted is that all that he told about fulfilling the desires is for the devotees, who had chosen the path of householders. On the other hand, sādhaka, who wants to live a singly single, God centered devoted life are advised not even to look at the picture of a woman. Thus, Rāmakṛṣṇa does not neglect any one of both the paths and recognize both. But he considers the desires as the disease to be cured. He says "He (God) will free us when the disease is cured." (GSR: 185)

(iii) God's Will Granting Liberation

We had seen earlier about the ethical transcendence and metaphysical immanence of God, in which it was cleared that all is done through the power of God only. Rāmakṛṣṇa believes that "Both worldliness and liberation depend on God's will. It is God alone who has kept man in world in a state of ignorance; and man will be free when God, of His own sweet will calls him to Himself...When the time comes for setting a man free, God makes him seek the company of holy man. Further, it is God who makes him restless for spiritual life." (GSR: 225)

Further he says, "A man becomes liberated even in this life when he knows that God is the Doer of all things...Not even leaf moves except by the will of God. Where is man's free will? All are under the will of God." (GSR: 159) The liberated one who will be free from the cycle of birth and rebirth. "When the embodied soul says: 'O God I am not the doer, Thou art the Doer. I am the machine and Thou art its operator', only then does its suffering of worldly life come to an end;

only then does it obtain liberation. It no longer has to be reborn in this world of action...If you find a person free from ego, then know for certain that he has seen God." (GSR: 45)

(iv) Qualification For Liberation

Rāmakṛṣṇa explains about the nature of the mind of a person who is qualified for the attainment of the vision of God, that is, liberation. He says, "He is unknowable by the mind engrossed in worldliness...But He is knowable by the pure mind and pure intelligence—the mind and intelligence that have not the slightest trace of attachment. Pure mind, Pure Intelligence, Pure Atman, is one and the same thing." (GSR: 524) Liberation is possible for a person whose mind has become pure. "The mind and intellect become pure the moment they are free from attachment to 'woman and gold'. The pure mind and pure intellect are one and the same. God is known by pure mind." (GSR: 726)

Further he clarifies the difference between pure and impure mind. The mind filled with the consciousness of woman and gold is impure mind and that must be died in order to attain liberation. "A man attains Brahmajñāna as soon as his mind is annihilated. With the annihilation of the mind dies ego, which says 'I', 'I'." (GSR: 776) Here the wicked ego should be annihilated, then only the liberation is possible. He says, "God is far far away from the worldly minded. But God is very near the man nay within a distance of three cubits – whose mind is free from worldliness." (GSR: 784)

(v) Nature and Attitude of Ego in Liberation

In the state of liberation also there remains the ego. But that is of the 'ripe ego'. "Only the ego that is attached to 'woman and gold' is harmful. But the ego of that feels it is the servant of God does no harm to anybody. Neither does the ego of a child, which is not under the control of any guna...With this kind of ego, one is able to love satcidananda. It is impossible to get rid of the ego. Therefore it should be made to feel that it is the devotee of God, His servant." (GSR: 788) This 'ripe ego' is not harmful to the self. Again he says, "The 'ego of knowledge' and the 'ego of Devotion' can do no harm; it is the wicked I' that is harmful. After realizing God a man becomes like a child. There is no harm in the 'ego of a child'." (GSR: 940)

Rāmakṛṣṇa believes that the attitude of one who has realized God is that he feels: "I am machine and Thou a lord; art the operator. I am house and thou art the indweller. I am the chariot and thou art the Driver. I move as Thou movest me I speak a Thau maketh me speak." (GSR: 211) God is not known until one leaves the ego. "Give up the ego that makes you feel, 'I am the doer. I am teaching people'... Give up 'wicked ego'...One does not develop the 'divine ego' as long as one retains the 'wicked ego'...There is a greater accumulation of divinity in man." (GSR: 405)

17. Bondage and Liberation

(i) Nature of a Bound Soul

According to Rāmakṛṣṇa, man is slave of three things and that is the bondage. "How can a man living in the midst of 'woman and gold' realize God? It is very hard for him to lead an unattached life. First, he is the slave of his wife, second of money and third, of the master whom he serves." (GSR: 710) Further, he defines bondage in different terms. "There are eight fetters with which man is bound: shame, hatred, fear, pride of caste, hesitation, the desire to conceal and so forth." He believes that there is lust and greed which are the basic causes of bondage. "Woman and gold is the cause of bondage. Woman and gold alone constitutes saṃsāra, the world. It is woman and gold that keeps one from seeing God...When it is removed one attains Chidananda, consciousness and bliss." (GSR: 438)

(ii) Nature of a Liberated Soul (a state of a jñānī)

Rāmakṛṣṇa narrated the nature of liberation in this way. "If one analyses oneself, one doesn't find any such thing as 'I'...In that state a man no longer finds the existence of his ego. And who is there left to seek it? Who can describe how he feels in that state–in his own pure consciousness about the real nature of Brahman? There is a sign of perfect knowledge. Man becomes silent when it is attained. Then the 'I', which may be likened to the salt doll, melts in the ocean of existence-knowledge-Bliss Absolute and becomes one with it. Not the slightest trace of distinction is left." (GSR: 148) Thus in the state of perfect knowledge, one feels identified with the supreme Brahman. "As a result of discrimination that Brahman alone is real and the world illusory, the aspirant goes into Samādhi. Then for him, the forms or attributes of God disappear altogether. Then he does not feel God to be a Person. Then he cannot describe in words what God is. And who will describe it? He who is to describe does not exist at all; he no longer finds his 'I'. To such a person Brahman is attributeless. In that state God is experienced only as consciousness, by man's inmost consciousness, He cannot be comprehended by the mind and intelligence." (GSR: 859) Explaining the state of a Vedānti, Rāmakṛṣṇa says, "According to Vedānta one has to know the real nature of one's own self. But such knowledge is impossible without the renunciation of ego...When the ego disappears in Samādhi, then one knows Brahman to be one's own inner consciousness...One must renounce the 'I'." (GSR: 387)

(iii) Nature of a Liberated Soul (a state of a vijñānī)

Here it is important to note that according to Rāmakṛṣṇa, this state of a jñānī is not the highest state of consciousness. The highest level is that of the state of vijñānī, in which a self has personal relation with God. Still, Rāmakṛṣṇa accepts the state of jñānī also as one type of the state of liberation. But there is also something ahead this state of consciousness. "That man is a true man whose mind dwells on God. He alone is a man whose spiritual conscious has been awakened and who is firmly convinced that God alone is real and all else illusory... So long as 'I-consciousness' exists, a man cannot go beyond the Relative. Through meditation he can negate the phenomena, following the process of 'Neti, Neti' and reach the Absolute; but nothing can really be denied as in the instance of the bel-fruit." (GSR: 851) Thus, in the highest state, he accepts all phenomena as the manifestation of the Ultimate Reality.

He classifies the state of consciousness in different levels. Initially one is aware of the 'I'. At that time the separation of self with the God is realized and jīva perform all the necessary functions for the attainment of liberation. He says, "As long as 'I-consciousness' exists, God reveals Himself to us as a Person." (GSR: 636) Then, comes the state of a jñānī, in which one feels identified with the supreme self. And lastly comes the state of a vijñānī, in which one talks with the Reality.

(iv) Nature of Jīvanamukta

According of Rāmakṛṣṇa those who have the mystical experience of self-realization and God-realization can continue to live in this world as a jīanmuktas, necessarily go beyond the sense of egoity and attachment for the worldly objects. Therefore, "Fully awakened souls are beyond virtue and vice. They realize that it is God who does everything." (GSR: 201) This however, does not mean that the mystic is allowed to do immoral actions without being responsible for them. Rāmakṛṣṇa has left no room for such misunderstanding, for he has clearly asserted that "Those whose spiritual consciousness has been awakened never make a false statement. They do not have to reason in order to shun evil. They are so full of love of God that whatever action they undertake is a good action. They are fully conscious that they are not the doers of their action but mere servants of God. They always feel: 'I am the machine and he is the Operator. I do as He does through me. I speak as He speaks through me. I move as He moves me." (GSR: 201) Thus Rāmakṛṣṇa accepts the possibility of the jīvanamukta after the achievement of egoless ness. "Māyā is nothing but the egotism of the embodied soul...If by the grace of God a man but once realizes that he is not the doer, then he at once becomes a jīvanamukta. Though living in the body, he is liberated." (GSR: 168-169)

Rāmakṛṣṇa defines the idea of jīvanamukta in this way. "If a man truly believes that God alone does everything, that He is the Operator and man the machine, then such a man is verily liberated in life... He who firmly believes that God alone is the Doer and he himself a mere instrument is a jīvanamukta, a free soul though living in a body." (GSR: 893) "The Pure Self is unattached. Both vidyā and avidyā are in it, but it is unattached. He who has attained this knowledge of Brahman is a jīanamukta; liberated while living in the body. He rightly understands that the Atman and the body are separate things. After realizing God one does not identify the Atman with the body. These two are separate." (GSR: 719)

"A man may keep this ego even after attaining Samādhi. Such a man feels either that he is a servant of God or that he is a lover of God. Shankarācārya retained the 'ego of knowledge' to teach men spiritual life. The 'servant ego', 'the knowledge ego', or the 'devotee ego' may be called the 'ripe ego'. It is different from the 'unripe ego', which makes one feel: 'I am the doer...After realizing God, a man becomes like a child five years ago. The ego of such a man may be called the 'ego of a child', the 'ripe ego'. The child is not under the control of any of the gunas. He is beyond three gunas." (GSR: 860)

The body of jīvanamukta remains because of the prārabdha karma. "The truth is that one must reap the result of the Prārabdha Karma. The body remains as long as the result of past actions does not completely wear away." (GSR: 276) Thus, the jīvanamukta passes his life either in worship and meditation upon God. "A man should reach the Nitya, the Absolute, by following the trail of the Līlā, the Relative...After realizing the Absolute, he should climb down to the Relative and live on that plane in the company of devotees, charging his mind with the love of God." (GSR: 257) Or a jīvanamukta keeps himself busy with such activities which would help as many people as possible to realize the true end of their life. "After attaining Samādhi, Narada, Sukadeva and others came down a few steps, as it were, to the plane of normal consciousness and broke their silence out of compassion for the suffering of others and to help them." (GSR: 276) Not only that "A perfect soul, even after attaining knowledge, practices devotion or observe religious ceremonies to set an example to others." (GSR: 543) "He who has realized God has obtained the fruit of Immortality. He is free from rebirth. God keeps some jñānīs in the world of māyā to be teachers of men. In order to teach others tho jñānī live in the world with the help of vidhyamāyā. It is God Himself who keeps the jñānī in the world for His work." (GSR: 669)

But it is important to note that the jnvanmukta is free from the fetters of new prārabdh karma. "The body survives with same so that they may work out their prārabdha karma or work for the welfare of others...present body remains alive as long as its momentum is not exhausted. The momentum of the actions of his previous birth, which has given rise to his present body. But future births are no longer possible." (GSR: 477) Rāmakṛṣṇa says, "Even after attaining knowledge through the guru's grace, one can very well live in the world as a Jīvanamukta." (GSR: 233) "A man can live in the world after attaining God. Then he can lead the life of detachment." (GSR: 523)

Rāmakṛṣṇa believes that when the body is there, one may have I-consciousness. But jīvanamukta has the ego, what he says, the 'ripe ego', which never harms in any way. "He who has attained God keeps only an appearance of ego; there remains in him only a semblance of anger and lust. He becomes like a child...Even after attaining Samādhi, some retain the 'servant ego' or the 'devotee ego'. The bhakta keeps this 'I – consciousness'." (GSR: 171) "There are some who come down, as it were, after attaining the knowledge of Brahman – after Samādhi–and retain the 'ego of Knowledge' or the 'ego of Devotion'...What appears in the Pure Mind is the voice of God. That which is Pure Mind is also Pure Buddhi, that again is Pure Atman, because there is nothing pure but God." (GSR: 178) Thus he asserts that "A man cannot be egoistic if he has true knowledge. In other words, in Samādhi, man becomes one with God and gets rid of his egotism...But if you see in anyone a trace of 'I-consciousness' after the attainment of true knowledge, then know that it is either the 'ego of knowledge' or the 'ego of devotion' or the 'servant ego'. It is not the 'ego of ignorance'." (GSR: 767)

(v) Characteristics of Jīvanamukta

Rāmakṛṣṇa describes the characteristics of a liberated who attains total equilibrium and balance of mind. "The man who has seen God become like a child. He is beyond the three gunas; he is unattached to any of them. He behaves like a ghoul, for he maintains the same attitude toward things holy & unholy." (GSR: 45)

Externally jīvanamukta behaves sometimes like a child, sometimes like a jñānī, and sometimes like a mad man. Rāmakṛṣṇa describes certain traits of a jīvanamukta. "Again, like a madman, he sometimes laughs and sometimes weeps. Now he dresses himself like a dandy and the next moment he goes entirely naked and roams about with his cloths under his arms. Therefore he seems to be a lunatic. Again at times he sits motionless Līlā an inert thing." (GSR: 451) Rāmakṛṣṇa says, "When a man attains the knowledge of Brahman he shows certain characteristics. The Bhāgavatam describes four of them: the state of child, of an inert thing, of a madman and of a ghoul." (GSR: 791)

4
Cosmology

1. Reality of the World

Rāmakṛṣṇa has described the impermanence of the worldly objects by saying "The real means that which is eternal, the Supreme Brahman, and the unreal means that which is non–eternal that is to say, the world." (GSR: 583) Again he has said, "The world is illusory, Brahman alone is real. The world is of the nature of magic. The magician is real but his magic is unreal." (585)

Any student of Indian Philosophy who is unaware of Rāmakṛṣṇa's comprehensive philosophical position would be led to believe on the basis of the above quoted words of Rāmakṛṣṇa, that Rāmakṛṣṇa did not believe in the reality of the world. It is therefore, very much necessary to clarity that like Indian philosophers who propound Kevāladvaita and Western Philosopher propounding Idealism, Rāmakṛṣṇa does regard the world as mere appearance of Ultimate Reality. In the above quoted passage of Rāmakṛṣṇa the word "illusory" means "impermanent". The following two passages from The Gospel of Śrī Rāmakṛṣṇa prove this point indubitably:

(1) "It (world) is unreal as long as one has not realized god. People are born and they die. This moment the world is and the next it is not. It is impermanent." (GSR: 325)

(2) According to Rāmakṛṣṇa the world is as real as the Ultimate Reality, God Himself. As he has said, "As long as one feels that Brahman exists, one must also be aware that the universe, living beings and the twenty four cosmic principles exists as well."(GSR: 343)

Thus, it is evidently clear that Rāmakṛṣṇa's philosophical position is fundamentally different from that of those Indian and Western philosophers who regard the world as unreal.

The real world is created, preserved and destroyed by God. From the point of view of God and only of God, God's activity of creation, preservation and destruction is nothing more than His play or Līlā. Rāmakṛṣṇa has clearly said, "As a child builds up his toy house and ten breaks it down, so god acts while creating, preserving and destroying the universe." (GSR: 176) Thus, according to Rāmakṛṣṇa "All this is his play, his Līlā." (GSR: 853) Again, he has said, "The līlā is real too." (GSR: 238)

Rāmakṛṣṇa believes that in the highest state of consciousness, one can not be an illusionist. But rather the world becomes the 'mansion of mirth' for a person who has realized the God. "After realizing God, one finds that He alone has become māyā. The universe and all living beings. This world is no doubt a framework of illusion, unreal as a dream. One feels that way when one discriminates following the process of 'Not this, not this'. But after the vision of God, this very world becomes 'a mansion of mirth'." (GSR: 836) Further he says, "As long as there is the ego, everything else exists. So long as the 'I' exists the Bhakta sees that it is god who has become māyā, the universe, the living beings and the twenty–four cosmic principles." (GSR: 939) Thus, according to Rāmakṛṣṇa the world is the real.

Rāmakṛṣṇa describes the reality of the world with reference to Purāṇa. He says, "There are two schools of thought. The Vedānta and the Purāṇa. According to the Vedānta this world is a 'framework of illusion'. That is to say, it is all illusory, like a dream. But according to Purāṇa, the book of devotion, god himself has become the twenty four cosmic principles...As long as god keeps the awareness of I in use, so long do sense objects exists, and we can not very well speak of the world as a dream...Hence the Bhakti scriptures describe this very world as a 'mansion of mirth'." (GSR: 243) And again he says, "This world may be a framework of illusion but it is also said that it is a mansion of mirth. Let the body remain. One can also turn this world into a mansion of mirth." (GSR: 298)

Rāmakṛṣṇa's views regarding the word as a real element, is clearly seen by considering this expression of Rāmakṛṣṇa. He says, "I accept all Brahman and also māyā, the universe and its living beings. If I accepted less, I should not get the full weight... Brahman is qualified by the universe and its living beings...he alone has become the twenty four cosmic principles." (GSR: 652)

As the activity of God with regard to the world is three-fold, (i) Creation (ii) Preservation, and (iii) Destruction of the world. In the words of Rāmakṛṣṇa, "God is engaged in three kinds of activities: Creation, Preservation and Destruction." (GSR: 209) We now proceed to explain Rāmakṛṣṇa's views on this three-fold activities one after the other.

2. Creation of the World

According to Rāmakṛṣṇa the cycle of this three-fold activities of God is "anādi" (beginningless). It can therefore, be starched into past infinitely without ever getting a stop. This being so, every time the world is created with a continuity with its past, that is, the last destruction of the world. Explaining this, Rāmakṛṣṇa has said, "All will be destroy at the time of dissolution nothing will remain. At that time the Divine Mother will gather up the seeds for the future creation... The Divine mother will take her seeds out again at the time of the new creation." (GSR: 209)

The Divine Mother mentioned in the above passage has been named as Akash by Rāmakṛṣṇa as under:

"All elements finally merge in akash. Again, at the time of creation, akash evolves into mahat and mahat into ahamkara. In this way the whole world system is evolved. It is the process of involution and evolution." (GSR: 395)

According to Rāmakṛṣṇa, "Both creation and destruction are God's māyā." (Gospel 768) Rāmakṛṣṇa defines māyā as the other form of God. He believes that as we can not separate hotness form the fire, we can not distinguish God from his māyā. God himself becomes māyā for the purpose of creation, preservation and destruction. "It is he alone who has become the universe, living beings and the twenty four cosmic principles." (GSR: 802) Twenty four cosmic principles are named as Prakṛti in Sāṅkhya Philosophy. Rāmakṛṣṇa also uses the same name. But the concepts of Prakṛti in Sāṅkhya and in Rāmakṛṣṇa are different. In Sāṅkhya, prakṛti is the material cause of the world and its existence is completely separate from Puruṣa. While in Rāmakṛṣṇa Prakṛti is the Śakti (Power) of God, which is not separate from God. "Brahman and Śakti are not different from each other."(GSR: 802)

According to Rāmakṛṣṇa, the Reality is one and the same. But when It is inactive, It is called Brahman, a formless God, while when It is active It is considered as a Śakti or Personal God or Saguṇa Brahaman, which is considered as Māyā, or primordial power by Rāmakṛṣṇa. "This divine māyā made up of three gunas...The three gunas are Sattva, Rajas and Tamas." (GSR: 218) Again he says, "Sattva preserves, rajas creates and tamas destroys. But Brahman is beyond the three gunas. It is beyond Prakṛti." (GSR: 267)

3. Order of Evolution

While describing the process of evolution of the world Rāmakṛṣṇa clearly admits that world is evolved from Divine māyā or Prakṛti made up of three gunas-Sattva, Rajas and and twenty four cosmic principles. On the basis of this we can say that Rāmakṛṣṇa would accept the following table indicating the Sāṅkhya theory of the creation or the evolution of the twenty four cosmic principles:

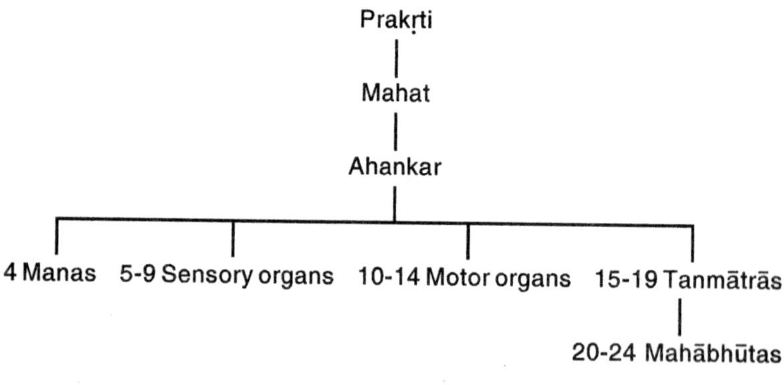

(The 25th is the Puruṣa, untouched by this evolution.)

It is important to note here that, as it is explained earlier that there is a difference between the concept of Prakṛti in Sāṅkhya philosophy and the Rāmakṛṣṇa's concept of it. The same applies to the concept of Puruṣa also. Rāmakṛṣṇa also believes that Puruṣa is untouched by the process of evolution. But the concept of Puruṣa is also different in Rāmakṛṣṇa as well as in Sāṅkhya philosophy. The concept of Puruṣa in Sāṅkhya is similar to that of the concept of self in Rāmakṛṣṇa. Rāmakṛṣṇa and Sāṅkhya both accept the plurality of jīva or self. While talking about the creation of the world Rāmakṛṣṇa uses both words, Prakṛti and Puruṣa, but there by 'Puruṣa' he means, One and the only one Brahman, which is not at all different from Prakṛti or Mahāmāyā. Where in Samkhy□s Prush and Prakṛti are fundamentally different from each other. They are their nature as well as their metaphysical status are different from each other. While even a shade of this kind of dualism is not found in Rāmakṛṣṇa' philosophy.

In addition to what has been said above about the basic difference in the philosophical position of Sāṅkhya and that of Rāmakṛṣṇa, the following description of the glory of God made by Rāmakṛṣṇa is also indicated the difference most strikingly:

(1) According to Rāmakṛṣṇa the physical things are created by God and man's psychological states are also governs by God for the preservation of the world. "God has created this universe. He has made the sun and the moon, men and beasts, and all other beings. He has provided means for their substance. He has given children parents and endowed them with love to bring them up. The lord has done so many things." (GSR: 80)

(2) And "He who has created the sun and the moon, who has put love for their children in parents, hearts, endowed noble souls with compassion, and holy men and devotees with divine love." (GSR: 108)

(3) "In this creation of god there is a variety of things, men, animals, trees, plants. Among the animals some are good, some bad. There are ferocious animals like the tiger, some trees bear fruit sweet as nectar and others bear fruit that is poisonous. Likewise among human beings, there are the good and the wicked, the holy and unholy. There are some who are devoted to god and others who are attached to the world." (GSR: 104)

4. Arguments for the Existence of God

Rāmakṛṣṇa was a mystic having intuitive vision of God and was not primarily interested in giving the arguments for the existence of God. In spite of this, we find that the following observation form sound argument for the existence of God comparable to the classical argument for the existence of God given in Western and Indian philosophy:

(1) Rāmakṛṣṇa believes that "The universe and its created beings and the twenty four cosmic principles, all exists because God exists. Nothing remains if god is eliminated." (GSR: 178) Thus, we see that Rāmakṛṣṇa refers to the existence of universe and the existence of God as the cause of the existence of the universe. This is clearly what is known as the cosmological argument for the existence of God.

(2) "One must accept the forms of God. Do you know the meaning of the image of Jagaddhātrī? She is the Bearer of the universe. Without Her support and protection the universe would fall from its place and be destroyed." (GSR: 270) This argument is very well comparable to the argument 'dhṛtyādeḥ' given a great Naiyāyika in his 'Nyāyakusumāñjali'.

In western philosophical tradition there are three well known arguments for the existence of God. (i) Ontological argument, (ii) Cosmological argument and (iii) Teleological argument. Of these, cosmological argument is clearly found in the observations of Rāmakṛṣṇa as indicated above. The Ontological argument proves the existence of God on the basis of the idea of God as a being than which nothing greater can be conceived. This basis is very much emphasized by Rāmakṛṣṇa while describing His infinitude and omnipotence. Thus, we find that Rāmakṛṣṇa has given clear basis on which can ontological argument can be formed by any good logician. The teleological argument is based on description of the systematic ongoing process of the world and purposive activities of human beings. Rāmakṛṣṇa certainly describes this basis of teleological argument which will be shown by us in the heading of the "Purpose and Preservation of the World". What will be said by us in this provides sufficient materials to give the teleological argument for the existence of God.

5. Purpose and Preservation of Creation

Rāmakṛṣṇa has indicated that God has created the world and preserves it in order to see that the purpose of creation is achieved. In his own words, "He who has created the sun and the moon, who has put love for their children in parents, hearts, endowed noble souls with compassion, and holy men and devotees with divine love." (GSR: 108)

God is regarded by Rāmakṛṣṇa as identical with His creative power, Praktiti, Māyā or Mother. Therefore, he has described the creation, preservation and purpose of the world by saying, "She (Mother) is the mother of the Universe. It is She who creates and preserves the world, who always protects Her children. And who grants whatever they desire: dharma, artha, kāma, mokṣa." (GSR: 321)

Of the four purposes namely, dharma, arth, kāma and mokṣa mentioned in the above passage, the most important purpose is mokṣa or liberation. And for attaining this is the performance of duties (dharma) is very necessary. Thus, according to Rāmakṛṣṇa the world is created and preserved in order that the human beings perform their duties as the expression of love for God and thereby destroy their prarbdha karma (potencies resulting into particular kind of fruit of one's freely perform actions in the past). Any self whose prarbdh karma are destroyed becomes free from the responsibility for remaining in the world for getting the fruits of freely performed past actions. This freedom is the attainment of liberation or mokṣa. As Rāmakṛṣṇa says, "This world is our field of activities. We are born here to perform certain duties." (GSR: 209)

6. Destruction of the World

It is important to note that it is not the destruction of the world but the involution of the created world in its Primal Cause from which it will again evolve at the time of evolution. Describing this Rāmakṛṣṇa has said, "It is the process of evolution and involution. The world, after its dissolution, remains involved in god, and god, at the time of creation, evolves as the world." (GSR: 328)

Thus, we see that Rāmakṛṣṇa accept the dictum "Ex Nihilo Nihil Fit." That is, "Nothings comes out of nothing". To put it differently, Rāmakṛṣṇa accepts the Satkāryavāda, according to which anything which is produced as effect, must be preexisting in its cause. This will be seen in his description of the process of creation (evolution) and destruction (involution) of the words. As he says, "After the destruction of the universe, my divine mother, the embodiment of Brahman, gathers together the seeds for the next creation. After the creation the Primal Power dwells in the universe itself. She brings forth this phenomenal world and then pervades it. God is the containers of the universe and also what is contained in it." (GSR: 135)

5
The Nature of Religion

Among all living beings, the religion is only for human beings. Human personality can be divided into three parts, thinking, feeling and willing. Accordingly in Indian tradition, it is believed that the aim of religious life can be achieved through the practice of three paths, which present one or the other aspect of human personality.

In India, aspirants who take to spiritual life seriously, and tread the path of God-realization are expected to follow one or the other of the paths, which is known as yogas.

The original meaning of the word yoga is union. In application to spiritual life it means 'union with God' or the union with the Divine'. They are generally described as three in number related to the three aspects of human personality - Jñāna yoga or the way of knowledge, Bhakti yoga or the way of devotion, and Karma yoga or the way of service. It is important to note that these three are not exclusive to each other, but are complemontary to each other. Thus, religion is a philosophy of life which is intimately concerned with active, reflective, and sensitive nature of man.

From the standpoint of Rāmakṛṣṇa, religion is not merely a matter of intellectual understanding, as it has been maintained by Hegelian philosophers. Nor is it true to say with Kant that religion is nothing more than the recognition of all our duties as divine commandments. Similarly, it is wrong to say, as it has been said by Schleiermacher, that pure religion is nothing but pure feeling which is totally disconnected from knowledge on the one hand, and from morality, on the other. Saloman Reinach was also wrong when he defined religion as, 'A sum of scruples which impede the free exercise of our faculties.' (Soloman Reinach, Orpheus, (E.T., 1909), 3. quoted from Yajnik J. A., 1972: 144)

According to Rāmakṛṣṇa, each one of the four above mentioned representative theories regarding the nature of religion renders very important service to the philosophy of religion by emphasizing one or the other essential element of religious life. The difficulty with all these thinkers is, however, that, as all of them have concentrated only upon one aspect of religious life to the exclusion of other equally important aspects, and their views are involved into the fallacy of being extremely one-sided and partial. Rāmakṛṣṇa accepted all the path, putting more emphasis on Bhakti yoga, especially in this age of kaḷiyuga.

1. Place of Jñāna in Religious Life

The knowledge which is regarded by Rāmakṛṣṇa as an essential element in religious life, pertains to the proper conception of metaphysical nature of the self, world and God. If a man is to lead a truly religious life, he must have firm faith in the truth of those metaphysical principles which are necessary for the possibility, and ultimately justification of religious life. The true knowledge, according to Rāmakṛṣṇa, is to know what is real and what is not real. This sat-asat viveka jñāna is a knowledge which is necessary for the realization. In Rāmakṛṣṇa's terminology, a realized soul is jñānī, but still higher stage of realization is that of a vijñānī. Therefore, it is necessary to explain both the stages of realization. We shall first try to concentrate on the concept of a jñānī. And then, proceed to the concept of a vijñānī.

The first thing to be noted about jñāna yoga is that the follower of this yoga or jñānī very much understands the distinction between knowledge and ignorance and tries to be free from ignorance. The distinction between knowledge and ignorance is clarifies by Rāmakṛṣṇa in the following way:

(i) Knowledge and Ignorance

Rāmakṛṣṇa believes that 'I and mine' is the ignorance and discrimination is necessary for the right knowledge. 'I' and 'mine'—that is ignorance. By discrimination you will realize that what you call

'I' is really nothing but Atman. (GSR:208, 609) The right knowledge is 'Thee and Thine'. The feeling of 'Thee and Thine' is the outcome of knowledge; 'I and mine' comes from ignorance. Knowledge makes one feel: 'O God, Thou art the Doer and I am Thy instrument. O God, to Thee belong all body, mind, house, family, living beings and the universe. All these are Thine. Nothing belongs to me...An ignorant person says, 'Oh, God is there very far off. The man of knowledge knows that God is right here, very near, in the heart, that he has assumed all forms and dwells in all hearts as their inner controller. (GSR: 265,425,568) Again, he classifies the characteristics of knowledge and ignorance in this way, He is the Master and the universe and all its living beings belong to Him – that is knowledge. And, I am the doer, I am the guru, I am the father – that is ignorance. This is my house, this is my family, this is my wealth, these are my relatives – this also is ignorance. (GSR: 307) As long as the upādhi exists, 'there is ignorance. I am a scholar, I am a jñānī, 'I am wealthy,', 'I am honorable. I am the master, father, and teacher – all these ideas are begotten of ignorance. 'I am the machine and you are the Operator' – that is knowledge. (GSR: 804) 'I' and 'mine' – that is ignorance. 'Thou' and 'Thine – that is knowledge. A true devotee says, 'O God, Thou alone art the Doer, Thou alone does all. I am a mere instrument; I do as Thou maketh me do. (GSR: 900) It is God Himself who has become both vidyā and avidyā. He remains deluded by the māyā of avidyā, ignorance. Again, with the help of the guru, He is cured by the māyā of vidyā, knowledge. (GSR: 436) He is beyond the gunas and māyā beyond both the 'māyā' of knowledge and the māyā of ignorance. 'Woman and gold' is the māyā of ignorance. Knowledge, renunciation, devotion and other spiritual qualities are the splendours of the 'māyā of knowledge'. (GSR: 943)

(ii) Nature of Jñāna Yoga Followed By Jñānī

Rāmakṛṣṇa defined jñāna-yoga in this way, Jñāna-yoga 'is the path by which a man can realize the true nature of his own self. It is the awareness that Brahman alone is his true nature.' (GSR: 680) Jñāna-yoga is essentially a discipline of keen intellectual analysis coupled with an intense spirit of discrimination and dispassion. The aspirant's object is to reject one aspect after another of the phenomenal world as unreal until he reaches a point where all discrimination between the real and the unreal stops, and Brahman is realized in samādhi. (Swami Tapasyananda, 1993: 100) The Jñānīs, who adhere to the non- dualistic philosophy of Vedānta, say that the acts of creation, preservation and destruction, the universe itself and all its living beings, are the manifestations of Śakti, the divine power. If you reason it out, you will realize that all these are as illusory as a dream. Brahman alone is the real and all else is unreal. Even this very Śakti is unsubstantial, like a dream. (GSR: 134) "To the jñānī the waking state is no more real than the dream state." (GSR: 236) According to Rāmakṛṣṇa, the study of scriptures is helpful for the realization of God. The fire of knowledge at first destroys such enemies of spiritual life as passion, anger and so forth. Then comes the turn of ego. And lastly a violent commotion is seen in the physical frame. (GSR: 322) There are two signs of knowledge, first, an unshakable buddhi. No matter how many sorrows, afflictions, dangers and obstacles one may be faced with, one's mind does not undergo change...And second, manliness – very strong grit. If lust and anger injure a man, he must renounce them once for all. (GSR: 410) Explaining the characteristics of a jñānī, Rāmakṛṣṇa says, a jñānī can not injure anybody. He becomes like a child...The anger and egotism of a jñānī are more appearances, they are not real..Perhaps he has many luxuries at home couch, chairs, painting, and equipage. But any day he may leave all these and go off to banaras...Acc to Vedānta ...Jñāna is the realization of self through the process of neti, neti. Not this, not this, one goes into samādhi. (GSR: 417)

(iii) Importance of The Study of The Scriptures

In order to cultivate discrimination and dispassion, one should study the scriptures. But after reaching a certain state of mind, one is not required to prolong the study. Thus, reasoning for the sake of reasoning is not desirable for the attainment of self; it is valueable as means. The study has the importance, but when one has cultivated the sense of discrimination, it is not necessary. Not to indulge in futile reasoning. "As long as a man argues about God, he has not realized him." (GSR: 735) Just argumentations and reasoning do not help a person to achieve his goal. Reasoning must be used to cultivate the attitude of detachment. "Though you reason all your life, unless you established in Samādhi, you cannot go beyond the jurisdiction of

Śakti. Even when you say I am meditating or I am contemplating, still you are moving in the realm of Śakti, within its power." (GSR, 134) Therefore, reasoning for discrimination of real & unreal is necessary.

One should hear the scriptures during the early stages of spiritual discipline. After attaining God there is no lack of knowledge. Then the divine mother supplies it without fail. (GSR: 200) Books, scriptures and things like that only point out the way to reach God. After finding the way, what more need is there of books and scripture. Then comes the time for action... What will it avail a man to have mere scholarship? A pundit may have studied many scriptures, he may recite many sacred texts, but if he is still attached to the world and if inwardly he loves 'Woman and Gold' then he has not assimilated the contents of the scriptures. For such a man the study of scriptures is futile. (GSR: 729) Therefore, when a man has realized God, he does not even need to know other thinks. Rāmakṛṣṇa expressed his views through the feeling of Hanuman that, I don't know anything about the day of the month, the position of the moon and stars, or any such things. I think of Rāma alone. (GSR: 260)

(iv) Limitation of Mere Scriptural Scholarship

He believes that Reasoning only injures the aspirant. (GSR: 377) Too much of study of the scriptures does more harm than good. The important thing is to know the essence of the scriptures. (GSR: 255) e says, It is not enough to know it. One must assimilate its meaning. (GSR: 350) One can not understand the meaning of the scriptures without practicing spiritual discipline. What will one gain by merely quoting or hearing the scriptures? One must assimilate them. (GSR: 524) Without knowing the essence the reading will not give fruits. It one does not have pure intellect or discrimination; one cannot find the true meaning of the scriptures. One doesn't really need to study the different scriptures. If one has no discrimination, one doesn't achieve anything through mere scholarship, even though one studies all the six systems of philosophy. (GSR: 292) So it is not the thing that without study of the scriptures one cannot get the realization. It is one thing to learn about God from the scriptures, and quite another to see Him. The scriptures only give hints. Therefore to read a great many scriptures is not necessary. It is much better to pray to God in solitude, (GSR: 587) hearing is better then reading, and seeing is better than hearing. (GSR: 863) Thus, though Rāmakṛṣṇa found the importance of the study of scriptures but he very well knew the limitations of that too. He believes that mere scholarship is futile activity. By reading the scriptures one may feel at the most that God exists. But God does not reveal himself to a man unless he himself dive deep...Scriptures and books–what can one achieve with these alone? Nothing can be realized without his grace. (GSR: 625)

(v) Scholarship Should be Supplemented by Love of God, Discrimination and Renunciation

Rāmakṛṣṇa says, "What will you achieve by mere reasoning? Be restless for God and learn to love him." (GSR: 610) Thus, the study of the scriptures should be combined with the sense of discrimination. This is also not sufficient but it should be combined with the faith and love for God. God can not be realized through mere scholarly reasoning. She can not be realized by means of mere scholarship One must have faith and love. (GSR: 106) You may speak of the scriptures of philosophy, of Vedānta , but you will not find God in aṇy of these. You will never succeed in realizing God unless your soul becomes restless for him. (GSR: 607) One cannot get the state of Oneness without that. Rāmakṛṣṇa said quoting Trailangswami that because a man reasons, he is conscious of multiplicity, of variety. (GSR: 245) The very reason for birth is to cultivate love for God. Those who have read a few books can not get rid of conceit...You have been born in this world as a human being to worship God, therefore try to acquire love for his lotus feet. Why do you trouble yourself to know a hundred others things? What will you gain by discussing philosophy? (GSR: 900) What will you gain by mere scholarship? The pundits hear many things and know many things – the Vedas, the Purnas, the Tantra. But of what avail is mere scholarship? Discrimination and renunciation are necessarily...He alone has understood the secret of the Gītā who has renounced his attachment to 'Woman and Gold' and has directed his entire love to God. It isn't necessary to read the whole of the Gītā. The purpose of reading the book is served if one practices renunciation. (GSR: 917) Rāmakṛṣṇa believes that the characteristic of a man of perfect knowledge is that he doesn't keep a single book with him. He carries all his knowledge on the tip of his tongue. (GSR: 341) God can not be realized through scholarship He is beyond the scriptures – the Vedas, purnas, and Tantras. If I see a man with even one book in his hand, I call him a rājarṣi, though he is a jñānī, But brahmarṣi has no outer sign whatsoever. (GSR: 882)

Rāmakṛṣṇa firmly believes that Mere pandits, devoid of divine love, talk incoherently. (GSR: 316) You may learn great deal from books, but it is all futile if you have no love for God and no desire to realize Him. A mere pandit, without discrimination and renunciation, has his attention fixed on 'Woman and Gold'. The vulture soars very high but its eyes are fixed on the charnel-pit...That alone is knowledge through which one is able to know God. All else is futile. (GSR: 368) He does not have any regard for mere scholarship He says, Mere dry reasoning – I spit on it! I have no use of it. (GSR: 272) Because, nothing can be achieved through mere talking. Rāmakṛṣṇa says, what can you achieve by mere lecturing and scholarship without discrimination and dispassion? God alone is real and all else is unreal. This is discrimination...There is no use in making noise if you want to establish the Deity in the Śrīne of your heart, if you want to realize God. First of all purify the mind in the pure heart, God takes his seat. (GSR: 125) Only reasoning does not give anything in respect to the God-realization. Rāmakṛṣṇa expressed his thoughts that, What will you gain by the mere study of scriptures? The pundits merely indulge in reasoning. (GSR: 836) Mere pandits are like diseased fruit that becomes hard and will not ripen at all. Vultures soar very high in the sky, but their eyes are fixed on rotten carrion on the ground. The book-learned are reputed to be wise, but they are attached to 'Woman and Gold'. Like the vultures they are in search of carrion. They are attached to the world of ignorance. Compassion, love of God and renunciation are the glories of true knowledge. (GSR: 101)

The aim of human life is the realization of God and that cannot be achieved only through mere scholarship in the depth of heart, one must feel deep devotion and love for God together with discrimination and renunciation. That is the only way of realization. Thus, God can not be realized through scholarship All should strive for devotion to the lotus feet of God. (GSR: 182) If a man but once tastes the joy of God, his desire to argue takes wing. What will you achieve by quoting from books? The pundits recite verses and do nothing else. (GSR: 844)

Rāmakṛṣṇa expressed that the metaphysical nature of Ultimate Reality is infinite. Therefore, the finite cannot totally conceive the whole of It. It is impossible to know the Ultimate Reality in its totality. But Rāmakṛṣṇa says that there is even no need to know it wholly. The love for It is sufficient for the soul especially in this age of kaḷiyuga. He says, Who can fully know the infinite God? And what is need is there of knowing the infinite? Having attained this rare human birth, my supreme need is to develop love for the lotus feet of God...The various states of mind of the Brahmajñānī are described in the Vedas. The path of knowledge is extremely difficult. One can not obtain jñāna if one has the least trace of worldliness and the slightest attachment to 'Woman and Gold'. This is not the path for the kaḷiyuga. (GSR: 150) The path of knowledge is very difficult. One can not obtain knowledge unless one gets rid of the feelings that one is the body. In the kaḷiyuga the life of a man is centered on food. He can not get rid of the feeling that he is the body and the ego. Therefore, the path of devotion is prescribed for this cycle. (GSR: 170)

(vi) Characteristics of Jñānī

He defined it is this way. It is bhakta and not the jñānī, who discriminates between holiness and unholines...In the state of jñāna organization and things like that become unreal, like a dream. (GSR: 782) The jñānī wants neither a form of God nor his Incarnation. (GSR: 766) The aim of the jñānī is to know the nature of one's own self. This is knowledge, this is liberation. The true nature of the self is that it is the supreme Brahman: I and the supreme Brahman are one. (GSR: 658) Even after attaining knowledge, the jñānī keeps his body. But this fire of knowledge burns away his lust and other passions... A jñānī loves to talk only about God. He feels pained if one talk about worldly things...The Vedas speaks of the seven plans of mind. When the jñānī's mind ascends to the fifth plane, he can not listen to anything or talk anything but God. At that stage only words of wisdom come from his lips. (GSR: 659)

(vii) Going Beyond Knowledge and Ignorance

There are two signs of knowledge. First absence of pride, and second, a peaceful nature...Once a man's inner spirit is awakened, once he succeeds in knowledge of God, he doesn't feel the desire even to know about all this rubbish. There are two characteristics of knowledge. A peaceful nature and absence of pride. Rāmakṛṣṇa says that 'Go beyond knowledge and ignorance: only then can you realize God.' To know many things is ignorance. Pride of scholarship Is also ignorance. The unwavering conviction that God alone dwells in all beings is jñānam, knowledge. To know him intimately is vijñāna, a richer knowledge. If a thorn gets into your foot, a second thorn is needed to take it out. When it is out, both thorns are thrown away. You have to procure the thorn of knowledge and ignorance. God is beyond both knowledge and ignorance. (GSR: 899) Whoever has knowledge has ignorance also. Whoever is conscious of light is also conscious of darkness. Therefore go beyond knowledge and ignorance. One attains that state through an intimate knowledge of God. This knowledge is called vijñāna...After removing the thorn of ignorance with the help of the thorn of knowledge, you should through away the thorns of both knowledge and ignorance...There are signs of perfect knowledge one is hat reasoning comes to an end. (GSR: 852) 716 One procures the thorn of knowledge to remove the thorn of ignorance, then one goes beyond both knowledge and ignorance. (GSR: 716)

(viii) Concept of Vijñāna

Rāmakṛṣṇa gave his unique idea of a vijñāna. His concept of vijñāna is a state of consciousness. It comes after the knowledge of the self that Is brahmajñāna. In the state of brahmajñāna, a person has achieved the consciousness of oneness. But the state of a vijñāna is further beyond that state. (What remains with a man when he goes beyond jñāna and ajñāna, knowledge and ignorance?) It is vijñāna, a special knowledge of God. To know many things is ignorance. To know that God dwells in all beings is knowledge. And what is vijñāna? It is to know God in a special manner, to converse with him and feel him to be one's own relative...You should procure the thorn of knowledge in order to remove the thorn of ignorance. After destroying ignorance, you should discard both knowledge and ignorance. Then you attain vijñāna. (GSR: 914)

How to achieve this state of consciousness, Rāmakṛṣṇa says that 781 In order to attain vijñāna one has to accept the help of vidyāmāyā. Vidyāmāyā includes discrimination -that is to say, God is real and the world illusory—and dispassion and also chanting God's name and glories, meditation, the company of holy persons, prayers and so forth. (GSR: 781)

In this state, soul has personal experience with God. Not only that, he can move from absolute to relative and the relative to the absolute plane. The Vijñānī always sees God. That is why he is so indifferent about the world. He sees God even with is eyes open. Sometimes he comes down to the Līlā from the Nitya and sometimes he goes up to the Nitya from the Līlā...The Jñānī reasons about the world through the process of Neti, Net. And at last reaches the Eternal and Indivisible Satcidānanda. He reasons in this manner. Brahman is not the living beings. It is neither the universe nor the twenty-four Cosmic Principles. As the result of such reasoning he attains the absolute. Then he realize that it is the absolute that has become all this – the universe, its living beings and the twenty four cosmic principles. (GSR, 477)

He says, it is only after attaining Brahmajñāna that one sees non-duality, the one-ness of Brahman and its Śakti. Brahman and Śakti are identical...But there is a stage beyond even brahmajñāna. After jñāna comes vijñāna. He who is aware of knowledge is also aware of ignorance. Rāma said. Go beyond both knowledge and ignorance. He who has knowledge has ignorance also. If a thorn has entered your foot, get another thorn and with its help take out the first and throw away the second also. (GSR: 281) On attaining vijñāna, he (self) discard both the thorns, knowledge and ignorance. (GSR: 404) Rāmakṛṣṇa defined the concept in this way, What is vijñāna? It is knowing God in a special way. To know by ones inner experience that God exists is jñāna. But to talk to Him, to enjoy Him as child, as friend, as master, as beloved is vijñāna. The realization that God alone has become the universe and all living beings is vijñāna. (GSR: 288)

According to Rāmakṛṣṇa in the state of perfect knowledge or of liberation, the soul thinks him as a machine and the Operator is God Himself. Thus, a soul doesn't have any desire to be fulfilled. A man sees a thing in one way through reasoning and in an altogether different way when God himself shows it to him. A man gets rid of all desires when he has perfect knowledge. (GSR: 346)

There are some external traits of differences between the two, which have been described. There is difference between a sādhu endowed with jñāna and one endowed with vijñāna. He is sometimes like an inert thing, sometimes like a ghoul, sometimes life a child and sometimes like a madman. (GSR, 404) Jñāna is the realization of self through the process of 'Neti, Neti', 'Not this, Not this'. One goes into samādhi through this process of elimination and realizes the Atman...But vijñāna means Knowledge with a greater fullness. Some have heard of milk, some have seen milk, and some have drunk milk. He who has merely heard of it is ignorant; he who has seen it is a jñānī. But he who has drunk it has vijñāna, that is to say, a fuller knowledge of it. After having the vision of God one talks to Him as if He were an intimate relative. That is vijñāna. (GSR: 417) God alone is the Master and again He is the Servant. This attitude indicates Perfect Knowledge. At first one discriminates, 'Not this, not this' and feels that God alone is real, and all else is illusory. Afterwards the same person finds that it is God Himself who has become all this – the universe, māyā, and the living beings. First Negation and then affirmation...First of all reach the indivisible Satcidānanda and then, coming down look at the universe. You will then find that everything it is its manifestation. It is God alone who has become everything. The world by no means exists apart from Him. (GSR: 395)

Rāmakṛṣṇa showed the difference between ignorance, knowledge and perfect wisdom. The jñānī sees that God alone exists and is the Doer that He creates, preserves and destroys. The vijñānī sees that it is God who has become all this. (GSR: 436) To know many things is ajñāna, ignorance. To know only one thing is jñāna, knowledge – the realization that God alone is real and that he dwells in all. And to talk to him is vijñāna, a fuller knowledge. To love God in different ways, after realizing Him, is vijñāna...To go up from Līlā to Nitya and come down again from Nitya to the līlā is nature. Bhakti. (GSR: 598)

There are other traits also described by him. The first sign of knowledge is a peaceful nature, and the second is absence of egotism...there are other indications of a jñānī, he shows intense dispassion in the presence of a sādhu, is a lion when at work, for instance, when he lectures and is full of wit before his wife... But the nature of vijñānī is quite different, as was the case with

Caitanyadeva. He acts like a child or a mad man or in inert thing or a ghoul. While in the mood of a child, he sometimes shows child like guileless, sometimes the trivolity of adolescence and sometimes, while instructing others, the strength of a young man. (GSR: 493) There is a sign of perfect knowledge. Man becomes silent when it is attained. Then the 'I' which may be likened to the salt doll, melts in the ocean of existence-knowledge-bliss-absolute and becomes one with it. Not the silent trace of distinction is felt. (GSR: 148) Reasoning stops when on sees God. But there are instances of people who have realized God and who still continue to reason. Again there are people who even after having seen God, chant his name with devotion and sing his glories. (GSR, 208)

In is explained in the chapter IX that Rāmakṛṣṇa believes in the concept of jīanamukta, that is, a person living in the world after realization for the welfare of others. After attaining vijñāna, one can live in the world as well. Then one clearly realizes that God himself has becomes the universe and all living beings, that he is not outside the world. (GSR, 418)

Rāmakṛṣṇa says that as the state of vijñānī is beyond the state of jñānī, a seeker should not stop at the state of jñānī. Because, to the vijñāna i, this world is a mansion of mirth. But to the jñānī, it is a framework of illusion...The vijñānī enjoys the bliss of God in a richer way. (GSR. 478) He says, how long one should one reason about the texts of the scriptures? So long as one does not have direct realization of God...But Jñānī will not talk about spiritual things without being asked...But the nature of vijñānī is different. He is unconcerned about anything...The man who knows that God exits, is called a jñānī. A jñānī is like one who knows beyond a doubt that a log of wood contains firs. But a vijñānī is he who lights the log, cooks over the fire and is nourished by the food. The eight fetters have fallen from the vijñānī, he may keep merely the appearance of lust, anger and the rest. (GSR: 476) Where there is knowledge, there is also ignorance, go beyond both...The jñānī says, 'this world is a framework of illusion', but he who is beyond both, knowledge and ignorance describes it as a 'mansion of mirth'. He sees that it is God Himself who has become the universe, all living beings and the twenty-four cosmic principles... He alone who, after reaching the Nitya, the Absolute, can dwell in the līlā, the relative and again climb from the līlā to the Nitya, has ripe knowledge and devotion. Sages like Narada cherished love of God after attaining the Knowledge of Brahman. This is called vijñāna. (GSR: 523) Thus, The vijñānī accepts both God with form and the Formless, both the Personal God and the Impersonal. (GSR: 802)

2. Place of Bhakti in Religious Life

Bhakti or love of God constitutes, what can be said the differentia of religious life. There can be no religious life without bhakti. Thus, the presence of bhakti in religious life is the most fundamental requirement of it.

(i) Nature of Bhakti or Love of God

Bhakti is defined by Rāmakṛṣṇa as the intense love for God. "Bhakti is the only essential thing. One obtains love of God by constantly chanting his name and singing his glories." (GSR: 158) Explaining the meaning of bhakti, Rāmakṛṣṇa says, "It is to adore God with body, mind and words, 'With body' means to serve and worship God with one's hand, go to holy places with one's feet, hear the chanting of the name and glories of God with one's ear and behold the divine image with one's eyes. 'With mind' means to contemplate and meditate on God constantly and to remember and think of His Līlā. 'With words' means to sing hymns to Him and chant His name and His glories. It means to chant constantly the name and glories of God." (GSR: 680) Thus, doing bhakti with detachment to the world and intense love for God is the bhaktiyoga. He says, "What is bhaktiyoga? It is to keep the mind in God by chanting His name and glories." (GSR: 468) Thus, bhakti is, to use John Hutchison's words, "a fulfillment of the 'I'-Thou relation which is at the heart of religion." (Hutchison J., 1956: 119) Describing the characteristics of the person who loves God intensely, Rāmakṛṣṇa has said that when one develops love of God, "one likes to talk only of God. If you love a person, you love to talk and hear about him." (GSR: 660) There is such a thing as love for love's sake. "It is very good if one can grow such love. Prahlad loved God for the sake of love. A devotee like Prahlad says: 'O God: I do not want wealth, fame, creature comforts or any such thing. Please grant me the boon that I may have genuine love for Thy lotus feet." (GSR: 866)

(ii) Classification of Devotees

Rāmakṛṣṇa classifies the devotees as superior, mediocre and inferior devotees. He says, "He who has seen God finds that God alone has become the world and all its living beings, it is he who has become all. Such a person is called a superior devotee...There is also the devotee of the mediocre class; he sees that God dwells in all beings as their inner guide. But the inferior devotees says, 'God exists, he is up there', that is to say, beyond the sky." (GSR: 678) Further he described as the answer to a question 'what is ekāngi bhakti, that, "It means one-sided love, there are other kinds of love, sadharani, samanjasa and samartha. In the first, which is ordinarily love, the lover seeks his own happiness; he doesn't care whether the other person is happy or not. In the second, which is compromise, both seek each others happiness. This is a noble kind of love. But the third is the highest of all. Such a lover says to his beloved, 'Be happy yourself, whatever may happen to me'." (GSR: 766)

(iii) Importance of Bhakti in Kaḷiyuga

According to Rāmakṛṣṇa bhakti is not only necessary, but also sufficient for the realization. In kaḷiyuga the best way is bhaktiyoga, the path of devotion–singing the praises of the Lord and prayer. The path of devotion alone is the religion for this age. (GSR: 143,181) If a person develops bhakti in him, then he does not need to do anything else. He told about his personal experience which reflects the importance of bhakit that, I used to weep, praying to the Divine Mother, 'O Mother, destroy with the thunderbolt my inclination to reason'...Why should I desire the knowledge of God's splendours? I am intoxicated with the little wine I have swallowed. (GSR: 482) Because everything can be achieved through bhakti alone. Those who want the knowledge of Brahman will certainly achieve that also by following the trail of bhakti. (GSR: 376) But as Rāmakṛṣṇa believes that a true lover of God never seek the knowledge but seek only love for God. Thus for a devotee, the knowledge of Brahman is the result of love for God and not the aim for a devotee.

Rāmakṛṣṇa has recognized the value of the path of knowledge but he considered it as a difficult path especially in this age when materialism is in its bloom. By realizing the divine Mother of the universe, you will get knowledge as well as devotion. You will get both. In bhāva Samādhi. You will see the form of God, and in nirvikalp Samādhiyou will realize Brahman, the Absolute Existence-Knowledge-bliss. In nirvikalpa Samādhiego, name and form do not exist. (GSR: 468) But he believes that for the kaḷiyuga the path of devotion is easiest. This is indeed the path for this age. Therefore he said that If a man acquires the firm knowledge that Brahman alone is real and the world illusory, then his mind merges in Samādhi. But in the kaḷiyuga the life of a man depends entirely on food. How can he have the consciousness that Brahman alone is real and the world illusory? In the kaḷiyuga it is difficult to have the feeling, 'I am not the body, I am not the mind, I am not the twenty four cosmic principles, I am beyond pleasure and pain, I am above disease and grief, old age and death'. However you may reason and argue, the feeling that the body is identical with the soul will somehow crop up from an unexpected quarter...One can not get rid of this identification with the body, therefore the path of bhakti is best for the people of the Kaḷiyuga. It is an easy path...people speak of the waves as belonging to the Ganges; but no one says that the Ganges belongs to the waves. The feeling 'I am He' is not wholesome. A man who entertains such an idea, while looking on his body as the Self, causes himself great harm. He cannot go forward in spiritual life; he drags himself down. He deceives himself as well as others. He cannot understand his own state of mind. (GSR: 172)

Thus, there is a path of knowledge which leads a devotee in the spiritual path. But it is difficult path. Rāmakṛṣṇa says, reasoning is one of the paths; it is the path of the Vedantists. But there is another path, the path of bhakti. "If a bhakta weeps longingly for the knowledge of Brahman, he receives that as well. These are the two paths jñāna and bhakti...One may attain the knowledge of Brahman by either path. Some retain bhakti even after realizing Brahman, in order to teach humanity...Since one can not easily get rid of the ego, a bhakta does not explain away the states of waking, dream and deep sleep He accepts all the states. Further, he accepts the three gunas–sattva, rajas and tamas. A bhakta sees that God alone has become the twenty–four cosmic principles, the universe, and all living beings. He also sees that God reveals himself to his devotees in a tangible form, which is the embodiment of spirit...The Bhakta takes shelter under vidyāmāyā. He seeks holy company, goes on pilgrimage and practice discrimination, devotion and renunciation...But a bhakta also attains the knowledge of oneness; he sees that nothing exists but God. He does not regard the world as a dream, but says that it is God himself who has become everything. ..But a man realizes this only when his devotion to God has matured. (GSR: 700)

Rāmakṛṣṇa believes that it is not easy to get rid of the 'I-consciousness. Therefore he says that if at all it remains, it should be like that of a child or a servant. That 'I' never harm to a devotee. He says, if the 'I' must remain, let the rascal remain as the 'servant'. As long as you live, you should say, 'O God, Thou art the Master and I am Thy servant. The 'I' that feels, I am the servant of God, I am His devotee does not injure one. (GSR: 170) Thus, it is assumed that God with attribute is accepted in the true religious life. That further results into the fact that God is very own for a devotee. Rāmakṛṣṇa says, The saguṇa Brahman is meant for the bhaktas. In other words, bhakta believes that God has attributes and reveals himself to men as a person, assuming forms. It is He who listens to our prayers. The prayers that you utter are directed to Him alone. It doesn't matter whether you accept God with form or not. It is enough to feel that God is a Person who listens to our prayers, who creates, preserves and destroys the universe, and who is endowed with infinite power...It is easier to attain God by following the path of devotion. (GSR: 149)

Here it should be noted that when a devotee experiences the attributes of God, that attributes are in the form of consciousness. According to the path of devotion, God has attributes. To a devotee Kṛṣṇa is spirit, His Abode is spirit and everything about Him is spirit. (GSR: 180,347,779)

(iv) Love for God as Ekāntika Bhakti

The word 'ekāntika' means the love pointed towards God only. That is, the single minded love for God. According to Rāmakṛṣṇa, the aim of human life is to attain Bhakti. (GSR: 161) Therefore, Rāmakṛṣṇa professed to pray to God for bhakti or love for God. The way is, earnestly praying to God. God is our very own. We should pray to him 'O God, what is Thy nature? Reveal Thyself to me. Thou must show Thyself to me, for why else hast Thou created me? (GSR:

96) Rāmakṛṣṇa defined bhakti or the love of God as Kierkegaard has put, 'Every moment is wasted in which he does not have God.' (Kierkegaard S., 1940: 179) Rāmakṛṣṇa believes that one may not accept the truth of the existence of Rādhā and Kṛṣṇa, but for the realization of God, one is required to cultivate intense yearning for God. So he says, whether, you accept Rādhā and Kṛṣṇa, or not, please do accept their attraction for each other. Try to create that same yearning in your heart for God. Yearning is all you need in order to realize Him. (GSR: 140) God can easily be realized through bhakti. The bliss of worship and communion with God is the true wine, the wine of ecstatic love. The goal of human life is love to God. Bhakti is the one essential thing. To know God through jñāna and reasoning is extremely difficult. Who is there that can understand what Mother Kālī is? Even the six darsans are powerless to reveal her...The one goal of life is to cultivate love for God, the love that milk maids, the milk men and the cowherd boys of Vrindavan felt for Kṛṣṇa. (GSR: 94) Thus, Bhakti, love of God, is the essence of all spiritual discipline. Through love one acquires renunciation and discrimination naturally. (GSR: 123)

This discrimination means all the attachments of the world and worldly people will be cut off and all affection will be centered in One Reality. Thus one can realize God. Rāmakṛṣṇa believes that God reveals himself to a devotee who feels drawn to him by the combined force of these three attractions: the attractions of worldly possessions for the worldly man, the child's attraction for its mother and the husband attractions for the chaste wife. It one feels drawn to Him by the combined force of these three attractions, and then through it one can attain Him. The point is, to love God even as the mother loves her child, the chaste wife her husband and the worldly man his wealth. Add together these three forces of love, these three powers of attraction and give it all to God. Then you will certainly see him. (GSR: 83,846)

(v) Types of Bhakta's Feelings towards God

In Indian tradition, there are two types of feelings for God have been recognized. One of these is known as mārjāranyāya, and the other is known as Markaṭanyāya

According to Rāmakṛṣṇa both the types of feelings are equally important. So, a devotee can choose any one of that as per one's own liking. With reference to this, Rāmakṛṣṇa said, "There are two classes (attitudes) of devotees. One class has the nature of the kittens. The kittens depends completely on his mother, devotees of this class give God the power of attorney and thus become free of all worry. Devotees of this class have an unwavering conviction that God is our mother and our father. (Marjara Nyaya) There is another class of devotees. They have the nature of the young monkey. The devotees who behave like the young monkey have a slight idea of being the doer. They feel: we must go to the sacred placed; we must perform worship with sixteen articles as prescribed by the śāstras, only then shall we be able to realize God; such is their attitude. (Markat Nyaya)" (GSR: 843)

(vi) Kinds of Bhakti

Rāmakṛṣṇa advices his devotees that "As long as I consciousness exists, one should have the attitude of a bhakta, one should not say, 'I am God'. A man aware of his body should feel that he is not Kṛṣṇa Himself, but His devotee. (GSR: 812) Therefore, one should assume a particular attitude toward God while praying to him – the attitude of friend or servant or son or hero. (GSR: 377) But the right attitude to be assumed is that of a complete surrender to God. According to Rāmakṛṣṇa a true devotee says: 'O God, Thou alone art the Doer. Thou alone doest all. I am a mere instrument; I do as Thou makest me do. All these–wealth, possessions, nay, the universe itself–belong to Thee. This house and these relatives are Thine alone, not mine. I am Thy servant; mine is only the right to serve Thee according to Thy bidding. (GSR: 900) (?)-But a devotee must assume toward God a particular attitude. God in His Incarnation as Rāma demonstrated śānta, dāsya, vātsalya and sakhya. But Kṛṣṇa demonstrated madhura, besides all these. (GSR: 957)

According to Rāmakṛṣṇa different attitudes a devotee can assume towards God. There is a concept of Navadhābhakti in Vaiṣṇava tradition. That is, there are nine types of attitudes of a devotee. Caitanya Mahāprabhu also, as a devotee, presents a particular attitude towards God. Both these have affected Rāmakṛṣṇa's thinking. As a result, he believes that a devotee may assume any of the nine attitudes. These nine are: śravaṇa (hearing the glories of God), Kirtana (singing the glories of God), Smaraṇa (remembering God), vandana (bow down to God), pādasevana (all types of services), dāsya (feeling of a servant of God), pūjana (doing rituals), saṅkirtana (chanting God's name), ātmanivedana (complete self-surrenderness). The Reality is infinite, so the ways to love Him is also infinite. So, Rāmakṛṣṇa recognized other attitudes like, madhurabhāva (loving God as one's beloved), mātṛ bhāva (loving God as one's own child) etc. His described the attitude of a lover of God is: 'O God, Thou art the Master I am the servant. Thou art the Mother, I am Thy child.' Or again 'Thou art my Father, and Mother. Thou art the Whole and I am a part.' (GSR: 133) Thus, Rāmakṛṣṇa says, they (believers in personal God) enjoy Him through many different attitudes: the serene attitude, the attitude of a servant, a friend, a mother, a husband or a lover. (GSR: 217)

(vii) Elements of Ecstatic Love

According to Rāmakṛṣṇa "there are two elements in this ecstatic love. 'I-ness and 'my-ness'. For instance Yaśodā used to think: 'Who would look after Gopāla if I did not? He will fall ill if I do not serve Him.' The other element is 'my-ness'. It means to look on God as one's own-'my Gopāla'... It is not possible to develop ecstatic love of God unless you love Him very deeply and regard Him as your very own. Rāmakṛṣṇa explained different attitude towards God by a story. In this story, when trouble came to three friends, each thought in different way. A person who said, 'we are lost', is defined by Rāmakṛṣṇa as an ignorant one. The other who told, 'Let us pray' is defined by his as a jñānī, because a jñānī knows that God is the cause of creation, preservation and dissolution. And a person who said, 'why should we trouble God about it' is called a bhakta by him. It is the very nature of such love that it makes a man think himself stronger than his Beloved. He is always alert lest his Beloved should suffer." (GSR: 229,360)

(viii)Sātvik, Rājasik and Tāmasik Bhakti

It is seen earlier in this chapter that according to Rāmakṛṣṇa Bhakti is the most essential thing in religious life. Rāmakṛṣṇa believes that the bhakti has different aspects: the sātvika, the rajasik and the tamasik. One who has sātvika bhakti is very modest and humble. But a man with tamasik bhakti is like a highwayman in his attitude toward

God. (GSR: 702) Describing the other characteristics of these three, Rāmakṛṣṇa says that, three kinds of Bhakti are found, according to the nature of the man: sātvika bhakti, rajasik bhakti and tamasik bhakti... Sātvika bhakti is known to God alone. It makes no outward display. A man with such devotion loves privacy. Perhaps he meditates inside the mosquito net, where nobody sees him. When this kind of devotion is awakened, one hasn't long to wait for the vision of God...A man with rajasik bhakti feels like making a display of his devotion before others. He worships the deity with 'sixteen ingredients', enters the temple wearing a silk cloth and puts around his neck a string of rudrākṣa beads interspersed here and there with beads of gold and ruby...A man with tamasik bhakti shows the courage and boisterousness of a highway robber. The devotee with tamasik bhakti also shouts like a madan, Hara! Hara! Vyom! Vyom! Victory to Kālī! He has great strength of mind and burning faith. (GSR: 146,494)

(ix) Concept of Prema-bhakti

It is seen in the chapter II that there is a state of a vijñānī, who is at the highest state of consciousness. After the practice of bhakti, one acquires the knowledge that all is God. Of course, this knowledge is different from that of a brahmajñānī, who has the knowledge that 'I am He.' According to Rāmakṛṣṇa there is a state which is beyond the state of a jñānī. That state is called by him a state of a vijñānī. A vijñānī can have the preme-bhakti. Rāmakṛṣṇa described the process leading to preme-bhakti in this way, "Niṣthā leads to bhakti; bhakti, when mature, becomes bhāva; bhāva when concentrated, becomes niṣthā-mahābhāva; and last of all is prema. Prema is like a cord; by prema God is bound to the devotee. He can no longer run away. An ordinary man can at best achieve bhāva. None but an Iśvarakoṭi (see ch.II) attains niṣthā-mahābhāva and prema. Chaitnayadeva attained them." (GSR: 680) In short, "Bhakti pales before bhāva. Bhāva ripens into niṣthā-mahābhāva and prem." (GSR: 436) Thus, "Bhakti matured becomes bhāva. Next is niṣthā-mahābhāva, then prema, and last of all is the attainment of God." (GSR: 255) This is the whole process of spiritual path of devotion. Rāmakṛṣṇa defined the concepts of bhakti, bhāva, prem etc. in this way, "Prema, ecstatic love of God, is a rare thing. First of all one requires bhakti. Bhakti is single—minded devotion to God, like the devotion a wife feels for her husband. It is very difficult to have unalloyed devotion to God. Through such devotion one's mind and soul merge in Him. Then comes Bhāva, intense love. Through bhāva a man becomes speechless. His nerve currents are stilled. Kumbhaka comes by itself...But pram, ecstatic love, is an extremely rare thing. When one has prema, one forgets all outer things. One forgets the world. One even forgets one's own body, which is so dear to a man." (GSR: 315)

One cannot realize God without prema-bhakti. Another name for prema-bhakti is raga-bhakti. God cannot be realized without love and longing. Unless one has learnt to love God, one cannot realize Him. There is another kind of bhakti, known as vaidhi–bhakti, according to which one must repeat the name of God a fixed number of times, fast, make pilgrimages, worship God with prescribed offering make so many sacrifices and so forth and so on. By continuing such practices a long time one gradually acquires raga-bhakti. God cannot be realized until one has raga-bhakti. One must love God. In order to realize God one must be completely free from worldliness and direct all of one's mind to Him. (GSR: 172)

(x) Characteristic of Prema Bhakti

Intense love, prema or niṣthā-mahābhāva is a divine ecstasy. It shakes the body and mind to their very foundation. (GSR: 747) There are two characteristics of prema or intense and ecstatic love of God. First if makes one forget the world. Second, one has no feeling of 'my-ness' toward the body, which is so dear to man. (GSR: 202,255,441) Prema or raga bhakti is pure love of God, a love that seeks God alone and not any worldly end. (GSR: 183) Thus, it is exclusively God centered love. Josiah Royce has laid special stress on this aspect of love by saying that "the child individuates the toy (only when he loves toy) with an exclusive love that permits no other." (Royce J., 1902: 261) There is another characteristic of prema described by Rāmakṛṣṇa is that a person who has attained prema or niṣthā-mahābhāva, looks nothing but God everywhere. After attaining niṣthā-mahābhāva and prema one realizes that nothing exists but God. (GSR: 436) Still another characteristic of that person, who has prema or raga bhakti, is that, he is not able to perform any type of ritual. One does not follow the injunction of ceremonial worship when one develops raga bhakti, when one loves God as ones own. (GSR: 196) It is like seeking

God alone, and not asking Him for wealth, fame, bodily comforts or anything else. This is called pure love...There is an element of joy in it, no doubt; but it is not a worldly joy; it is the joy of bhakti and prema, devotion to God and ecstatic love of Him...But there is a state higher than this. When a man attains it, he moves about aimlessly, like a child. (GSR: 894)

(xi) Prema Bhakti With Reference to Urjita Bhakti and Vaidhi Bhakti

Describing, further the characteristic of preme bhakti with reference to urjita bhakti and vaidhi bhakti, Rāmakṛṣṇa says, there is another kind of love, known as urjita bhakti, an ecstatic love of God that overflows, as it were. When it awakened, the devotee laughs and weeps and dances and sings. (GSR: 698) When prema is awakened the devotee not only feels the world to be unreal, but forgets even, the body, which everyone loves so intensely...The mature stage of bhakti is bhāva. When one attains it one remains speechless, thinking of Satcidānanda. (GSR: 502-3)

There is another type of bhakti described by Rāmakṛṣṇa. That type of bhakti is called vaidhi-bhakti, a devotion expressed through certain rituals. When the devotee develops raga-bhakti, passionate love of God, he realizes Him. But one loses vaidhi–bhakti, formal devotion as easily as one gains it. This is formal devotion: so much japa, so much meditation, so much sacrifice and homa, so many articles of worship and the recitation of so many mantras before the Deity. Such devotion comes in a moment and goes in a moment...But there is no falling away from raga–bhakti. (GSR: 659) Thus, according to Rāmakṛṣṇa, all rituals will stop when one attains love for God. A devotee observes many rites because of the injunctions of the scriptures. Such devotion is called vaidhi bhakti. But there is a higher from of devotion known as raga–bhakti, which springs from yearning and love for God. Prahlad had such devotion. When the devotee develops that love, he no longer needs to perform prescribed rites. (GSR: 588,655)

(xii) Relation between devotee and God

The preme bhakti is defined as the love of God, which means a devotee loves God. Besides this, it has been also to be noted, with regard to the relation between a devotee and God, that God in His part also intensely loves His devotee. Thus, according to Rāmakṛṣṇa there is a reciprocal relationship between a devotee and God. This is clarified through the following sentences:

God has infinite splendor; yet he is under the control of his devotees. (GSR: 792) That is why He can be tamed only through love. (GSR: 322)

Describing further the love of God for His devotee, Rāmakṛṣṇa has said, "God will give you everything–more than you asked for, perhaps more than you deserve, because there are no laws in the domain of His grace. If there were laws, they would be His laws and He could break them. If God notices your intense longing He may break the law." (GSR: 230) Actually, a true devotee never wants an occult powers or anything like that. He only loves God. A true lover does not seek anything from God. He prays only for pure love. He doesn't want any powers or miracles. (GSR: 547) 591 If one believes that God out of his grace may grant wealth and riches as well as knowledge and devotion, then, that thinking is not proper according to Rāmakṛṣṇa. He says, I call I this impure devotion to God. Pure devotion has no desire behind it. (GSR: 591)

Rāmakṛṣṇa gave so much importance and value to the path of devotion that he says, a man may not know the right path but if he has bhakti and the desire to know God, then he attains him through the force of sheer bhakti. (GSR: 858) Not only this, he says, that what is the use of going to Benares if one does not feel restless for God? And if one feels that longing, then this very place is Benares. (GSR: 306)

3. Place of Karma in Religious Life

Rāmakṛṣṇa has used the word 'dharma' in the sense of duty or morality and not in the sense of religion of which morality is only one of the aspects. This has been defined by Rāmakṛṣṇa as the religious acts enjoined by the scriptures, such as charity, śraddhā, feeding the poor and the like. The performance of this dharma is called the path of karma (action). (GSR: 617)

From the standpoint of Rāmakṛṣṇa, morality, though not the whole of religion, is an important ingredient of religious life. Because, spiritual consciousness is not awakened unless, certain duties have been performed. (GSR: 504) Like jñāna yoga and bhakti yoga, Rāmakṛṣṇa also accepts karma yoga, a path of action in the religious life. Path of action is a path which leads one to the realization by the performance of one's duties in a detached manner. Though he believed the love of God as the essential element in religious life, he did not reject the benevolent actions. To surrender to God the fruit of all action is also called karma yoga according to Rāmakṛṣṇa. (GSR: 849) In his opinion, all actions should be performed after the possession of knowledge and devotion. Otherwise it may be harmful. Hence, this path should be followed very carefully and with consciousness.

This karma yoga is not easy path according to Rāmakṛṣṇa. The path of karma is extremely difficult. Therefore one should pray: O God, make my duties fewer and fewer. May I have no desire to be involve in many activities...It is not possible to give up work all together. Even to think or to meditate is a kind of work. As you develop love for God your worldly activities become fewer and fewer of themselves. And you lose all interest in them. (GSR: 451) Actually, the aim of life is the attainment of God. Work is only a preliminary step, it can never be the end. Even unselfish work is only a means. It is not the end...the aim of this life of yours is the attainment of God and not the building of hospitals and dispensaries. Suppose God appeared and ask for boon, would you say–build hospitals etc...furthermore, after realizing God. One feels that he alone is the doer and we are but his instruments. Then why should we forget him and destroy ourselves by being involved in too many activities. His grace becomes his instrument. In building many hospitals and dispensaries...Therefore, I say again that work is only the first step, It can never be the goal of life. Devote yourself to spiritual practice and go forward. Through practice you will advance more and more in the path of God. At last you will come to know that God alone is real and all else is illusory, and that the goal of life is the attainment of God. (GSR: 451)

(i) Attitudes in Performing Duties

(1) Detached way

In the Bhagvad Gītā it is said that the efficiency in doing actions or in performing one's duties is called yoga. ('Yogaḥ karmasu kauśalam') In the light of this definition of yoga, we can say that this kind of yoga is rightly known as karma yoga. But the question arises that what is the true meaning of 'efficiency' in performance of action? Rāmakṛṣṇa in his natural simple language revealed the truth regarding this. He says, Do all your duties, but keep your mind on God. Live with all–with wife and children, father and mother–and serve them. Treat them as if they were very dear to you, but know it in your heart of hearts that they do not belong to you. (GSR: 81) This is the basic attitude one should remember while performing one's duty in life. But you must remember that nothing can be achieved except in its proper time. Some persons must pass through many experiences and perform many worldly duties before they can turn their attentions to God; so they have to wait a long time. Even while one is performing one's duties, the mind should be left with God. (GSR: 162) When one is conscious of doing work, one should establish with God the relationship of servant and master. (GSR: 280)

"When a man develops pure sattva, he thinks only of God. He does not enjoy anything else. Some are born with pure sattva as a result of their prārabdha karma. Through unselfish action, one finally acquires pure sattva. Sattva mixed with rajas diverts the mind to various objects. From it springs the conceit of doing good to the world. To do good to the world is extremely difficult for such an insignificant creature as man. But there is no harm in doing good to others in an unselfish spirit. This is called unselfish action. It is highly beneficial for a person to try to perform such action. But by no means all succeed, for it is very difficult. Everyone must work. Only one or two can renounce action. Rarely do you find a man who has developed pure sattva. Through disinterested action sattva mixed with rajas gradually turns into pure sattva...No sooner does a man develop pure sattva than he realizes God" (GSR: 895)

In Indian tradition four stages of life has been accepted. They are called āśramas: Brahmacaryāśrama, Gṛhasthāśrama, Vānaprasthāshrama and Sannyāsāshrama. Of these four āśramas, Rāmakṛṣṇa has referred only two āśramas: Gṛhasthāśrama and Sannyāsāshrama. He explains their duties as indicated in the following passages:

"If a householder gives in charity in a spirit of detachment, he is really doing good to himself and not to others. It is God alone that he serves-God, who dwells in all beings; and when he serves God, he is really doing good to himself and not to others. If a man thus serves God through all beings, not through men alone but through animals and other living beings as well; if he doesn't seek name and fame, or heaven after death; if he doesn't seek any return from those he serves; if he can carry on his work of service in this spirit-then he performs truly selfless work, work without attachment. Through such selfless work he does good to himself. This is called karmayoga. This too is a way to realize God. But it is very difficult and not suited to the kaḷiyuga. Therefore, I say, he who works in such a detached spirit–who is kind and charitable–benefits only himself. Helping others, doing good to others-this is the work of God alone, who for men, has created the sun and moon, father and mother, fruits, flowers and corn. The love that you see in parents is God's love. He has given it to them to preserve His creation. The compassion that you see in the kind–hearted is God's compassion. He has given it to them to protect the helpless. Whether you are charitable or not, He will have His work done somehow or other. Nothing can stop His work. What then is man's duty? What else can it be? It is just to take refuge in God and pray to him with a yearning heart for his vision. If you entangle yourself in many activities, you will be attached to them in a way unknown to yourself. You may think you have no motive behind your work, but perhaps there has already grown a desire for fame and the advertising of your name. Then again, if you are entangled in too many activities, the pressure of them will make you forget God. Those who build hospitals and dispensaries and get pleasure from that are no doubt good people; but they are of a different type. He who is a real devotee of God seeks nothing but God. If he finds himself entangled in too much work, he earnestly prays, 'Lord, be gracious and reduce my work." (GSR: 671)

"It will be good if you can do these works (build schools, hospitals and dispensaries, roads and so forth) in a selfless spirit. But it is extremely difficult to perform unselfish action. Desire for fruits comes from nobody knows where. Suppose God appears before you; will you pray to him, then for such things as schools and dispensaries and hospitals? he who has knowledge has ignorance also." (GSR: 780)

"Those who felt, they must do their duties in a detached spirit...

There is no harm in doing work after the attainment of bhakti. But it is very hard. One needs tapasyā...It is God who does everything we are His instrument." (GSR: 791)

"Householders practice yoga through karma, the performance of duty. There are four stages of life: brahmacārya, gārhasthya, vānaprastha and sannyāsa. Sannyāsis must renounce those karmas which are performed with special ends in view, but they should perform the daily obligatory karmas, giving up all desire for results, Sannayasis are united with God by such karmas as the acceptance of staff, the receiving of alms, going on pilgrimage, and the performance of worship and japa. It doesn't matter what kind of action you are engaged in. You can be united with God through any action provided that, performing it, you give up all desire for its result." (GSR: 578-9)

(2) Unselfish way

Rāmakṛṣṇa says that "perform your duties in an unselfish spirit. Always try to perform your duties without desiring any result. Even to chant the name and glories of God is work, as is the meditation of the non–dualist on 'I am He'. Breathing is also an activity. There is no way of renouncing work, altogether. So do your work but surrender the result to God." (GSR: 113) "Work is by no means the goal of life. Go forward and then you will be able to perform unselfish work, but again I say that it is most difficult to perform unselfish work." (GSR: 454) "But people act according to their inherent tendencies...Love without any selfish motive is best." (GSR: 459)

Again Rāmakṛṣṇa says, "God can be realized when a man acquires sattva. Householders engage in philanthropic work, such as charity, mostly with a motive. That is no good. But actions without motives are good. Yet it is very difficult to leave motives out of ones actions...after realization of God all such desire are left behind...God alone is the doer (What can I do I am nothing). The great souls deeply affected by the sufferings of men, show them the way to God." (GSR: 379)

Rāmakṛṣṇa believes that work without any selfish motive is good. It does not create any worry. But it is very difficult to be totally unselfish. We may think that our work is selfless, but selfishness comes, unknown to us, from no one knows were. But if a man has already undergone great spiritual discipline, then as a result of it he may be able to do work without any selfish motive. After the vision of God a man can easily to unselfish work. In most cases, action drops away after the attainment of God. Only a few, like Narada, work to bring light to mankind. (GSR: 314)

(ii) Actions Necessary at Initial Stage of Religious Life

A man can not renounce action as long as he desires worldly enjoyment. (GSR: 792) Therefore Rāmakṛṣṇa advised a devotee to perform actions in initial stage of religious life. "Some persons must perform selfless work a long time before they can practice dispassion and direct their minds to the spiritual ideal and at last be absorbed in God." (GSR: 267) Through actions, one acquires knowledge. The guru instructs the disciple to perform certain works and refrain from others. Again he advises the pupil to perform action without desiring the result. The impurity of the mind is destroyed through the performance of duty. (GSR: 185) "But remember that work is only the first in spiritual life. God can not be realized without sattva–love, discrimination, kindness, and so on. It is very nature of rajas to involve a man in many worldly activities. That is why rajas degenerate into tamas. If a man is entangled in too many activities he surely forgets God. He becomes more and more attached to 'Woman and Gold'... But it is not possible for you to give up work together. Your very natures will lead you to it whether you like it or not. Therefore, the scriptures ask you to work in a detached spirit, that is to say, not to crave of the works result (people's recognition or increase merit). To work in such a spirit of detachment is known as karmayoga. But it is very difficult. You may worship in temple or arrange a grand religious festival or feed many poor and starving people. You may think you have done all this without hankering after the result. But unknown to yourself the desire for name and fame has some how crept into your mind. Complete detachment from the result of action is possible only for one who has seen God." (GSR: 452)

Rāmakṛṣṇa has advised to the persons who are practicing karma yoga, to reduce their activities concerning different rites and rituals. In his words, "You may ask people to practice scriptural rites and rituals but when prescribing the rituals, remove the 'head and tail'. I tell people not to bother about the elaborate rituals of the sandhyā as enjoined in the scriptures. I say that it will be enough for them to repeat the Gāyatrī alone. If you must give instruction about scriptural ceremonies, do so only to a very few" (GSR: 464)

According to Rāmakṛṣṇa a karma yogi who has the consciousness of body and external world, he should perform duties. But performing in unselfish way, when he makes sufficient progress, God himself takes the responsibility of his work. Rāmakṛṣṇa says, "As long as you look after your own body, you must look after you mother too...But it is quiet different when you completely forget your body. Then God himself assumes your responsibilities." (GSR: 813)

(iii) Karma Yoga in The Form of Benevolent Actions

It is believed that Rāmakṛṣṇa was not interested in any worldly activities, whether it is good or bad. As Rāmakṛṣṇa went on advising people to go in solitude and completely abandon the work, people believed that he was not at all interested in any kind of activities. But the following passages clearly show that he had advocated the need for benevolent actions as a form of karma yoga.

Rāmakṛṣṇa believes that the work doing for the well-being of others is good. "Compassion springs from sattva. Though work for the good of others belongs to rajas, yet this rajas has sattva for its basis and is not harmful. Shuka and other sages cherished compassion in their minds to give people religious instruction, to teach them about God. You are distributing food and learning. This is good too. If these activities are done in a selfless spirit, they lead to God. But most people work for fame or to acquire merit. Their activities are not selfless." (GSR: 101) Further he says, "It is good to help those who yearn for God. Thus one makes good use of one's money." (GSR: 515) "Those who have money should give in charity." (GSR: 696) Again, he clarifies that "Although a jñānī living in the world may have a little blemish, yet this does not injure him...After realizing God, some souls perform work in order to teach men. Janaka, Narada and others like them, belong to this group But one must possess power in order to be able to teach others. The sages of old were busy attaining knowledge for themselves. But teachers like Narada went about doing good to others. They were real heroes." (GSR: 857) Regarding work for the goodness for other he says, "Even after having attained perfect knowledge teachers like Narada retained love of God in their minds for the welfare of others." (GSR: 858)

(iv) Love of God Causing Gradual Drop of Actions

Though Rāmakṛṣṇa believes that initially the path of action is helpful for a devotee. But after reaching at the certain level of consciousness, a devotee will feel to reduce the activities. Because, he believes that our only duty or the only purpose of life is to realize God. (GSR: 273) One characteristics of God realization is that the activities of a man with such realization gradually drop away. (GSR: 308) When love of God is awakened, work drops away of itself. If God makes some men work, let them work. (GSR: 315) Rāmakṛṣṇa says, If a man comes to love God, he need not trouble himself much about these activities. The activities that you are engaged in are good. It is very good if you can perform them in a selfless spirit, renouncing egotism giving up the idea that you are the doer. Through such action one envelops love and devotion to God and ultimately realizes him...The more you come to love God, the less you will be inclined to perform action...If you can do them (philanthropic activities) disinterestedly, your mind will become pure and you will develop love of God. As soon as you have that love you will realize him...Man can not really help the world. Good alone does that... The man who works for others, without any selfish motive really does good to himself...Once you are aware of it (what is in your heart) all these activities of your will lesson. (GSR: 108) God dwells within us. If one knows that, one feels like giving up all activities and praying to God with a yearning soul. (GSR: 112)

(v) Limit of Performing Actions For Householders

According to Rāmakṛṣṇa the path of action is basically meant for the householders. They are supposed to perform all their duties to the extent when their children become independent. After that they should stop worldly activities and concentrate their minds on God alone. Once Mahendranath asked Rāmakṛṣṇa that how long a man feel obliged to do his duty towards his wife and children? Rāmakṛṣṇa answered, As long as they feel pinched for food and clothing. But one need not take the responsibility of a son when he is able to support himself. One doesn't have to do one's duty after the attainment of God, nor does one feel like doing it them. As you advance nearer and nearer to God,

He will reduce your activities little by little. Have no fear. (GSR: 114) Like Lord Kṛṣṇa says Arjuna, 'Ma shucha', Rāmakṛṣṇa also said his disciple.

(vi) Drop Even Religious Activities

Rāmakṛṣṇa believes that not only duties and actions drop away, but any outer signs of devotion also disappear after the realization. After a man has attained Samādhi, all his actions drop away. All devotional activities, such as worship, japa and the like, as well as all worldly duties, cease to exist for such a person. At the beginning there is much ado about work. As a man makes progress toward God, the outer display of his work becomes less and less-so much so that he can not even sing the name and glories of God. (GSR: 151) Thus, such actions as japa and austerity drop away when one spontaneously feels love and attachment for God. (GSR: 173) At the beginning of religious life, a man makes much ado about work, but as his mind dives deeper into God, he becomes less active. Last of all, comes the renunciation of work, followed by Samādhi. (GSR: 152) When a man shed tears at the name of Hari, Kālī or Rāma, then he has no further need of the sandhyā and other rites. All actions drop away of themselves. The fruit of action does not touch him. (GSR: 251) How long should one perform devotions? So long as one's mind does not merge in God while repeating Om. (GSR: 487) How long should a man perform his duties? As long as he identifies himself with the body, in other words, as long as he thinks he is the body. That is what the Gītā says, To think of the body as the Atman is Ajñāna, ignorance. (GSR: 582) All actions drop away when a man reaches the stage of the Paramahaṃsa. He always remembers the ideal and meditates on it. He is always united with God in his mind. If he even performs the actions, it is to teach man. (GSR: 579)

As long as a man has worldly desires, he must perform actions and consequently sufferer from worry, anxiety and restlessness. No sooner does he renounce these desires, then his activities fall away and he enjoy peace of soul...But work without any selfish motive is good. (GSR: 314) Formal worship drops away after the vision of God. (GSR: 396) It is by no means necessary for a man always to be engaged in his duties. Actions drop away when one realizes God...He who has realized God no longer performs religious duties such as the sandhyā. In this case the sandhyā merged in the Gāyatrī. When that happens, it is enough for a person to repeat just the Gāyatrī mantra. Then the Gāyatrī merges in Oum. After that, one no longer chants even the Gāyatrī, it is enough then to chant simply Oum. (GSR: 335) 585 You don't have to perform duties all your life. As you develop unalloyed love and longing for God, your duties become fewer and fewer. After the realization of God they completely drop away...The sandhyā merges in the Gāyatrī, the Gāyatrī in Om. (GSR: 585) How long should a man perform his duties? As long as he has not attained God. Duties drop away after the realization of God. Then one goes beyond good and evil...How long should a devotee perform daily devotions such as the sandhyā. As long as his hair does not stand on end and his eyes do not shed tears at the name of God. These things indicate that the devotee has realized God. From these one knows that he has attained pure love of God. (GSR: 367) Without having realized God one cannot give up rituals altogether... You will know that your ritualistic worship has come to an end when your eyes become filled with tears as you repeat 'Om Rāma'. Then you do not have to continue your sandhyā or other rituals...The sandhyā merges in the Gāyatrī, the Gāyatrī is Om and Om in samādhi. (GSR: 465) When you cry by simply utterance of the name of hari, no need of rituals high state of devotion – rituals will drop away themselves. (GSR: 77)

In the initial stage it is necessary. With the realization of Satcidānanda, one goes into Samādhi. Then duties drop away. But it will not do for the sādhaka to renounce duties. He should perform his duties, such as worship japa, meditation, prayer and pilgrimage. (GSR: 111) It is necessary to do certain work, amount of work, this is a kind of discipline. But one must finish it speedily. (GSR: 209) One should pass through these disciplines (rites & rituals) in the beginning later one doesn't need the rituals of formal worship or to follow the injunction. (GSR: 217)

A true seekers, according to Rāmakṛṣṇa, does not seek anything but liberation. There are four fruits; dharma, artha, kāma and mokṣa. The jñānī seek the fruits of liberation, and the bhaktas, love of God, love without any motive behind it. They seek neither dharma nor arth nor karma. (GSR: 820) Rāmakṛṣṇa says that it is not the thing that a person who has attained realization will not do any rituals, but it is not possible to do anything for him, as he looks at everything as God. So, he simply is not able to perform any rituals. He cannot remember anything but God. Rāmakṛṣṇa observes that when a man is inebriated with divine love, he doesn't abide by the injunctions of the Vedas. He picks durvā grass for the worship of the deity, but he doesn't clean it. He picks whatever he lays his hands on. While gathering tulasī – leaves he even breaks the branches. When one develops love of God, one needs nothing else.

(vii) Need of Command of God For Fruitful Preaching

Rāmakṛṣṇa clearly believes that any person cannot start, on his own, the activities of the welfare of others. People listen instruction only when it is given by a sādhu who has truly renounced the world. They are not much impressed by the writings or the words of a mere scholar. (GSR: 737) Man cannot teach by his own power. One can not conquer ignorance without the power of God. (GSR: 407) Without practicing sufficient disciplines in the path of liberation, one should not start teaching and preaching others. First of all invoke the Deity and then give lectures to your hearts content. Then you may do other things. They learn a few words and immediately start to deliver lectures. It is difficult to teach others. Only if a man gets a command from God, after realizing Him, is he entitled to teach. (GSR: 125)

Not only that, no one will obey him if he is not qualified. Without the command from within, one is not qualified to become preacher. And if at all one tries to do that, no one will hear him. People will listen to them who have command form God. Not only that, he has nothing to say, people will on their own, will come to him. The preacher who has a commission from God need not invite people to hear him. He does not have to announce the time of his lecture. He possesses such irresistible attraction that people come to him on their own accord. People of all classes, even kings and aristocrats gather around him. Such a preacher may not be a scholarly person, but don't conclude from that that he has any lack of wisdom. Does book-learning make one wise? He who has a commission from God never runs short of wisdom. That wisdom comes from God; it is inexhaustible. As he teaches people, the divine mother Herself supplies him with fresh knowledge from behind. That knowledge never comes to an end. A teacher of men must have great power. (GSR: 466)

Rāmakṛṣṇa says, "it is extremely difficult to teach others. A man can teach only if God reveals Himself to him and gives the command. Narad, Shukadeva and sages like them had such a command from God, and Sankara had it too. Unless you have a command from God, who will listen to your words? But it won't do if a man only imagines that he has God's command. God does reveal himself to man and speak. Only then may one receive his command. How forceful are the words of such a teacher! They can move mountain. But mere lectures? People will listen to them for a few days and then forget them. They will never act upon mere words. To teach others, one must have a badge of authority; otherwise teaching becomes a mockery. A man who is himself ignorant, starts out to teach others—like the blind leading the blind! Instead of doing good, such teaching does harm. After the realization of God, one obtains an inner vision. Only then can one diagnose a person's spiritual malady and give instruction. Without the commission from God, a man becomes vain. He says to himself, 'I am teaching people'. This vanity comes from ignorance, for only an ignorant person feels that he is the doer. First realize God, see Him by means of spiritual discipline. If He imparts power then you can do good to others; otherwise not. I may think I am doing unselfish work, but it turns out to be selfish. People who carry to excess the giving of alms, or the distributing of good among the poor, fall victims to the desire of acquiring name and fame. Undertake only those works that present themselves to you and are of pressing necessary and those also in a spirit of detachment. It is not good to become involved in many activities. That makes one forget God." (GSR: 141-2) Thus, "one can teach others if one receives that command from God after seeing him. Before that one should not lecture." (GSR: 158)

Rāmakṛṣṇa believes that while doing the activities like preaching and teaching, from somewhere comes the ego, which is harmful. He defined it as an unripe ego. But when a person doing all these with the command form within, then his ego will be a ripe ego, which is not harmful. It is very difficult to preach religion. It is not possible to do so without receiving the commandment of God. The permission of God is necessary. If, after realizing God, a man gets his command and becomes a preacher or teacher, then that preaching or teaching does not harm. His 'I' is not 'unripe', it is 'ripe'. (GSR: 269) 465 There is no harm in teaching others if the preacher has a commission from the lord. Nobody can confound a preacher who teaches people after having received the command of God. (GSR: 465)

(viii) The Highest Form of Karma Yoga: Going Beyond Virtue and Vice and Becoming Perfectly Moral

Rāmakṛṣṇa says that dharma means good actions, like giving in charity. If you accept dharma, you have to accept adharma too. If you accept virtue, you have to accept sin. If you accept knowledge, you have to accept ignorance. If you accept holiness, you have to accept unholiness. If a man is aware of one, he is aware of many too. If he is aware of good, he is aware of evil too. (GSR: 902) But according to Rāmakṛṣṇa a person who has realized God is beyond virtue and vice. When a person becomes egoless then the differentiations will vanish. If God keeps the ego in a man, then he keeps in Him the sense of discrimination and also the sense of virtue and sin. But in a rare few He completely effaces the ego and these go beyond virtue and sin, good or bad. As long as a man has not realized God, he retains the sense of differentiation and the knowledge of good and bad. (a person who has realized God) Such a devotee enjoys only spiritual talk and spiritual deeds. He does not enjoy the company of ungodly people. He does not care for any work that is not of a holy nature. (GSR: 328) Thus, realizing God one goes beyond virtue and vice. (GSR: 367) In the beginning of spiritual life, a man should think about sin and how to get rid of it. But when, through the grace of God, devotion and ecstatic love are awakened in his heart, then he altogether forgets virtue and sin. Then he leaves the scriptures and their injunctions far behind. Thoughts of repentance and penance do not bother him at all. (GSR: 403)

A realized one is beyond virtue and vice does not mean that he has nothing to do with morality. Rather he is ever perfect in morality. The one who has attained perfection, realized God, can not commit sin. (GSR: 369) Rāmakṛṣṇa believes that a true seeker does not need to try to speak the truth, he simply cannot do the reverse. A devotee who has realized God will never take a false step If a man has the firm conviction that God alone is the doer and he is his instrument, then he cannot do anything sinful. (GSR: 220) A man who has true devotion to God never makes a false step, never gives others trouble. (GSR: 281) Rāmakṛṣṇa has said that the moral laws which are divine commandments can never be violated by a bhakta, who really loves God, for, loving necessarily involves acting in accordance with the liking of the lover. Thus, to be immoral is not to be in love with God. That is, immorality and religion are incompatibles.

It may be noted that as the love of God is the basis of the morality for a religious man, his morality differs from that of an atheist in being concerned not only with cognition and conation, but also with affection. We, thus, see that although Matthew Arnold's assertion that "Religion is morality touched with emotion" wrongly identifies morality with the whole of religion, it rightly brings out the fact that religious morality is necessarily 'touched with emotion' for in religious morality, to use Dr. Martineau's phrases, "the life of Law" is converted into "the life of love". (Yajnik J. A., 1972: 146)

Rāmakṛṣṇa believes that those whose spiritual consciousness has been awakened never make a false step If man is firmly convinced that God alone is the Doer and that he himself is nothing, then he will never make a false step (GSR: 379) They do not have to reason in order to shun evil. They are so full of love of God that whatever action they undertake is a good action. They are fully conscious that they are not the doers of their actions, but mere servants of God. They always feel: 'I am the machine and He is the Operator. I do as He does through me. I speak as He speaks through me. I move as He moves me...Fully awakened souls are beyond virtue and vice. They realize that it is God who does everything. (GSR: 201) He says, 208 when you acquire knowledge of the self and you go beyond attributes, then you will realize that you have never been the doer of any action, that you have been free from virtue and faults alike, that you are beyond righteousness and unrighteousness. (GSR: 208)

4. Superiority of the path of devotion

All the paths are the ways to reach the ultimate goal. Sincerely following any of the paths leads one to the same destination. A man can reach God, if he follows one path rightly. Then he can learn about all the other paths. (GSR: 372) But Rāmakṛṣṇa says that pure knowledge and pure love are one and the same thing. Both lead the aspirants to the same goal. The path of love is much the easier. (GSR: 278,811) Thus, all the paths leading to the same goal, but according to Rāmakṛṣṇa the path of devotion is easy and especially relevant in the kaḷiyuga. In the Kaḷiyuga the life of a man depends on food. The path of devotion prescribed by Narad is best for this age. (GSR: 175) The path of knowledge leads to truth, as does the path that combines knowledge and love. The path of love, too, leads to this goal. The way of love is as true as the way of knowledge. All paths ultimately lead to the same truth. But as long as God keeps the feeling of ego in us, it is easier to follow the path of love. There is nothing in mere scholarship. The object of study is to find means of knowing God and realizing Him. A holy man had a book. When asked what it combined, he opened it and showed that on all the pages were written the words Oṃ Rāma and nothing else. What is the significance of the Gītā? It is what, you find by repeating the world ten times. It is then reversed into 'tagi', which means a person who has renounced everything for God. And the lesson of the Gītā is: 'O man, renounce everything and seek God alone. (GSR: 104)

Thus, Rāmakṛṣṇa advocates more for the path of devotion. Further he gave an additional argument in the favor of the path of devotion. He says, "One should not reason too much; it is enough if one loves the lotus Feet of the Mother. Too much reasoning throws the mind into confusion." (GSR: 186) defining the confusion, he observes, 'I am He', 'I am the pure Self'-that is the confusion of the jñānī. But the bhaktas say 'The whole universe is the glory of God'. Who would recognize a wealthy man without his power and riches? But it is quite different when God Himself, gratified by the aspirant's devotion, says to him, 'You are the same as Myself'. (GSR: 248)

Rāmakṛṣṇa gave warning to the devotees to keep themselves away from the brahmavādis who do not even believe in the incarnation of God. Brahman alone is real and the world is illusory–that is reasoning. And everything but Brahman is like a dream. But this is an extremely difficult path. To one who follows it even the divine play in the world becomes like a dream and appears unreal; his 'I' also vanishes. The followers of this path do not accept the divine incarnation. It is a very difficult path. The lovers of God should not hear much of such reasoning. (GSR: 355)

(i) Highlighting Superiority of Bhakti Yoga Through Showing Limitations of Jñāna Yoga and Karma Yoga

Rāmakṛṣṇa has nicely narrated the characteristics of all the three paths and showed the superiority of the path of devotion in his Gospel. He says that there are the paths of jñāna, of karma and of bhakti. What is jñānayoga? The jñānī seeks to realize Brahman. He discriminates, saying, not this not this. He discriminates, saying Brahman is real and the universe illusory. He discriminates between the real and the unreal. As he comes to the end of discrimination, he goes into Samādhi and attains the knowledge of Brahman. What is Karmayoga? Its Aim is to fix ones mind on God by means of work. That is what you are teaching. It consists of breath–control, concentration, meditation and so on, done in a spirit of detachment. If a house–holder performs his duties in the world in a spirit of detachment, surrendering the results to God and with devotion to God in his heart, he too may be said to practice karmayoga. Further, if a person performs worship, japa and other forms of devotion, surrendering the results to God, he may be said to practice karmayoga. Attainment of God alone is the aim of karmayoga. What is Bhaktiyoga? It is to keep the mind on God by chanting his name and glories. For the kaḷiyuga the path of devotion is easiest. This is indeed the path for this age.

The path of karma is very difficult. First of all, as I have just said, where will one find the time for it nowadays? Where is the time for a man to perform his duties as enjoined in the scriptures? Man's life is short in this age. Further, it is extremely difficult to perform one's duties in a spirit of detachment, without craving the result. One cannot work in such a spirit without first having realized God. Attachment to the result somehow enters the mind, though you may not be aware of it.

To follow jñānayoga in this age is also very difficult. First, a man's life depends entirely on food. Second, he has a short span of life. Third, he can by no means get rid of body-consciousness; and the knowledge of Brahman is impossible without the destruction of body-consciousness. The jñānī says,: 'I am Brahman; I am not the body. I am beyond hunger and thirst, disease and grief, birth and death, pleasure and pain.' How can you be a jñānī if you are conscious of disease, grief, pain, pleasure, and the like?

Therefore, bhaktiyoga is prescribed for this age. By following this path one comes to God more easily than by following the others. One can undoubtedly reach God by following the paths of jñāna and karma, but they are very difficult paths. Bhaktiyoga is the religion of this age. (GSR: 467,479,862)

Rāmakṛṣṇa has talked about the path of action, but according to him, that path is relevant only in the initial stage of sādhanā. When a person grows, his activities will be fewer and fewer. Therefore, he has much talk and compare between the two paths, the path of knowledge and the path of devotion. He has shown the different nature of the path of knowledge and the path of devotion in this way: The heart of the devotee is the abode of God. He dwells, no doubt, in all beings, but He especially manifests himself in the heart of the devotee. The jñānī, sticking to the path of knowledge, always reasons about the Reality, saying, 'Not this, not this'. What Brahman is can not be described. One can not even say that Brahman is a Person. This is the opinion of the jñānī, the follower of Vedānta philosophy. But the bhaktas accept all the states of consciousness. They take the waking state to be real also. They don't thing the world to be illusory, like dream. They say that the universe is a manifestation of God's power and glory. (GSR: 133,652) and Jñāna and bhakti are twin paths. Whichever you follow, it is God that you will ultimately reach. The jñānī look on God in one way and the bhakta looks on him in another way. The God of the jñānī is full of brilliance and the God of the bhakti is full of sweetness. (GSR: 768)

Over and above discussing them as twin path, Rāmakṛṣṇa has shown the superiority of the path of devotion by saying that the followers of this path also attain the highest stage of jñāna yoga, that is, bhrahmajñāna. As he said, It is to be noted that according to Rāmakṛṣṇa the devotees of God may have achieved the knowledge of Brahman, but they do not wish to have that. They want a personal relationship with God. The jñānī experience God-consciousness within himself. To him the whole universe is illusory, like a dream. He is always established in the Reality of self. But with the lover of God the case is different. His feeling does not flow in only one direction. He laughs and weeps and dances and sings in the ecstasy of God. The lover of God likes to sport with him. The jñānī seeks to realize

Brahman. But the ideal of bhakta is the Personal God, a God endowed with omnipotence and with the six treasures. (GSR: 277) One can attain the knowledge of Brahman, too by following the path of bhakti. God is all-powerful. He may give His devotee Brahmajanan also, if He so wills. But the devotee generally doesn't seek the knowledge of the Absolute. He would rather have the consciousness that God is the Master and he the servant or that God is the Divine Mother and he the child. (GSR: 171,776) The ṛṣis followed the path of Jñāna. Therefore they sought to realize Brahman the Indivisible Existence-Knowledge—Bliss Absolute. But those who follow the path of devotion seek an incarnation of God, to enjoy the sweetness of bhakti. (GSR: 189)

(ii) All the three paths combined in the state of a vijñānī

We have seen the views of Rāmakṛṣṇa on all the three paths leading to the ultimate goal. They are independent of each other and enable a sādhaka to reach the final destination of self-realization or God-realization. But there is a state of consciousness in which the culmination of all the three paths is achieved. That is the state of a vijñānī. Thus, a vijñānī has the knowledge that nothing exist but God, as well as he is so perfect that he cannot step false, and with this, he has so intimate relation with God that he talks with God. Thus, there is a state of consciousness which is beyond jñāna yoga, bhakti yoga and karma yoga. Through the path of bhakti a man may attain them both. (jñāna & bhakti). It is necessary; God gives him the knowledge of Brahman. But a highly qualified aspirant may develop both jñāna and bhakti at the same time. Such is the case with the Iśvarakoṭi s. In an incarnation of God one sees at the same time the sun of knowledge and the moon of love. (GSR: 351)

In this passage, Rāmakṛṣṇa has talked only of the combination of the highest stage of jñāna yoga and bhakti yoga. But it is very necessary to note in this connection that those who have attained the highest stage of jñāna yoga and bhakti yoga, go beyond good and evil. And as clarified earlier that this going beyond good and evil means becoming naturally and perfectly moral. Thus, the highest stage of karma yoga is also achieved by vijñānī.

Describing in detail the state of a vijñānī, Rāmakṛṣṇa has said,

"When a man does all sorts of worldly things, he should not say, 'I am Brahman'. Those who can not give up attachment to worldly things, and who find no means to shake off the feeling of 'I' should rather cherish the idea, 'I am God's servant', 'I am His devotee'. One can also realize God by following the path of devotion. The jñānī gives up his identification with worldly things, discriminating, 'not this, not this'. Only then can he realize Brahman. It is like reaching the roof of a house by leaving the steps behind, one by one. But the vijñānī, who is more intimately acquainted with Brahman, realizes something more. He realizes that the steps are made of the same materials as the roof: bricks, lime and brick-dust. The vijñānī sees that the Reality which is nirguṇa, without attributes, is also saguṇa, with attributes." (GSR: 103)

Rāmakṛṣṇa finally concluded that don't read books any more. But you may read books on devotion. The whole thing is to love God and taste His sweetness. (GSR: 305) The sum and substance of the whole thing is to cultivate devotion for God and love him. (GSR: 339)

6
The Concept of Guru

In the past, Indian philosophy is blamed as an irrational by western people. But that is not true, it is proved by many. In the same way, the concept of guru is also extremely misunderstood by the westerners. They gave the definition of guru in a way that any Indian would see the very lack of right meaning of guru in that. Rāmakṛṣṇa has very clearly defines the meaning, types and functions of a guru or a spiritual teacher. The German Indologist Axel Michaels in his 1998 book on Hinduism, called "guruism, a form of modern hinduism" (arising since 1850). He described it as a Western-oriented and especially active proselytizing form of Hinduism founded by charismatic persons with a corpus of esoteric writings, predominantly in English." This definition of guru would be immediately rejected as misconception of the concept of guru by any true disciple of a true guru in India.

Rāmakṛṣṇa accepts and explains the meaning and implication of the words of the well-known Hindu prayer: Kṛṣṇaṃ vande jagadguru. (I bow down to Lord Kṛṣṇa, who is the World-Teacher.) God is the World-Teacher because, He is all-pervasive as well as He is the inner Guide as the Antarayāmin. Explaining this, Rāmakṛṣṇa has said, "He who is the Lord of the Universe will teach us everyone. He is our inner guide...Suppose there is an error in worshipping the clay image; doesn't God know that through it He alone is being invoked? He will be pleased with that very worship He is Omniscient and Omnipresent. So He is witness to our every up and down. Accordingly He Guides us at every step" (GSR: 80) Explaining the requirement for getting the guidance from God as guru, Rāmakṛṣṇa says, "God is the Inner Guide. He sees the longing of our heart and the yearning of our soul." (GSR: 112) According to Rāmakṛṣṇa all good seekers sincerely believe that one can have the vision of God only by the grace of guru. Rāmakṛṣṇa says, "If by the grace of the Guru one's ego vanishes, then one sees God." (GSR: 169)

Rāmakṛṣṇa believes that the guru whose grace enables the disciple to have the vision of God is the embodiment of Satcidānanda. Explaining this, Rāmakṛṣṇa has said, "Satcidānanda alone is the Guru. If a man in the form of a Guru awakens spiritual consciousness in you, then know for certain that it is God, the Absolute who has assumed that human form for your sake. The Guru is like a companion who leads you by the hand. After the realization of God, one loses the distinction between the guru and the disciple. That creates a very difficult situation; there the guru and the disciple do not see each other...For the distinction between the teacher and the disciple attains to Brahman. The relationship between them remains as long as the disciple does not see God." (GSR: 217)

Almost all seekers are interested in having a guru. Therefore, some seekers go on searching for guru and trying to choose between persons who can be chosen as guru. With reference to this Rāmakṛṣṇa has said that a man can not choose the guru for him. The guru's spiritual state is much higher than an ordinary person. Hence, he can not apprehend the whole of the guru's character. So, a man should not wonder into the search of a guru. But one should pray to God. "Have faith in the guru's wards and work. If you have no guru, then pray to God with a longing heart. He will let you know what he is like." (GSR: 645)

1. Nature of Firm Faith in Guru

Rāmakṛṣṇa believes that a devotee should consider the Guru in the human body as the form of God. It is God himself who come in the form of Guru. This perception is necessary for the spiritual upliftment. "Many need a guru. But a man must have faith in the guru's words. He succeeds in spiritual life by looking on his guru as God himself." (GSR: 241) "Faith in the guru's words. One attains God by following the guru's instructions step by step" (GSR: 524) Rāmakṛṣṇa shows the reason why one should put firm faith in guru. Because he is realized one and who remembers God all the time. "One should trust in the words of holy men and great souls, those who have realized

God. They constantly think of God." (GSR: 864) Thus to achieve the goal, the faith is guru is necessary.

Rāmakṛṣṇa has very much emphasized the disciple's firm faith in guru. This firm faith must be based on disciple's clear conviction that guru is a realized soul. Because, only a realized soul deserves firm faith. According to Rāmakṛṣṇa this kind of firm faith is there, then, the disciple will not look into guru's character in ordinary way. He will continue to see divinity in each and every behaviour of his guru, even if the behaviour is objectionable from the ordinary point of view. In the words of Rāmakṛṣṇa, "A man should have faith in the words of his guru. He doesn't have to look into his guru's character. Though my guru visits the grogs-shop still he is the Embodiment of Eternal Bliss." (GSR: 658) Rāmakṛṣṇa explains how the guru and the God are one and identical. "He who is the Iṣa appears in the form of the guru. The aspirant practices meditation on a corpse. When he obtains the vision of his chosen Ideal, it is really the guru who appears to him and says, 'This is that,' that is to say, he points out to the disciple his Iṣa. The disciple no longer sees the guru. In the state of perfect jñāna, who is the guru and who is the Shishya? That creates a very difficult situation; there the teacher and the disciple do not see each other...The further you advanced, the more you will realize that God alone has become everything. He alone does everything. He alone is the Guru and he alone is the Iṣa. He alone gives us knowledge and devotion." (GSR: 843)

2. Need for the Guru

It is needed to study properly the scriptures for the sādhanā. The scriptures are full of mystical statements. To understand its proper meanings, the true guru is needed. "The scriptures contain a mixture of sand and sugar...It is extremely difficult to separate the sugar from the sand. Therefore one should learn the essence of the scriptures from the teacher or from a Sādhu...and then practice Sādhanā." (GSR: 543)

It is true that the Ultimate Reality is the Guru who is all-pervading substance. But as we are under the spell of māyā, and the path of spirituality is mysterious, the empirical self needs a spiritual teacher. It is Rāmakṛṣṇa's contention that the Guru and the Reality are identical.

"One must have faith in the guru's words. The guru is none other than Satcidānanda. God himself is the Guru. If you believe his words like a child, you will realize God." (GSR: 673) "One must get instruction from a guru... It is Satcidānanda that comes to us in the form of the guru. If a man is initiated by a human guru, he will not achieve anything if he regards his guru as a mere man. The guru should be regarded as the direct manifestation of God. Only then can the disciple have faith in the mantra given by the guru. Once a man has faith he achieves all." (GSR: 292) "All the knots of ignorance come undone in the twinkling of an eye, through the guru's grace." (GSR: 298) Rāmakṛṣṇa finds the need for the guru. Instructions and guidance from guru is inevitable for the liberation of the ignorant soul. The empirical self is bound by eight fetters. That can be removed by the grace of guru. "Shame, hatred, fear, caste, lineage, good conduct, grief, and secretiveness–these are eight fetters. And they cannot be unfastened without the help of a guru." (GSR: 243) It is important to note that a disciple must have faith in the guru. Without faith in him, one can not achieve the goal. "Though my guru visits the tavern, still to me he is the Nityananda." (GSR: 424)

3. Who can be a Guru?

The basic thing in Rāmakṛṣṇa is that he very forcefully says that without direct instruction to become a guru, from inside, from God, one is not eligible to become a guru. A man can not decide on his whether or not he is a guru. It is the command from inside, that decide it. If one tries to do the function of guru on his own, then, according to Rāmakṛṣṇa, no one will actually hear him. Without God's will, all functions done by a man will be completely futile. "It is only a man's vanity that makes him think of preaching. A man is but an insignificant creature. It is God alone who will preach – God who has created the sun and moon and so illumined the universe. Is preaching such a trifling affair? You cannot preach unless God reveals Himself to you and gives you the command to preach... otherwise, who will listen to you?" (GSR: 668) Not only that, Rāmakṛṣṇa says that the person who has not got the command from God can not be even consistent in his thinking and speaking. "One cannot teach men without the command of God. After attaining knowledge, Shankarācārya retained the 'ego of knowledge' in order to teach mankind. But to lecture without realizing

God! What good will that do?...The instruction of a man who has not seen God, does not produce the right effect. He may say one thing rightly, but he becomes confused about the next." (GSR: 875) To clarify his views Rāmakṛṣṇa says that to become a guru is not a profession. "It is not good to be a guru by profession. One cannot be a teacher without a command from God. He who says he is a guru is a man of mean intelligence...He who is spiritually higher than others does not consider himself a guru. Everyone wants to be a teacher, but a disciple is hard to find." (GSR: 794)

"The task of a religious teacher is indeed difficult. One cannot teach men without direct command from God. People won't listen to you if you teach without such authority. Such teaching has no force behind it. One must first of all attain God through spiritual discipline or some other means. Thus armed with authority from God, one can deliver lectures...After receiving the command from God one can be a teacher and give lectures anywhere. He who receives authority from God also receives power from him. Only then can he perform the difficult task of a teacher...Man is an insignificant creature. He cannot fulfill the difficult task of a teacher without receiving power direct from God...How is it ever possible for one man to liberate another from the bondage of the world? God alone, the Creator of this world-bewitching māyā, can save men from māyā. There is no other refuge but that great Teacher, Satcidānanda. How is it ever possible for men who have not realized God or received his command, and who are not strengthened with divine strength, to save others from the prison house of the world?...A man's ego is destroyed, after three croaks, as it were, if he gets into the clutches of a real teacher. But if the teacher is an 'unripe' one, then both the teacher and the disciple undergo endless suffering. The disciple cannot get rid either of his ego or of the shackles of the world. If a disciple falls into the clutches of an incompetent teacher, he doesn't attain liberation." (GSR: 168)

The guru should lead the exemplary life of a renunciate. In spite of his mental detachment he is supposed to lead that life externally too. Otherwise he can not claim to be a guru. "Like teacher, like disciple. Even if a Sannyāsi renounces 'woman and gold' mentally, but lives with them outwardly, he cannot be a teacher of man." (GSR: 580) Rāmakṛṣṇa further says, "But the renunciation of the world is needful for those whom God wants to be teachers of men. One who is an ācārya should give up 'woman and gold'. Otherwise people will not take his advice. It is not enough for him to renounce only mentally; he should also renounce outwardly. Only then will his teaching bear fruit." (GSR: 579) Everything to be taught by a guru should be practiced by him. The task of a guru is very difficult because very small and subtle behaviour of a devotee should be corrected. Rāmakṛṣṇa talked about his own pattern. One day he said to his disciple, "One should not sit before a sādhu with one leg over the other. That increases one's rajas." Rāmakṛṣṇa says, "as soon as he and his friends would arrive, I would salute them before they bowed to me. Thus, they gradually learnt to salute a holy man, touching the ground with their foreheads." (GSR: 433)

Rāmakṛṣṇa distinguishes the difference between the guru and the scholar in scriptures. The teachers of the scriptures can not be a guru. Only realized souls are qualified to be a guru. "A worldly person should also receive instructions from a sadguru, a real teacher. Such a teacher has certain signs...one should not receive instruction from a pandit who has not realized the world to be unreal. Only if a pandit has discrimination and renunciation is he entitled to instruct." (GSR: 780)

4. Three Types of Religious Teacher

Rāmakṛṣṇa has explained the quality of a good guru with reference to his behaviour with his disciple. Here, he distinguishes between three types of guru and suggest the best type among them he says, "There are three types of religious teachers. The inferior teacher only gives instruction to the disciples but makes no inquiries about their progress. The mediocre teacher, for the good of the student makes repeated efforts to bring the instruction home to him, begs him to assimilate it and shows him love in many other ways. But there is a type of teacher who goes to the length of using force when he finds the student persistently unyielding; I call him the best teacher." (GSR: 148) He re-uttered the same thing at different place in the Gospel. "There are three classes of religious teachers. The inferior teacher is content with merely giving spiritual instruction; he doesn't bother about the student of after that. The mediocre teacher explains the teaching again and again for the good of the student, that he may assimilate it; he persuades the student through love and kindness to follow it. But the superior teacher uses force, if necessary, on the stubborn student." (GSR: 866) This views are expressed differently in this way. "There are three classes of physicians. The physicians of one class feel the patient's pulse and go away, merely prescribing medicine...There are physicians of another class, who prescribe medicine and ask the patient to take it...reason with him...Lastly, there are the physicians of the highest class, if the patient does not respond to their gentle persuasion, they even exert force upon him." (GSR: 469-470) According to Rāmakṛṣṇa the last type of guru is the best person, through whom one will certainly reach the goal.

5. Choosing The Disciples

Rāmakṛṣṇa believes that a guru is supposed to take all responsibility of the spiritual progress of his disciples. Therefore, a guru should be very critical in choosing a person as a disciple. Rāmakṛṣṇa criticizes the person who makes many disciples. "Those who goes about making disciples belong to a very inferior level...it is very hard for such people to have pure love for God." (GSR, p903) Further, without studying the nature of a person, one should not make him a disciple. Once he told to Keshab Sen that "Why don't you study their nature?..Is there any God in making anybody and everybody a disciple?" (GSR, p269) To make disciples is a very responsible job. Guru will take all the responsibility of a disciples' spiritual progress. With reference to guru's responsibility of a disciple's spiritual progress, it is to be noted that guru can take the responsibility only when the disciple completely surrenders to guru. In this connection, Rāmakṛṣṇa has said, "The guru said to the disciple, 'Give me your mind and I shall give you knowledge'." (GSR: 776)

The Indian traditional views of the adhikārī bheda is accepted by Rāmakṛṣṇa. 460 "You may impart thousands of instructions to people, but they will not bear fruits except in proper time."

7

Fundamental Unity of all Religions

It is believed that there has not been a single culture and civilization without having one or the other form of religion as its basic constituent. Thus, on the one hand, religion constitutes the hard-core of culture, and on the other hand, we find that almost all quarrels and wars occur under the name of religion only. The global issue of terrorism is nothing but the outcome of the misapprehension of true religion. This shows that in contemporary age, mankind needs true religious understanding whereby he can practice his own religion thoroughly, and at the same time, he may develop truly universal attitude towards other religions too. Modern man, living in the age of anxiety, stress, and competition, can't afford to be an atheist and sacrifice the healing and supporting power of religion under the name of secularism, nor can he afford to become fanatic to survive with scientific temper in the 21st century of globalization. Thus the knowledge and respect for other religions together with the practice of the universally applicable tenets of one's own religion (upāsanā) are very relevant and inevitable in modern age for peaceful co-existence.

Rāmakṛṣṇa's theoretical understanding and practice of different religions of the world needs to be very much highlighting under the circumstances indicated by Swami Ranganathananda in the following two passages:

"Religions which seemed to have worked well in the places of their birth are found to be failures in their careers outside. Sentiments like love, brotherhood, and peace give place to those of hatred, scorn, and strife. In the name of religion, countries have been devastated, great cultures have been destroyed, and masses of men have been massacred-all with the 'pious' idea of extending the empire of the 'one true God'. Little does the fanatical religionist realize that that is not the way to establish the 'Kingdom of Heaven' on earth." (Swami Ranganathananda, 1988: 54) So there is the need for the universal religion. This idea of universality in nicely put by Swami Ranganathanada in this way.

"The idea of universal religion is not something new in the world. There have been two senses in which it has been understood. (1) When a religion steps out of its local boundaries and starts on a career of conquest and annexation, adding new recruits, much in the same way as an empire extends by the accession of new territories, it styles itself a universal religion. Such a religion keeps before itself the alluring ideal of becoming a world-religion sooner or later and believes itself to be the only fit candidate to that estate...this ideal of universal religion is self-destructive. Not through conquest and the use of might is the way to universal religion...And when there are two claimants, both equally strong, zealous, and fanatical, this idea of universalism is seen to defeat itself. (2) The second idea of universal religion is seen in the eclecticism...A still greater criticism is that it has a tendency to become a closed system in itself, which defeats its very purpose. It says, 'There are so much sectarianism in the world; it must be destroyed; so let us start a new sect'. This sounds like the famous wartime sentiment-a war to end all wars. But just as not one among the older sects is entitled legitimately to claim universality, by the same inexorable logic, no new sect also can lay claim to that position...From the previous analysis we have come to this-that no religion can aspire individuality to become universal. Unity in variety is the test of universality and not a dull and dead uniformity."

After explaining misconception an its horrifying results, Swami Ranganathananda explains Rāmakṛṣṇa's ideal of universal religion, the very great contemporary relevance of which had been indicated by us in the beginning of this chapter. Swami Ranganathananda has showed Rāmakṛṣṇa's ideal of universal religion in sharp contrast to misconception, narrated by him in the above mentioned passage. This views of Swami Ranganathananda is expressed in the following passage:

"In sharp contrast to the previous two conceptions stands Śrī Rāmakṛṣṇa's ideal of a universal religion. The very first principle of this ideal is: 'If one religion is true, then by the very same logic all other religions are also true', the verification of which is found in the fact that 'holiness, purity, and charity are not the exclusive possessions of any church in the world and that every system has produced men and women of the most exalted character'. Hence this great teacher left every religion undisturbed; neither did he start a new religion. Yet his life was the greatest vindication of true religion. Nay, it was a veritable Parliament of Religions." (Swami Ranganathananda, 1988: 57-58)

1. Rāmakṛṣṇa on Quarrels Between Religions and Their Fundamental Unity

Rāmakṛṣṇa says, "I see people who talk about religion constantly quarrelling with one another. Hindus, Mussalmans, Brahmos, Saktas, vaiṣṇavas, śaivas, all quarrel with one another. They haven't the intelligence to understand that He who is called Kṛṣṇa is also Siva and the Primal Śakti and that it is He again who is called Jesus and Allah. There is only one Rāma and He has a thousand names...Truth is one; only It is called by different names. All people are seeking the same Truth; the variance is due to climate, temperament and name...But this very thing is at the root of the friction among sect, their misunderstandings and quarrels. This is why people injure and kill one another and shed blood, in the name of religion. But this is not good. Everyone is going toward God. They will realize Him if they have sincerity and longing of heart....All scriptures – the Vedas, the Purāṇas, the Tantra–seek Him alone and no one else, only that one Satcidānanda. That which is called Satcidānanda Brahman in the Vedas is called Satcidānanda Siva in the Tantra. Again it is He alone who is called Satcidānanda Kṛṣṇa in the Purāṇas." (GSR: 423) Not only the different sect of Indian traditions talks of the same Reality, but according to Rāmakṛṣṇa this applies the any religion of the world. He says. "Rāma is one, but He has a thousand names. He who is called 'God' by the Christians is addressed by the Hindus as Rāma, Kṛṣṇa, Iśvara and by other names." (GSR: 922)

According to Rāmakṛṣṇa the basic point in sādhanā is the yearning for God. All paths lead to the same goal. "It is not good to feel that one's own religion alone is true and all others are false. God is one only and not two. Different people call on Him by different names. Some as Allah, some as God and others as Kṛṣṇa, Siva and Brahman... Opinions are but paths. Each religion is only a path leading to God." (GSR: 264) Therefore, one should not be narrow in thinking that his own religion is true. He says, "One should not think, 'My religion alone is the right path and other religions are false'. God can be realized by means of all paths. It is enough to have sincere yearning for God. Infinite are the paths and infinite the opinions." (GSR: 158) Rāmakṛṣṇa was talking to Kālī. He said, "Mother, everyone says. 'My watch is right'. The Christians, the Brahmos, the Hindus, the Mussalmans. All says, 'My religion alone is true'. But Mother, the fact is that nobody's watch is right. Who can truly understand Thee? But if a man prays to thee with a yearning heart, he can reach Thee, through Thy grace, by any path." (GSR: 93) He himself has practiced several religious traditions. "There are various paths to reach God. Each view is a path...Many views, many paths – and I have seen them all." (GSR: 572)

2. Rāmakṛṣṇa's Whole-hearted Practice of Different World Religions and Various Sects of Hinduism

Rāmakṛṣṇa says, "I have practiced the disciplines of all these paths, each for a few days. Otherwise I should have found no peace of mind...I respect the śāktas, the Vaiṣṇavas and also the Vedāntists... Why should I be one-sided?" (GSR: 538) While serving as a priest at Dakṣiṇeśvara, in the year 1861 he came in the contact with a lady saint Bhairavi Brahmani. She initiated Rāmakṛṣṇa in the Tāntric tradition. Then in the year 1865, Rāmakṛṣṇa was initiated in the Vaidic tradition by Totapuri. Then he met Govindārāy, a Sufi saint and Rāmakṛṣṇa practiced Islam tradition. Then in the year 1872, through Shambhucharan Mallik, he knew about Christian tradition and practice that tradition. Not only that, he also practiced several Indian sects like vaishnavism etc. too. He says, "I had 'to practice' each religion for a time Hinduism, Islam, Christianity. Furthermore, I followed the paths of the Saktas, Vaisnavas and Vedāntists. I realized that there is only one God toward whom all are traveling; but the paths are different." (GSR: 129) and advised that "One should follow various paths. One should practice each creed for a time." (GSR: 128) Thus, his philosophy does not remain only in theory, but he himself have practiced almost all the ways of sādhanā. It is nicely put by Swami Lokeswarananda in this way, "Śrī Rāmakṛṣṇa returned to Dakṣiṇeśvara soon after his marriage with Mother Kālī's consent, he now started practicing different branches of Hinduism one after another. For each branch, a guru arrived just as he was about to start. In the shortest possible time, he reached the goal that each branch had in view. Hinduism's most difficult path is non-dualism. Few ever attempted it or succeeded if they do attempt it. Śrī Rāmakṛṣṇa, however, mastered within three days what his teacher Totapuri, on his own admission, had taken forty years to accomplish. Once Śrī Rāmakṛṣṇa had reached the goal in a particular system, he seemed to know more about it than his teacher. The roles between teacher and student were often then reserved... Śrī Rāmakṛṣṇa next turned to other religions, both major and minor. Whatever religion he chose to practice, qualified teachers were on hand to teach. The mystic experiences Śrī Rāmakṛṣṇa had through the practice of those religions convinced him that religions were like paths leading to the same goal. Religious differed in details, but their goal was one and the same. You might like your own religion better than another, but you have no right to think that your religion is the best or the only true religion. Holiness is not the monopoly of any particular religions; every religion has produced great Saints and Sages." (Swami Lokeswarananda, 1997: XI)

"Rāmakṛṣṇa differed from his predecessors in two essential respects:

(1) He maintained that the practices of each religion with its rituals and disciplines give its essence more really and vitally than its theoretical dogmas or creeds; and

(2) It is not by selective eclecticism but by syncretism and the whole-hearted acceptance of a religion that its full value and worth could be realized and experienced.

Rāmakṛṣṇa held that selective extracts would kill the vital element in each religion. He would be a Hindu with the Hindu, a Moslem with the Moslem and a Christian with the Christian in order to experience the whole truth and efficacy of each of these religions. But he would not practice different religious disciplines or hold different creeds at one and the same time. The observances, practices, and rituals of each religion are organic to it. He would tentatively accept the whole creed and ritual of the Moslem (or of the Christian Catholic), in order to experience its religious efficacy and truth. In all this there might be temptations or pitfalls, but one must be as an innocent child or babe, and pass unscathed through fire. It was thus that the Paramahaṃsa passed successively through Christian and Moslem experiences. Such was the Paramahaṃsa's Syncretism." (Brajendra Nath Seal, Studies on Śrī Rāmakṛṣṇa (1988), Article-Śrī Rāmakṛṣṇa: Above Time, Above Space, 7-8) Again comparing him with his contemporary, Bijendranath says, "What we want is not merely Universal Religion in its quintessence, as Rammohan sought it in his earlier days,- not merely an eclectic religion by compounding the distinctive essences, theoretical as well as practical, of the different religions, as Keshabchandra sought it, but experience as a whole as it has unfolded itself in the history of man, and this can be realized by us, as Rāmakṛṣṇa taught, by synergetic practice of Religion by being a Hindu with the Hindu, a Moslem with the Moslem, a Christian with the Christian and a Universalist with the Universalist, and all this as a stepping stone to the ultimate realization of God-in-Man and Man-in-God." (Seal B. N., 1988: 9) "Thus he was called "The Massiah of Spiritual Democracy."(Swami Paramananda, 1988: 18)

In all the practices, he got the culmination. He came to the conclusion that "God can be realized through all paths. All religions are true. You may say that there are many errors and superstitions in another religion. I should reply: Suppose there are. Every religion has errors. Every one thinks that his watch alone gives the correct time. It is enough to have yarning for God. It is enough to love Him and feel attracted to Him. Don't you know that God is the Inner Guide? He sees the longing of our heart and the yearning of our soul...the devotees call on God alone, though by different names. They call on one person only. God is one, but His names are many." (GSR: 111-112) He puts it this way, "Some address the Reality as 'Allah' some as Brahman, some as Kālī and other by such names as Rāma, Jesus, Durga, Hari." (GSR: 135) "He is Brahman to the followers of the path of knowledge, Paramātman to the yogi and Bhagavāna to the lovers of God." (GSR: 134) He spoke the same truth in different way. "The truth established in the Vedas, the Purāṇas and the Tantras is but one Satcidānanda. In the Vedas it is called Brahman, in the Purāṇas. It is called Kṛṣṇa, Rāma and so on, and in the Tantras it is called Siva. The one Satcidānanda is called Brahman, Kṛṣṇa and Siva." (GSR: 265) Again he says, "All religions and all paths call upon their followers to pray to one and the same God. Therefore one should not show disrespect to any religion or religious opinion. It is God alone who is called Satcidānanda Brahma in the Vedas, Satcidānanda Kṛṣṇa in the Purāṇas and Satcidānanda Siva in the Tantra. It is one and the same Satcidānanda...In reality there are not two. There is only one. A man may call on God by any name." (GSR: 306) "Liberal-minded devotees accept all the forms of God : Kṛṣṇa, Kālī, Siva, Rāma and so on." (GSR: 307) Thus, "The Mother reveals Herself to Her devotee in different forms." (GSR: 175)

"Most people are one-sided. But I find that all opinions point to the one. All views – the śāktas, the Vaiṣṇavas, the Vedānta – have that one for their centre. He who is formless is again endowed with form. It is He who appears in different forms. The attributeless Brahman is my father. God with attributes is my Mother. Whom shall I blame? Whom shall I praise? The two pans of the scales are equally heavy... He who is described in the Vedas is also described in the Tantras and the Purāṇas. All of them speak about the one Satcidānanda. The Nitya and the Līlā are the two aspects of the one Reality. It is described in the Vedas as Om Satcidānanda Brahman', in the Tantras as 'Om Satcidānanda śīva', the ever-pure śīva and in the Purāṇas as, 'Om Satcidānanda Kṛṣṇa'. All the Scriptures, the Vedas, the Purāṇas and the Tantras, speak only of one Satcidananda. It is stated in the Vaiṣṇava Scriptures that it is Kṛṣṇa Himself who has become Kālī." (GSR: 490)

3. Rāmakṛṣṇa's Explanation of Multiplicity of Religions

Rāmakṛṣṇa says, "God is infinite and infinite are the ways to reach Him." (GSR: 506) "It is by the will of God that different religions and opinions have come into existence. God gives to different people what they can digest." (GSR: 540) As it is said in Shivamahima Stotra that 'Ruchinam vaichitryat rujukutil nanapathjusham-there are many paths according to the different choices of different people. Rāmakṛṣṇa has actually practices this in his life. "People worship God according to their tastes and temperaments." (GSR: 188-189) "There are innumerable pathways leading to the ocean of immortality. The essential thing is to reach the ocean. It doesn't matter which path you follow...There are the paths of Jñāna, of Karma and of Bhakti." (GSR: 467)

"Both negation (path of knowledge) and affirmation (path of devotion) are ways to realize one and the same goal. Infinite are the opinions and infinite are the ways...While preaching, eliminate the 'head and tail', (Sectarian rituals), that is to say, emphasize only the essentials." (GSR: 485) "There are different temperaments. There are differences in the capacity to comprehend." (GSR: 486) He says, "If you ask me which form of God you should meditate upon, I should say, fix your attention on that form which appeals to you most; but know for certain that all forms are the forms of one God alone." (GSR: 184) "One can realize God through all religions. The Vaiṣṇavas will realize God, and so will the Saktas, the Vedantists and the Brahmos. The Mussalmans and Christians will realize Him too. All will certainly realize God if they are earnest and sincere. Some people indulge in quarrels, saying, 'One cannot attain anything unless one worships our Kṛṣṇa', or 'Nothing can be gained without the worship of Kālī, our Divine Mother' or one cannot be saved without accepting the Christian religion'. This is pure dogmatism. The dogmatist says, 'My religion alone is true. And the religions of others are false'. This is a bad attitude. God can be reached by different paths. Further some say that God has form and is not formless...One can rightly speak of God only after one has seen Him. He who has seen God, knows really and truly that God has form and that He is formless as well He has many other aspects that cannot be described." (GSR: 191)

Quoting Swami Vivekananda, Swami Lokeswarananda put this point is nicely in this way, "Swamiji once said about the Christian religion, 'You have one coat for everyone. All people – little or big, man or woman – must wear this same coat'. But Hindus are very accommodating. In Hinduism there are different kinds of coats for different kinds of people. There are various paths in Hinduism, but they all lead to one goal – God...Swamiji said, 'In all religions the super conscious state is identical. Hindus, Christians, Mohammedans, Buddhist and even those of no creed, all have the very same experience when they transcend the body'. (C.W.Vol. VII, 1964, 43)...The highest state, the Absolute Truth, is always One. But our minds and intellect are limited; we cannot grasp the whole truth, and we accept a partial truth, the relative truth. Each person has his own mental make-u That is why truth is different to different people. But the final experience of the highest stage is the same for everyone." (Swami Lokeswarananda, 1997: 353) Different faiths are not the problem in the world. Nor even one world religion should be there. According to Swami Vivekananda the differences of religion is rather good thing for all. "Swamiji said: To many it is disturbing that there are so many religious beliefs in the world. But I am glad of that because many people thus have an opportunity to approach God. I would be even happier if there were as many religious, sects on earth as there are people – each person following his own religion according to his own mental tendencies'." (Bani O Racana, Vol. III p 178-79, 1980) (Swami Lokeswarananda,1997: 354)

4. Rāmakṛṣṇa on The Single-minded Sādhanā of Any One Religion Preserving The Respect For Other Religions

Rāmakṛṣṇa is very liberal with reference to other religions. But simultaneously he put emphasis on the individual upāsanā for sādhanā. Rāmakṛṣṇa professed that one should not speak about one's own religion as only true way of living. His true spirituality led him towards universal anti-sectarian attitude, which underlies both- intense devotion towards one's own religion and respect for other religions too. He himself was thoroughly committed to Mother Kālī's worship and at the same time he maintained due respect for other religions. His openness led him to the extent that he practiced the cardinal principles of almost all major religions of the world. He actually lived all the major religions in a totally participatory and empathic manner, and thereby he showed on the basis of his own experiences that the goal of all religions is the same. He lived all religions universally without any overt claim. Ramkṛṣṇa's anti-sectarian attitude was not devoid of faith rather it was erected on the basis of true faith in God only. His liberal attitude towards other religions is quite comparable to that of Mahatma Gandhi's attitude for religions. Mahatma Gandhi said that by studying other religions, I came to understand my own religion in better form. Rāmakṛṣṇa says, "The worshippers of Vishnu and the worshippers of Śakti will all ultimately reach one and the same goal, the ways may be different. The true Vaiṣṇavas do not criticize the

Saktas... You should undoubtedly bow before all views. But there is a thing called unswerving devotion to one ideal. True, you should salute everyone. But you must love one ideal with your whole soul. That is unswerving devotion." (GSR: 370-371)

Further emphasizing the importance of the individual upasans, he says, "You must stick to one path with all your strength... But he cannot reach the roof if he sets foot now on one and now on another... But you must regard other views as so many paths leading to God. You should not feel that you path is the only right paths and that other paths are wrong." (GSR: 514) Giving the importance to the individual upāsanā, he says, "I keep men's own ideal intact. I ask a Vaiṣṇavas to hold his vaiṣṇava attitude and a śākta to his. But this also I say to them 'Never feel that your path alone is right and that the paths of others are wrong and full of errors'. Hindus, Mussalmans and Christians are going to the same destination by different paths. A man can realize God by following his own path if his prayer is sincere." (GSR: 596) Further he says, "If you believe that God is formless, then stick to that belief with firm conviction. But don't be dogmatic. Never say emphatically about God that He can be only this and not that." (GSR: 634)

Thus, it does not mean that one should be rigid to his own faith. "It is wrong to imagine that a deep-seated love for one's own religion must spell a corresponding hatred and ill-feeling towards the faiths of other communities. On the other hand, as the life of Śrī Rāmakṛṣṇa conclusively shows, deepest spirituality and broadest catholicity are not contradictory, but can stand synthesized in one and the same personality.... Higher intuition takes account of the natural differences of things and seeks to combine them in the ample unity of the whole.... Śrī Rāmakṛṣṇa therefore urged that to realize God an aspirant must stick to his own faith but at the same time look upon all other faiths as so many paths, and shall never dogmatize that his is the only true faith, and all else is wrong." (Swami Tejasananda, 1988: 83)

Rāmakṛṣṇa says, "One may have that single-minded devotion to one's own religion; but oné should not on that account hate other faiths. On the contrary, one should have a friendly attitude toward them." (GSR: 223) He distinguished between the belief and truth. The truth is that the Reality is the only One. And people may have different view or beliefs regarding the form of that Reality. He put great emphasize upon the clarity of this thinking. "It is not good to say that what we ourselves think of God is the only truth and what others think is false;...can a man really fathom God's nature?" (GSR: 422) Rāmakṛṣṇa himself is well known for his universal feelings towards other religion. And it is seen that he also see importance of individual upāsanā. This attitude is well seen in his utterance about his own upāsanā. He says, "The Hindu religion alone is the Sanātana Dharma. The various creeds you here of nowadays have come into existence through the will of God and will disappear again through His will. They will not last forever. Therefore I say, 'I bow down at the feet of even the modern devotees'. The Hindu religion has always existed and will always exist." (GSR: 642) It is by no means that he was rigid for his Hindu faith. But he shows that respect for all religions and devotion for one's own religion is the key to reach to liberation. Fundamentally, every path leads to the same goal. "Whether you follow the ideal of the Personal God or that of the Impersonal Truth, you will realize God alone, provided you are restless for Him." (GSR: 867) He favoured Hinduism in its very universal form and not with the feeling of narrowness. Thus, he was a true Hindu, without being fundamentalist Hindu. "Rāmakṛṣṇa, like Rammohan himself, was a composite personality. In contemplation truth from the absolute (nirupādhi) point of view, he negatived all conditions and modes (upādhi), but from the relative or conditional (sopādhi) point of view he worshipped Kālī, the Divine Mother, as well as other modes and adumbrations of the Deity. He worshipped the one in all, and the all in one, and he saw no contradiction but only a fuller reality in this. So also he reconciled sākāra and nirākāra upāsanā (iconic and un-iconic worship). For him there was nothing in the form of the Deity but God manifesting Himself. The antagonism between matter and spirit no longer existed for him." (Seal B. N., 1988: 4-5) Swami Lokeswaranand rightly says, "He favoured no particular creed or dogma; no particular ritual or practice; he rejected none either." (Swami Lokeswarananda,1997: XII)

The basic thing to be cultivated is the love for God. "That restlessness is the whole thing whatever path you follow – whether you are a Hindu, a Mussalman, a Christian, A śākta, a Vaiṣṇava or a Brahmo – the vital point is restlessness. God is our Inner Guide. It doesn't matter if you take a wrong path – only you must be restless for

Him. He Himself will put you on the right path." (GSR: 673) He believes that as the Reality is infinite, any single path will not totally apprehend the whole of the Reality. Giving the famous example of blind people and an elephant, he clarified that the different paths are many aspects of the one Reality. No path can present the whole Reality. "Besides, there are errors in all paths. Everyone thinks his watch is right; but as a matter of fact no watch is absolutely right." (GSR: 673) Each path contains partial truth, but God or Reality is beyond that, because It is Infinite.

"I say that we are all calling on the same God. Jealousy and malice need not be. Some say that God is formless and some that God has form. I say, let one man meditate on God with form if he believes in form and let another meditate on the formless deity if he does not believe in form. What I mean is that dogmatism is not good. It is not good to feel that my religion alone is true and other religions are false...Kabir used to say, 'God with form is my Mother, the formless is my father. Which shall I blame? Which shall I praise? The two pans of the scales are equally heavy'...Hindus, Mussalmans, Christians, śāktas, śaivas, Vaiṣṇavas, the Brahmajñānī of the time of the ṛṣis and you (Vijay) the Brahmajñānīs of modern times, all seek the same object...Do you know what the truth is? God has made different religions to suit different aspirants, times and countries. All doctrines are only so many paths; but a path is by no means God Himself. Indeed, one can reach God if one follows any of the paths with whole-hearted devotion. Suppose there are errors in the religion, that one has accepted, if one is sincere and earnest then God Himself will correct those errors...If there are errors in other religions, that is none of our business. God, to whom the world belongs, takes care of that...dogmatism is not good." 578 "The attitude that my religion alone is right and all other religions are false, is not good. I see that God Himself has become all these: men, images, and śāligrāma. I see one alone in all these; I do not see two. I see only one." (GSR: 558)

5. Rāmakṛṣṇa's Criticism of One-sidedness in Religious Texts

Rāmakṛṣṇa criticized the thinking which lacks the fundamental understanding of the metaphysical existence of the only One Reality. He disliked the narrowness of a person who thinks that his own belief is the only way for liberation. It is misunderstanding about the God when people say that 'the preserver Vishnu is different from that of Siva. "Do you know where those who speak of the formless God make their mistake? It is where they say that God is formless only, and those who differ with them are wrong." (GSR: 291) Regarding a book 'Bhaktamālā' which contains the stories about Vaiṣṇava saints, Rāmakṛṣṇa says, "But it is one-sided...the Bhāgavatama also contains some statements like that...Each sect magnifies its own view...Besides how vain people are about their own sects! There are weavers in the villages near Kamarpukur. May of them are Vaiṣṇavas and like to talk big. They say: 'Which Vishnu does he worship? The Preserver? Oh, we wouldn't touch him!' Or: 'Which Siva are you talking about? We accept the ātmārāma Siva.' Or again, 'Please explain to us which Hari you worship' They spin their yarn and indulge in talk like that." (GSR: 489) Again in spite of being a true Vaiṣṇava, he says regarding the book 'Bhaktamālā' that "The book contains nice stories about devotees. But it is one-sided. Also, it abuses those who differ with its views." (GSR: 333)

6. Swami Vivekananda on Variety and Unity of All Religion

All that we have said in this chapter about Rāmakṛṣṇa's theory and practice of unity of all religions together with maintenance of variety or multiplicity of religions has been very effectively and widely presented to the world by his great disciple Swami Vivekananda. This will be clear by (1) what Swami Tejasananda had said on Swami Vivekananada and (2) Swami Vivekananda's last speech in the World Parliament of Religions, 27th September, 1893.

(1) "Swami Vivekananda has significantly remarked: 'Then arises the question, How can all these varieties be true? If one thing is true, its negation is false. How can contradictory opinions be true at the same time?...But I will first ask you, Are all the religions of the world really contradictory? I do not mean the external forms in which great thoughts are clad....But I mean the internal soul of every religion. Every religion has a soul behind it, and that soul may differ from the soul of another religion; but are they contradictory? Do they contradict or supplement each other?-that is the question...I believe that they are not contradictory; they are supplementary. Each religion, as it

were, takes up one part of the great universal truth and spends its whole force in embodying and typifying that part of the great truth.... System after system arises, each one embodying a great idea, and ideals must be added to ideals. And this is the march of humanity. Man never progresses from error to truth, but from truth to truth; from lesser truth to higher truth-but it is never from error to truth." (Swami Tejasananda, Studies on Śrī Rāmakṛṣṇa, Article-Śrī Rāmakṛṣṇa and The Unity of Religion, 78)

(2) "The world's parliament of Religions has become an accomplished fact, and the merciful Father has helped those who laboured to bring it into existence, and crowned with success their most unselfish labour.

My thanks to those noble souls whose large hearts and love of truth first dreamed this wonderful dream and then realized it. My thanks to the shower of liberal sentiments that has overflowed this platform. My thanks to this enlightened audience for their uniform kindness to me and for their appreciation of every thought that tends to smooth the friction of religions. A few jarring notes were heard from time to time in this harmony. My special thanks to them, for they have by their striking contrast, made general harmony the sweeter.

Much has been said of the common ground of religious unity. I am not going jus now to venture my own theory.

But if any one here hopes that this unity will come by the triumph of any one of the religions and the destruction of the other, to him I say, "brother, yours is an impossible hope." Do I wish that the Christian would become Hindu? God forbid. Do I wish that Hindu or Buddhist would become Christian? God forbid.

The seed is put in the ground, and earth and air and water are placed around it. Does the seed become the earth, or the air, or the water? No. It becomes a plant, it develops after the law of its own growth, assimilates the air, the earth, and the water, converts them into plant substance, and grows into a plant.

Similar is the case with religion, the Christian is not to become Hindu or Buddhist, not a Hindu or a Buddhist to become a Christian. But each must assimilate the spirit of the others and yet preserve his individuality and grow according to his own law of growth.

If the Parliament of Religions has shown anything to the world it is this: It has proved to the world that holiness, purity, and charity are not the exclusive possessions of any church in the world, and that every system had produced men and women of the most exalted character. In the face of this evidence, if anybody dreams of the exclusive survival of his own religion and the destruction of the others, I pity him from the bottom of my heart, and point out to him that upon the banner of every religion will soon be written, in spite of resistance: "Help and not Fight.", "Assimilation and not Destruction", "Harmony and Peace and not Dissension."

In the above passage, Swami Vivekananda appreciates his 'warm welcome' by the audience of the World Parliament of Religion. With reference to this it is very necessary to note that the editor of the proceedings of the World Parliament of Religions has said that this speech of Swami Vivekananda had not any warm welcome but most of the members of the audience were in the mood of fundamental disagreement with what Swami Vivekananda had propounded in this speech.

This also indicates the fundamental difference between the Indian approach of Sanātana Dharma and other religions having fundamentalist approach. The Sanātana Dharma (mostly known as Hinduism) of India has been very much deep rooted since centuries in the heart of even a simple religious practitioner in India. They sincerely believe and practice the Vaidic dictum of "Ekam sat vıpra bahudhā vadanti."

Rāmakṛṣṇa was so liberal about the religious faith that the paths which are not well praised are also not criticized by him. "Some people practice the Sahaja Sādhanā 'the easy discipline'. It is called easy, but how difficult it is! It involves spiritual practices in the presence of members of the opposite sex and other kinds of objects of enjoyment. One must resist the attraction of all these. Swamiji and other young disciples were one day criticizing these practices in the presence of the Master, but Rāmakṛṣṇa told them that they should not criticize even these things, for some people have realized God following this method also. But he warned them, 'This path is dangerous. There are two entrances to a house, the front door and the rear door where the scavengers enter to remove the garbage, etc. this path is like the rear door, but even by this door people enter the house. However, this path is not pure; it is not for you'." (Swami Lokeswarananda, 1997: 351)

Rāmakṛṣṇa's message to the world about the unity and variety of different religions has been nicely expressed by Francis Younghusband in this way, "(Rāmakṛṣṇa) expounded the great yet simple principle of not merely toleration to other religions, but deeply appreciating them and penetratingly entering into them." (Younghusband F., 1988: 22) "All mankind is very greatly indebted to Śrī Rāmakṛṣṇa for having spread and intensified this doctrine and lived up to it in his own life. In this doctrine we come across one great principle which is a very simple principle too, by which the whole universe is governed, and that is of the 'Unity in diversity.' The diversity will always exist, and each one of us is different from the other as each particle in the universe is different from the other. We have to maintain our own individuality, but we should also realize that deep down there is this fundamental unity which unites us all." (Younghusband F., 1988: 23)

"Dr. Rādhākṛṣṇan emphasizes this point in his book 'The Future of Civilization': 'The Supreme presents itself in a variety of aspects to the human mind. The bewildering variety of Hindu theism and pantheism, the Buddhist developments of an impersonal law and a personal saviour, the old classical paganism with its personal gods and goddesses, the Hebrew faith in an inflexible Lord or righteousness, the Catholic Christianity with its somewhat distant personal deity and more immediate minor divinities from the Madonna to the Patron Saints,... the Muslim creed of one and only God are the different ways in which men have tried to orient their relations to the Unseen Reality conceived as something higher, better, and more sovereign than the individual self. If we admit the diversity of human nature, we can easily understand this variety of the appeal of God to it and the utter futility of reducing all dogmas to one. Underlying all the diversity of dogmas is the undefined and indefinable conception of an Ultimate Reality.'"(Swami Tejasananda, 1988: 76)

"H. H. Wilson also sighs to the very same tune when he remarks in his Essays and lectures: 'Contrarieties of belief and diversities of religion are part of the scheme of Providence; for, as a painter gives beauty to the picture by a variety of colours, or as a gardener embellishes his garden with flowers of every hue, so God appointed to every tribe its own religion that man might glorify Him in diverse modes, all having the same end and being equally acceptable in His sight.'" (Swami Tejasananda, 1988: 76)

"The message of harmony or the unity of religions thus delivered by Śrī Rāmakṛṣṇa at the present age to bring about peace and goodwill amongst the different sects and creeds of India and of the outside world is reflected in most of his illuminating and inspired utterances." (Swami Tejasananda, 1988: 81)

8

Analysis of the wide range and depth of the different aspects of Sādhanā

Rāmakṛṣṇa advocates the path of devotion for most of the people. It is his contention that the path of knowledge, in which one has to contemplate on the formless God, is difficult in this age of Kali, when everyone is dependent on food etc. This does not mean that he altogether negates the path of knowledge, but he asserts that the path of knowledge requires complete lack of any kind of worldliness. In the words of Rāmakṛṣṇa "It is possible to practice the discipline of the formless God. But it is very difficult to follow that path. One cannot follow it without renouncing 'woman and gold'. There must be complete renunciation, both inner and outer. You can not succeed in this path if you have the slightest trace of worldliness." (GSR: 354) Thus, the path of devotion is meant for almost all aspirants. Therefore, according to Rāmakṛṣṇa the goal of human life is to love God, which is the most central thing in spiritual life. While giving the guidance to all seekers Rāmakṛṣṇa has covered a very wide range and gone very deep in explaining different aspects of necessary sādhanā. In this chapter an attempt has been made to expound Rāmakṛṣṇa's views about different aspects of sādhanā under the following headings and sub-headings.

1. Spiritual Discipline

(i) Vigilance in Spiritual Discipline

It is seen that according to Rāmakṛṣṇa the vision of God is the only goal of human life. Without the rigorous practice one cannot achieve that goal. Rāmakṛṣṇa assures the aspirant that "through the vigilant spiritual disciplines, one can certainly get the realization of God." (GSR: 331) For this purpose to be fulfilled, Rāmakṛṣṇa says, "one must have strong determination; then alone is spiritual practice possible. One must make a firm resolve." Rāmakṛṣṇa makes a devotee cautious about the danger of the distraction of mind from God. Lust and greed are the great obstacles in the journey to the ultimate goal. Only genuine person having strong sense of detachment and vairāgya, can perform constant discipline with perseverance. "He only can achieve the goal. Therefore through the practice of spiritual discipline one can always fix his mind on God. And thereby achieve the ultimate goal. Rāmakṛṣṇa says, always keep your mind fixed on God. In the beginning you must struggle a little, later on you will enjoy your pension." (GSR: 210)

(ii) Necessity of Discipline

For the achievement of human goal, Rāmakṛṣṇa shows the necessity and value of spiritual discipline. According to him, even the study of scriptures or the study of six systems of Indian Philosophy failed to help in achieving the ultimate goal of God realization. "Mere studying the scriptures, nothing can be achieved. One must practice intense spiritual discipline. Can one see God by merely repeating, 'God exists'? One needs sādhanā." (GSR: 608) The only thing, which requires, is the rigorous spiritual discipline. He says, "there are many scriptures like the Vedas. But one can not realize God without austerity and spiritual discipline. God can not be found in the six systems, the Vedas or the Tantra. But one should learn the contents of the scriptures and then act accordingly to their injunctions." (GSR: 475) Thus, to reach to the ultimate state, spiritual discipline is necessary. (GSR: 368,418,690)

(iii) Remaining Away From the Delusion by Māyā

Rāmakṛṣṇa believes that people are deceived by the māyā. Māyā would make one feels the illusion of 'I and mine.' Under the spell of māyā, one faces the delusion. Unless one practices spiritual discipline, one cannot get rid of such delusion. Rāmakṛṣṇa says, "it is māyā that deludes. Only a few become spiritually awakened and are not deluded by the spell of māyā. One must practice spiritual discipline laboriously, in order to avoid the clutches of māyā." (GSR: 206) Thus, Spiritual discipline is necessary in order to see God. (GSR: 238)

(iv) Negation and Affirmation

The spiritual discipline underlies both, the complete detachment from the pleasures of senses and intense love for God. Giving the example of ṛṣis of old age, Rāmakṛṣṇa clarify the Indian concept of real spiritual disciplines. He says, "After intense austerities the ṛṣis of olden times realized God as their innermost consciousness and experienced the real nature of brahman. But how hard they had to work! They went out of their dwellings in the early morning and all day practiced austerities and meditation. Returning home at nightfall they took a light supper of fruit and roots. But an aspirant can not succeed in this form of spiritual discipline if his mind is stained with worldliness even in the slightest degree. The mind must withdraw totally from all objects of form, taste, smell, touch and sound. Only thus does it become pure. The pure mind is the same as the pure Atman. But such a mind must be altogether free from 'woman and gold'. When it becomes pure, one has another experience. One realizes: 'God alone is the Doer and I am His Instrument.' It is the thought of worldly objects that prevents the mind from going into samādhi." (GSR: 350)

(v) Ingredients of Spiritual Discipline

Rāmakṛṣṇa gave so much importance to spiritual discipline that if one is seen having achieved certain high level of consciousness, then he would assumed that he may have done practices in his previous births. He says, "One must inherit good tendencies to realize God. One must have done something, some form of tapasyā, either in this life or in another." (GSR: 542)

Rāmakṛṣṇa's concept of sādhanā is complex of the development of whole spiritual personality. It covers various human aspects of spiritual discipline. Widely speaking, Rāmakṛṣṇa's sayings can be classified under certain aspects of the spiritual life of a seeker. It is like, meditation, significance of solitude, importance of yearning, sense of discrimination and dispassion, idea of love and faith, value of prayer, company of holy persons and repeating the name of God, necessity of purity and truthfulness in day-to-day living, dangers of lust and greed etc. Here are Rāmakṛṣṇa's preaching regarding all such aspects, which are necessary of the achievement of the ultimate goal. The constant spiritual practices, which are required for the realization of God, are greatly benefited for the sādhaka. To be able to realize God, one must practice absolute continence. A man controlling the seminal fluid for twelve years develops special powers. He grows a new inner nerve called the nerve of memory. (GSR: 411)

2. Meditation

The meditation means to concentrate one's mind on God. The method of meditation, according to Rāmakṛṣṇa is that first mind should be merger in buddhi and that again in Atman. Then one acquires consciousness. Quoting another person, Rāmakṛṣṇa says, 658 "Nagta used to teach how to establish oneself in the true self, saying, 'Merge the mind in the buddhi and the buddhi in the Atman; then you will be established in your true self." (GSR: 658) Again, the same truth in different way he says, "When a man merges his buddhi, his intelligence, in Bodha, consciousness, then he attains knowledge of Brahman, he becomes Buddha-enlightened. Nagta used to say that the mind merges in the buddhi, and the buddhi in Bodha, Consciousness." (GSR: 430)

(i) Meditation on the Form of God

This concentration can be possible through the constant practice. In the initial stage, a seeker is required the practice to contemplate on one or the other form of God. Because Rāmakṛṣṇa believes that "Mind can not be fixed, all of a sudden, on the formless aspect of God. It is wise to think of God with form during the primary stage." (GSR: 127) In the same tune, he further says, "In order to mediate on God, one should try at first to think of Him, as free from upādhis, limitations. But it is very difficult to achieve perfection in this form of meditation. But it is easy to meditate on an incarnation-God born as man." (GSR: 365) This does not mean that in meditation, he does not accept any type of formless meditation. He compare the joy of formless meditation with the joy of floating fish in the vast ocean. He says, "Look at the fish. Meditating one the formless God is like swimming joyfully like this fish, in the ocean of bliss and consciousness." (GSR: 256) Thus, Rāmakṛṣṇa accepts the meditation on the formless God, but he believes that to meditating on the God with form gives the speed to the sādhanā. "By meditating on God with form one speedily acquires devotion then one can meditate on the formless God." (GSR: 353)

For this reason, Rāmakṛṣṇa recommended and put emphasis on the meditation of God with form.

(ii) Control of senses

Together with it, it is necessary to withdraw the senses from its natural tendencies. That is, all the senses have the tendencies of going outside to get their object. A seeker has to control and withdraw them in order to achieve the goal of human life. Rāmakṛṣṇa believes that after reaching a certain state of consciousness, one will not like any talk but of God's talk. It means that at that level, one's all senses will turned away from their objects and fixed to God only. Therefore, initially, before reaching that state, it is required for a seeker to withdraw his senses from their objects. This will result into the steadiness in the postures also. For the real concentration, fix posture is required, and to remain for long time in fix posture requires the control over mind, and control over mind is possible through the withdrawal of sense. Therefore, Rāmakṛṣṇa says that "The yogi seeks to realize the Paramātman, the Supreme Soul. His ideal is the union of the embodied soul and the Supreme Soul. He withdraws his mind from sense–objects and tries to concentrate it on the Paramātman. Therefore during the first stage of his spiritual discipline, he retires into solitude and with undivided attention practices meditation in a fixed posture." (GSR: 134)

According to Rāmakṛṣṇa the basic cause of sound meditation is the control of senses and mind. The complete non-awareness of the outer world is the sigh of true concentration. Rāmakṛṣṇa says, "A person can achieve such single mindedness in meditation that he will see nothing, hear nothing. He will not be conscious even of touch. A snake may crawl over his body, but he will not know it. Neither of them will be aware of the other. In deep meditation the sense organs stop functioning; the mind does not look outward. There are five objects of the senses: form, taste, smell, touch and sound. They are all left outside. At the beginning of meditation the objects of the senses appears before the aspirant. But when the meditation becomes deep, they not longer bother him. They are left outside." (GSR: 745)

Rāmakṛṣṇa believes that the ultimate goal of human life is the union of self with God. The achievement of this goal is only possible when the mind becomes quiet through the control of it. He says, "No matter what path you follow, yoga is impossible unless the mind becomes quiet. The mind of a yogi is under his control, he is not under the control of his mind. When the mind is quiet, the prāna stops functioning. Then one gets kumbhaka. One may have the same kumbhaka through bhaktiyoga as well. The prāna stops functioning through love of God too." (GSR: 248) When the mind becomes quiet, then one has only one thought, a thought of God. In that state, one likes to talk only about God. To reach to this state, Rāmakṛṣṇa advice a seeker to meditate on the form of God. "Have faith in God's form. Meditate on that form of God which appeals to your mind. The soul becomes restless for God when one is through with the enjoyment of worldly things. Then a person has only one thought-how to realize God. He listens to whether anyone says to him about God." (GSR: 272)

Rāmakṛṣṇa frequently uses the word 'dive deep'. Its meaning that he tells a seeker to go in deep in meditation. He says, In mediation one must be absorbed in God. By merely floating on the surface of the water, can you reach the gems lying at the bottom of the sea? ((GSR: 124)

(iii) Mind Progressingly Reaching the Seventh Plane

Rāmakṛṣṇa believes that during spiritual practices, one's mind dwells at different planes. The characteristic behaviour of a person, whose mind resides on different planes are different. He describes it as under: "Where does the mind of a man ordinarily dwell? In the first there planes. These are at the organs of evacuation, and generation and at the navel. Then the mind is immersed only in worldliness, attached to 'woman and gold'. A man sees light of God when his mind dwells in the plane of heart. He sees the light and exclaims: 'Ah! What is this? What is this?' The next plane is at throat. When the mind ascends to the next he likes to hear and talk only of God. When the mind ascends to the next plane, in the forehead, between the eyebrows, he sees the form of satchidanand and desires to touch and embrace It. But he is unable to do so. When the mind reaches to this seventh plane, then the ego vanishes completely and the man goes into samādhi. What happens when the mind reaches to the seventh plane cannot be described." (GSR: 169)

(iv) Rāmakṛṣṇa's views on the rules for meditation in scriptures

Rāmakṛṣṇa warns a seeker that he should not bound him by the rules in the scriptures. Here, it should be noted that Rāmakṛṣṇa respects all the scriptures. But as usual, he believes that as the Reality is infinite, the ways to reach him are also infinite. So, one should not narrow one's belief. Therefore he says, "The heart is a splendid place. One can meditate there or in the sahasrāra. These are rules for meditation given in the scriptures. But you may meditate wherever you like. Every place is filled with Brahman, Consciousness. Is there any place where It does not exist? There are two kinds of meditation, one, on the formless God and the other, on God with form. But the meditation on the formless God is extremely difficult. In that meditation you must wipe out all that you see or hear. You contemplate only on the nature of your Inner Self. Meditating on His Inner self, Siva dances about. He exclaims: 'What am I! What am I!' This is called the siva yoga. While practicing this form of meditation, one directs ones look to the forehead. It is meditation on the nature of one's Inner Self after negating the world, following the vedāntika method of 'Neti, Neli'. There is another form of meditation known as the Vishnu Yoga. The eyes are fixed on the tip of the nose. Half the look is directed inward and the other half outward. This is how one meditates on God with form. The sound Oum is Brahman. After attaining perfection one hears the sound of this eternal word, rising spontaneously from the navel. By following the trail of Om, you attain Brahman, of which the word is the symbol. But such vision is not possible as long as you are conscious of your ego. A man realizes Brahman only when he feels neither 'I' nor 'you', neither 'one' nor 'many'. Through spiritual discipline the individual soul can get the vision of supreme soul. He removes the thorn of ajñāna, ignorance by means of the thorn of jñāna, knowledge. But on attaining vijñāna, he discards both thorns, knowledge and ignorance. Then he talks with God." (GSR: 403) Thus, he believes that for different persons, there are different types of meditation. At another place he describes the nature of meditation in this way: "The kuṇḍalini, rising above the visudhh cakra, enables one to see everything as akasa. One attains the Absolute by going beyond the universe and its created beings conjured up by māyā. By passing beyond the Nada one goes into samādhi. By repeating 'Om' one goes beyond the Nada and attains samādhi." (GSR: 263) After reaching that state, all rituals and other activities will disappear. He says, "The yogi following in the trail of the sound Om, gradually merges himself in the Supreme Brahman. His Sandhyā and other ritualistic duties disappear in samādhi. Thus the duties of the Jñānī come to an end." (GSR: 465) Rāmakṛṣṇa says, "In such a state the breathing stops and one experiences kumbhaka. Another characteristic of God vision is that a great spiritual current rush up along the spine and goes towards the brain. If then the devotee goes into samādhi, he sees God." (GSR: 316)

(v) Uninterrupted Meditation

After the control of mind and senses, one can contemplate on God. Here, it is not important which way one uses, because all ways lead to the same goal. Rāmakṛṣṇa says that one's concentration should be completely uninterrupted. There should not be any wave of thought which may disturb the concentration. To describe this, Rāmakṛṣṇa says, "The thing is somehow to unite the mind with God. You must not forget Him, nor even once. Your thought of His should be like the flow of oil, (Tailadhārāvat) without any interruption. If you worship with love even a brick or stone as God, then, through His grace you can see Him. Once the mind has become mature, one doesn't have to continue formal worship for long. The mind then always remains united with God, meditation and contemplation become a constant habit of mind." (GSR: 432) Practicing meditation, one becomes so steady and calm that one will looks like an inert thing. Referring to his own practice, Rāmakṛṣṇa says, 604 "I used to meditate on the flame of a light. I thought of the red part as gross, the white part inside the red as subtle and the stick like black part which is the innermost of all as the casual. By certain signs you can tell when meditation is being rightly practiced. One of them is that a bird will sit on your head, thinking you are an inert thing. One can meditate even with eyes open. One can meditate even while talking." (GSR: 604)

(vi) Ideal Time for Meditation and importance of constant practice

This rigorous practice of meditation should be practices daily as well as in the quiet hour of the day. As Rāmakṛṣṇa says, "It is good to meditate in the small hours of the morning and at dawn. One should also meditate daily after dusk." (GSR: 258) If these practices will be performed constantly then the achievement of goal is in hand. "There is such a thing as abhyāsayoga. Yoga through practice. Keep up the practice and you will find that your mind will follow in whatever direction you lead it." (GSR: 539) Rāmakṛṣṇa says that always one should think positively. Because, daily and constantly whatever one thinks, he will become that only. Rather one should have faith that the name of God is so powerful that it will destroy all tendencies which are the obstacles to the realization. He says, "To feel that one is a free soul is very good. By constantly repeating 'I am free'. I am free, a man verily becomes free. On the other hand, by constantly repeating 'I am bound, I am bound', he certainly becomes bound to worldliness. The fool who say only, 'I am sinner, I am a sinner', verily drowns himself in worldliness. One should rather say, 'I have chanted the name of God. How can I be a sinner? How can I be bound?'" (GSR: 274) In this way not only one becomes free but also acquires the nature of God. "If you meditate on an ideal you will acquire its nature. If you think of God day and night, you will acquire the nature of God." (GSR: 657) Further Rāmakṛṣṇa believes that feminine and masculine, both qualities are there in each human being. It is the fact that one is called man because he has high masculinity and low femininity. And a person is called female, because she had high femininity and low masculinity. But the real saints are those who have high femininity and high masculinity. Which is called the Androgynous personality. To achieve this androgyny, one is required to conquer the lust for the opposite sex. Rāmakṛṣṇa says that if one assumes the nature of the opposite sex while meditating on God, then he will be able to achieve the state of androgyny, which is free from the lust etc. and helpful for the realization. Rāmakṛṣṇa says, "One acquires the nature of the object one meditates upon. He can get rid of a passion like lust by assuming the feminine mood." (GSR: 176) Further he says that God can not be realized without guileless.

(vii) Final Stage of Meditation

Thus, Rāmakṛṣṇa asserts that whatever aspect of the God one can choose as per one's own aptitude, ultimately he will reach at the same goal. Thus, as mentioned earlier that the separation of self remains at the highest level of consciousness, which Rāmakṛṣṇa called a state of a vijñānī. In that state, one can talk to God. Rāmakṛṣṇa says, "She is formless and again, She has form. If you believe in the formless aspect, then meditate on Kālī as that. If you meditate on any aspect of Her with firm conviction, She will let you know Her true nature. Then you will realize that not merely does God exists, but He will come near you and talk to you as I am talking to you." (GSR: 634)

3. Yearning for God

It is stated above how to practice meditation. But Rāmakṛṣṇa is very kind that he gave instructions to those who can not be particular in that. He advised to surrender to God completely and whole-heartedly. He says, "There are some aspirants who cannot practice spiritual discipline by calculating about japa or the period of meditation. All that they do is cry to God with yearning hearts. God hears their cry and can not keep himself away. He reveals himself to them. Surrender everything at the face of God. Give him the power of attorney." (GSR: 369) Not only that, those who can meditate on any aspect of God are also required to develop whole-hearted longing for God. Longing or yearning for God is the basic element of a devotee. Rāmakṛṣṇa says, "Be firm in one ideal, either in God with form or in the formless God. Learn to love God. He who seeks God with a longing heart can see Him, talk to Him as I am talking to you." (GSR: 624)

(i) Nature of Yearning

To show the exact meaning of yearning, Rāmakṛṣṇa gave the illustration of the worldly people, who have immense attractions for worldly things as well as one's own relatives. If all the attractions concentrated in God, then only one is qualified to have His vision. He says, "God reveals Himself to a devotee who feels drawn to him by the combined force of these three-attractions the attraction of worldly possessions by worldly man, the child's attraction for its mother and the husband's attraction for the chaste wife." (GSR: 83) Further he says in the same tune and assures that, "He can surely be seen. One can see His forms, and His formless aspect as well. Can you weep for Him with intense longing of heart? Men shed a jug full of tears for the sake of their children, for their wives, or for money. But who weeps for God?" (GSR: 149) Therefore, Rāmakṛṣṇa advised that, "Pray to God in secret and with yearning, that you may have that passionate attachment and devotion to Him. Shed tears for Him. A man shed a jug full of tears because his wife is sick or because he is loosing money or because he is worrying about getting a job. But tell me, who, ever weeps for God. Give God the power of attorney." (GSR:

627-628) Further, to explain the nature of yearning Rāmakṛṣṇa gave the example of the women, who performs all her duties, but her mind always dwells on the person to whom she love most. He says, "If an aspirant has yearning, that is enough for him to realize God. Live in the world like an unchaste woman. She performs her household duties with great attention, but her mind dwells day and night on her paramour. Perform your duties in the world but keep your mind always fixed on God." (GSR: 488)

In addition to this, Rāmakṛṣṇa illustrated through a story the real nature of yearning. A story goes thus, a disciple asked his teacher how he would get the vision of God. The teacher "took him to a lake, and both of them got into the water. Suddenly the teacher pressed the disciple's head under the water. After a few moments he released him and the disciple raised his head and stood u The guru (teacher) asked him, 'How did you feel?' the disciple said, 'Oh! I thought I should die; I was panting for breath.' The teacher said, 'When you feel like that for God, then you will know you haven't ling to wait for His vision." (GSR: 674,937)

(ii) The Means to Have The Vision of God.

Thus, Rāmakṛṣṇa gave much importance to the yearning for the vision of God. He says, "Weep at least once to see God. These are the two means: practice and passionate attachment to God, that is to say, restlessness of the soul to see Him." (GSR: 182) Through this, one can get the capacity to realize God. That is, one can get the divine eyes who can behold God. But for that "One must develop passionate yearning for God and practice discrimination and renunciation." (GSR: 183) Rāmakṛṣṇa believes that "God reveals Himself to the devotee if only he calls upon Him with a longing heart." (GSR: 306) Thus, for the realization of God, yearning for all the time and with all of body and mind is necessary. Rāmakṛṣṇa believes, "Longing is the means of realizing Atman. A man must strive to attain God with all his body, with all his mind and with all his speech. By thinking day and night of God one acquires the nature of God." (GSR: 429)

(iii) Exclusiveness of Yearning

This yearning is so important that one neither needs to study different scriptures, nor he needs to visit any holy places. That yearning and surrender to God will automatically develop in man the sense of discrimination and feeling of dispassion. Rāmakṛṣṇa says, "And we Pray to God, 'O God, keep my mind away from woman and gold.' And dive deep One doesn't really need to study the different scriptures. If one has no discrimination, one doesn't achieve anything through mere scholarship, even though one studies all the six systems of philosophy. Call on God, crying to Him secretly in solitude. He will give all that you need. The less people know of your spiritual life, the better it will be for you. Devotees endowed with sattva, meditate in a secluded corner or in a forest, or withdraw into the mind. Some times they meditate inside the mosquito net. Have faith in the name of the God. Then you won't need even to go to holy places." (GSR: 292) Thus, according to Rāmakṛṣṇa first of all, one should develop the love for God and then comes all other things like study, reasoning, pilgrimages etc. Rāmakṛṣṇa says, "Therefore, like Valmiki, one should at first renounce everything and cry to God in solitude with a longing heart. The first thing necessary is the vision of God, then comes reasoning about the scriptures and the world." (GSR: 376)

4. Importance of Solitude

Rāmakṛṣṇa, in his preaching, frequently advices his devotees to practice spiritual disciplines in solitude. He believes that to remain away from the world one is able to realize one's own nature. He professed the eternal truth of Aratijanasaṃsadi, that is, a real seeker will prefer to remain away from the people. It is especially necessary in the initial stage of sādhanā. He gave an illustration of milk and butter. He says that if we put curd in the milk, and keep it in 'solitude', then only we get the curd. Not only that, if we get the butter, then we can put it in water, it will not melt. In the same way, it one acquires the vision of God in solitude, then he can live in the world, nothing will touch him, like mud-fish. He says, At the beginning the aspirant should go into solitude now and then. One should go into solitude now and then. (GSR: 82,139,293,368,434,587,627,646,853) Further, he advised to one of his devotees that "For many years you have devoted yourself to various worldly things, you will not be able to think God and meditate on him in this confusion of the world. A little solitude is necessary for you, otherwise your mind will not be steady. Therefore you must fix a place for meditation at least half a mile away from your house." (GSR: 911) According to Rāmakṛṣṇa the solitude in necessary for sādhanā for all the persons, the householders or the renunciates. He believes, "A man can realize God even in the world. But at the beginning he must spend a few days in solitude he must practice spiritual discipline in a solitary place." (GSR: 626) Therefore he many times told his devotees that "Renounce everything for a few days retire into solitude and call on God with all your soul." (GSR: 589)

5. Discrimination and Dispassion

Discrimination and renunciation are the basic means to achieve the ultimate goal of human life. Rāmakṛṣṇa defines both in this way: Discrimination means to know the distinction between the real and the unreal. Renunciation means to have dispassion for the things of the world. (GSR: 179)

(i) To Direct inner allegories towards God

It is necessary to conquer one's inner obstacles for the attainment of God-realization. It is very difficult to conquer them, but through the feeling of surrender, one can sublimate them by directing everything to God. "One cannot completely get rid of the six passions: Lust, anger, greed and the like. Therefore one should direct them to God. If you must have desire and greed, then you should desire love of God and be greedy to attain Him. If you must be conceited and egotistic, then feel conceited and egotistic thinking that you are the servant of God, the child of God. A man can not see God unless he gives his whole mind to him. The mind is wasted on 'woman and gold'. As long as there is bhoga, there will be less of yoga." (GSR: 125,427-428) Unless one become free from all such human limitations, one cannot get liberation. "One can not have the vision of God as long as one has these three shame, hatred and fear is very true. Shames, hatred, fear, caste, pride, secretiveness and the like are so many bonds. Man is free, when he liberated from all these." (GSR: 315)

The meaning of discrimination, according to Rāmakṛṣṇa is: "Discrimination is the reasoning by which one knows that God alone is real and all else is unreal, real means eternal and unreal means impermanent. He who has acquired discrimination knows that God is the only substance and all else is non existent. With the awakening of this spirit of discrimination a man wants to know God. On the contrary, if a man loves the unreal such things as creature comforts, name, fame and wealth – then he doesn't want to know God, who is of the very nature of Reality. Through discrimination between the real and the unreal one seeks to know God. By turning the mind within oneself, one acquires discrimination and through discrimination one thinks of Truth. ...going near to God, you can without any effort gather four fruits, namely, dharma, artha, kāma and mokṣa." (GSR: 321)

(ii) Discrimination Between The Real and The Unreal

Rāmakṛṣṇa says that the world is the mixture of vidyā and avidyā. That is, the world is the mixture of good and evil. One should always think and try to discriminate between the two. God alone is the real and all else is not permanent. "By discriminating thus, one should shake off impermanent objects from the mind." (GSR: 81)

Rāmakṛṣṇa is known for his contention that God is the doer and man is just an instrument. With the discrimination between real and the unreal, Rāmakṛṣṇa advices the devotees to practice discrimination that we are just an instruments, and the real Doer is God only. The one who realize this, is the sign of his liberation. Rāmakṛṣṇa says, "A man verily becomes liberated in the life if he feels. 'God is the doer. He alone is doing everything. I am doing nothing. Man's sufferings and worries spring only from his persistent through that he is the doer. (GSR: 142)

(iii) Process of Attaining Discrimination

Rāmakṛṣṇa describes the process for the attainment of discrimination and dispassion or renunciation. 320 "During the period of struggle one should follow the method of discrimination. Not this, not this.. and direct the whole mind to God. But the state of perfection is quiet different. After reaching God one reaffirms what formerly one denied. After realizing God, one knows definitely that It is He who has become everything. In the beginning, when a man reasons following the vedāntika method of not this, not this, he realizes that Brahman is not the living beings, not the universe, not the twenty – four, cosmic principle all these things become like dreams to him. Then comes the affirmation of what has been denied. And he feels that God himself has become the universe and all living beings. (GSR: 345)

Rāmakṛṣṇa clearly says the only in the initial stage, one should negate all things. But after the realization, one will certainly know that all things are nothing but God. Not only that, that person will also be able to talk with God. They constantly discriminate, saying, 'Brahaman alone is real, and the world illusory. But this is an extremely difficult path. If the world is illusory, then you too are illusory. The teacher who gives instructions is equally illusory. His words too are as illusory as a dream. (GSR: 266) Because, Rāmakṛṣṇa believes that, "The wave is part of water, but the water is not part of the wave... When the master loves his servant. He may say to him come, sit by my side, there is no difference between you and me. But if the servant comes forward of his own will to sit by the master, will not the master be angry? (GSR: 290) Thus, Rāmakṛṣṇa advices all to practice discrimination with the sense of complete surrender.

(iv) Egolessness

The main cause of ego is ignorance. Through ignorance man forgets God and speaks of 'I' and mine. He sinks down and down, entangled in māyā, deluded by woman and God. Māyā robs him of his knowledge. (GSR: 325)

Sense of complete surrender will certainly lead a person to the achievement of the state of egolessness, which is very necessary for the realization. Discrimination will result into the knowledge. But according to Rāmakṛṣṇa, just to get knowledge is not enough. "One must come out of egotism. The mind must completely merge itself in knowledge but that is not enough. The principle of 'I' must vanish too. Then alone does one get the knowledge of Brahman." (GSR: 268) Because, 'I' and 'mine' is the result of ignorance or māyā. Rāmakṛṣṇa says, "Māyā is nothing but the egotism of the embodied soul." (GSR: 168) And, to realize that God as the Doer is the knowledge. When the ego completely vanishes, then only one gets the knowledge that God is the Doer.

Further he says that one should not be entangled in the ego for the worldly possessions. When this sense of ego vanishes, one can get the vision of God. Rāmakṛṣṇa says, "A man is able to see God as soon he gets rid of ego and other limitation. He sees God as soon as he is free from such feelings as 'I am a scholar', 'I am the son of such and such a person', 'I am wealthy', 'I am honorable' and so forth." (GSR: 363)

The ego is so subtle and deceiving that one will not understand form where it comes in the way. And without the elimination of it, one cannot have the realization. Rāmakṛṣṇa says, "It is on account of the ego that one is not able to see God. Likewise, the ego seems to vanish this moment, but it re-appears the next. Unless one renounces the ego, one does not receive the grace of God." (GSR: 790) However, Rāmakṛṣṇa believes that there is no harm in the sense of the ego of a devotee or of a child. He says, "Man can not see God on account of his ego. But there is no harm in the 'ego of a child'. On the contrary, this ego is helpful." (GSR: 678)

(v) Dispassion Leads to Renunciation

It is well said that according to Rāmakṛṣṇa the ultimate goal of human life is the attainment of the vision of God, or to develop love for God. For the achievement of this goal, the practice of intense renunciation is very necessary. The true renunciation is dispassion for worldly possessions, other than God, and intense love for God. Rāmakṛṣṇa believes that to develop this kind of sense of renunciation, the power of discrimination is very helpful. It once it is clear by discrimination what is real and what is not, one must renounce what is unreal. He says, One succeeds (in spiritual life) if one develops a strong spirit of renunciation. Give-up at once, with determination, what you know to be unreal. (GSR: 246)

Rāmakṛṣṇa asserts that the play of māyā will remain and become obstacles to a man, unless, the knowledge is acquired. Not knowing the nature of māyā is ignorance. When one recognizes its nature, all the play of it will disappear for him. "One can realize God if one feels intense dispassion for worldly thing. Woman and gold is māyā. If māyā is once recognized, it feels ashamed of itself and takes to flight." (GSR: 336)

Explaining the types of renunciation, Rāmakṛṣṇa says that "There are two kinds of renunciation: Intense and feeble. Feeble renunciation is a slow process. Intense renunciation is like the sharp edge of a razor, it cuts the bondage of māyā easily and at once." (GSR: 410) Rāmakṛṣṇa does not give much value to the person who renounce everything because of some unhappiness occur in his life. The only valuable thing is if one feels to renounce everything out of single-pointed love for God. Thus, Rāmakṛṣṇa believes that, "The truth is that you can not attain God if you have even a trace of desire. Subtle is the way of dharma. No matter how much sādhanā you practice, you will not realize the goal as long as you have desire. One can not realize God without renunciation." (GSR: 769)

Rāmakṛṣṇa believes that without renunciation, there is not peace or happiness. Giving the example of a saint Dattatreya, who learnt many things from the worldly objects and thereby considers that things as his spiritual guides. Rāmakṛṣṇa says, "The avadhuta learnt this lesson from the kite, that as long as a man has the fish, that is, worldly desires, he must perform actions and consequently suffer from worry, anxiety and restlessness. No sooner does he renounce these desires than his activities fall away and he enjoys peace of soul." (GSR: 314)

(vi) The Result of Discrimination and Dispassion

The outcome of the practice of discrimination which results into the total renunciation is the vision of God. The realized person acquires the purity of mind. Purity of mind is a mental state where there remain no desires for any worldly objects. Through this mind, absolutely free from the desires, God can be known. "God cannot be known by the sense-organs or by the mind, but he can be known by the pure mind, the mind that is free from worldly desires." (GSR: 328) Thus, Rāmakṛṣṇa advices his devotees to develop dispassion and discrimination, through which one can get the purity of mind. Then only the goal of human life can be achieved.

The outcome of the one who becomes free from desire will maintain that state even while leading a life of a householder. "Once a man realizes God through intense dispassion, he is no longer attached to woman. Even if he must lead the life of a house—holder, he is free from fear to and attachment to woman. (GSR: 167)

As it is seen that, man are considered as an ignorant because, there is a beginningless association of self with body, which is the outcome of ignorance. After attaining knowledge one can see that body and self are different. Rāmakṛṣṇa says, "After realizing God one does not identify oneself any more with the body. Then one knows that body and soul are two different things." (GSR: 319)

Another outcome of the vision of God is, according to Rāmakṛṣṇa "man is overpowered with bliss. He becomes silent." (GSR: 218) And, "Through the help of vidyāmāyā one cultivates such virtues as the taste of holy company, knowledge, devotion, love and renunciation." (GSR: 216)

6. Love of God

(i) Different types of Attitudes of a Devotee for God

It is very well accepted in the Indian devotional tradition that for the vision of God, a seeker should assume any one particular attitude towards God. Rāmakṛṣṇa preaches this traditional value of the path of devotion to his devotees. He says, "In order to realize God, one must assume one of these. Attitudes, Santa' dāsya, sakhya, vātsalya or madhur. One sees nothing but God everywhere when one loves him with great intensity." (GSR: 115, 610,681,700)

(ii) Importance of The Path of Devotion

Rāmakṛṣṇa put great emphasis on the path of devotion that is seen in his devotion towards the Mother worship. He advocates mother worship because he believes that, "Brahman alone is addresses as the Mother. This is because a Mother is an object of great love. One is able to realize God just through love. Ecstasy of feeling, devotion, love and faith-these are the means. What is needed is absorption in God. Loving him intensely." (GSR: 108) Further explaining the importance of the path of devotion for sādhanā, Rāmakṛṣṇa says that the renunciation and discrimination, which are necessary for God-realization can be developed through the love of God. In his own words, "Bhakti, love of God, is the essence of all spiritual discipline. Through love one acquires renunciation and discrimination naturally." (GSR: 123,497)

According to Rāmakṛṣṇa the purpose of the very birth as a human being is to cultivate love for God. Therefore, he says, "You have been born in this world as a human being to worship God, therefore try to acquire love for his lotus feet. Why don't you give your power of attorney to God rest all your responsibilities on him." (GSR: 841,900)

(iii) All Other Form of Sādhanā are for the Cultivation of Love of God

Further, Rāmakṛṣṇa says that mere scholarship can not be helpful in the development of the love for God. There must be some austerity and craving for God in life. Rāmakṛṣṇa believes that one should cry for the vision of God. Taking Caitanya Mahāprabhu's example Rāmakṛṣṇa says, Caitanya used to shed tears of joy at the very mention of Kṛṣṇa's name. God alone is the real substance, all else is illusory. Man can realize God if he wants to, but he madly craves the enjoyment of woman and gold. God alone is the highest good, the Eternal Substance, and that all else is transitory. One can not grasp this without tapasyā and the company of holy men. What can be accomplished by a mere lecture? It is austerity that is necessary. But that alone can one appear hand. (GSR: 157)

(iv) Love of God is Beyond All Other Virtues

Rāmakṛṣṇa says, "Mother, here is Thy virtue, here is The vice. Take them both and grant me only pure love for Thee. Here is Thy knowledge, here is Thy ignorance. Take them both and grant me only pure love for Thee. Here is Thy purity, here is Thy impurity. Take them both and grant me only pure love for Thee. Here is Thy dharma, here is Thy adharma. Take them both and grant me only pure love for Thee." (GSR: 138) Here, it should be noted that Rāmakṛṣṇa gave great importance to the love of God than purity, knowledge or dharma, but he could not say this with reference to truth. As truth and honesty is the part of love, they cannot be separated from it.

(v) Pure Mind is Required For The Love For God

According to Rāmakṛṣṇa the process of acquiring love for God is that, first of all, one must practice austerity with the practice of vaidhi bhakti. Because Rāmakṛṣṇa believes that "Unless the soul is pure, one cannot have genuine love of God and single-minded devotion to the ideal." (GSR: 710) Therefore, to get the purity of heart, one needs to perform vaidhi bhakti. The vaidhi bhakti includes japa, worship, pilgrimages, sacrifices etc. Through vaidhi bhakti and austerity, one can achieve prema bhakti or raga bhakti. And that is the real means to realize God. Rāmakṛṣṇa says, "One must love God. In order to realize God, one must be completely free from worldliness and direct all of one's mind to Him. One can not realize, God without 'Prema-bhakti...

God can not be realized without love and longing unless one has learnt to love God, one can not realize him. God cannot be realized until one has raga – bhakti. One must love God. In order to realize God, one must be completely free from worldliness and direct all of one's mind to Him. One practices japa, austerity and fasting in order to acquire love of God." (GSR: 172)

(vi) All The Passions Should be Directed Towards God

Rāmakṛṣṇa advices his devotees how to practice self-surrender in order to get the love for God. He advices, "Give your power of attorney to God." "Direct the six passions to God. The impulse of lust should be tuned into the desire to have intercourse with atman. Feel angry at those who stand in your way to God. Feel greedy for him. If you must have the feeling of 'I and mind', then associate it with God. If you must have pride, then feel like Bibhishana who said. 'I have touched the feet of Rāma with my head, I will not bow this head before anyone else." (GSR: 209,220,861) The basic thing is that if one attain little of the love for God, then nothing will there in the world which can attract him. Rāmakṛṣṇa says, "When a man is intoxicated with ecstatic love of God, he doesn't take delight in anything else. (GSR: 372)

In the world a person may feel for others as his own people, but actually, no one is his. On one is there in the world to whom one can say his own except God. Therefore, Rāmakṛṣṇa says, "There is only one whom you may call your own, and that is God. Therefore a man should act in such a way that he may have bhakti for the lotus feet of God and love God as his very own." (GSR: 610) Thus, one should direct one's feeling of affection towards God only.

(vii) Characteristics of a Person Having Attained The Love For God

The defining characteristic of the love for God is that if one will realize God, his senses and mind will be withdrawn from the world. Rāmakṛṣṇa says, "When this mind is united with God, one sees him very near, in one's own heart. But you must remember one thing. The more you realize this unity, the further your mind is withdrawn from worldly things." (GSR: 916) Because Rāmakṛṣṇa believes that love for God and attachment towards world are two polar opposite elements. The more one loves God, the less will be his attachment to world and the more there is an attachment for worldly objects, the less will be the love for God. He says, "Attribute to yourselves the bliss of God consciousness, then you too will experience ineffable joy. The less you are attached to the world, the more you love God. The nearer you approach to God, the more you feel his love. The less you are attached to the world, the more you love God. (GSR: 277)

Those who surrender their hearts and soul to God, those who are devoted to him and have taken refuge in him, do not worry much about money. This is what the Gītā describes as 'accepting what comes of its own accord'. (GSR: 506)

7. Need of Firm Faith in God

Rāmakṛṣṇa believes that the cause of all sufferings and unhappiness is due to lack of faith in God. Rāmakṛṣṇa agrees to the truth that 'Faith is the possession of the things unseen.' That is, if one wants to get salvation, one should have faith that God will certainly grant him His vision. For this purpose of life can be fulfilled if one thinks always positively. Thinking is so powerful that it can decide one's character. Hence, Rāmakṛṣṇa put much emphasis on that. He says, "The wretch who constantly say, 'I am bound', 'I am bound' only succeeds in being bound. He who says, I am a sinner, I am a sinner verity becomes sinner. (one must have faith that) I have repeated the name of God and can sin still cling to me?" (GSR: 138,538,679) In the same tune he further says, "The man who says he will not succeed will never succeed. He who feels he is liberated in indeed liberated, and he who feels he is bound verity remains bound. He who forcefully says, 'I am free' is certainly free, and he who says day and night, 'I am bound' is certainly bound. (GSR: 706) Rāmakṛṣṇa says that when a man sincerely prays to God, he is able to fix his mind on God and develop real love for His lotus feet. He advices, "Give up all such notions as: 'Shall we be cured of our delirium?' 'what will happen to us?' 'We are sinners!' One must have this kind of faith: 'Once I have uttered the name of Rāma, can I be sinner any more? (GSR: 820) Thus, according to Rāmakṛṣṇa one must faith to the extent that even for a moment one remembers God, he will free from bondage "Union with God even for one moment surely gives a man liberation." (GSR: 819)

Rāmakṛṣṇa's thoughts on faith are clearly seen in the following sentences:

"You may believe in God with form or in God without form, but your faith must be sincere and whole–hearted. Unless one is guideless and broadminded, one cannot have such faith." (GSR: 234) "worthless people do not have any faith. They always doubt. But doubts do not disappear completely till one realizes the self." (GSR: 252)

8. Prayer, Chanting a Name of God and Company of Holy Men

(i) Prayer

Rāmakṛṣṇa told about prayers at many places but the essence is in his this utterance that, "Take refuge in Chitsakti, Mahāmāyā.... say to God with a guideless heart, O God! Reveal Thyself to me." (GSR: 291) This is the highest and honest prayer. The finite cannot apprehend it, still in whatever way one worship the God, but one should always pray like this. Rāmakṛṣṇa says that God is our own, so for discrimination, for love of God, for detachment, for everything one should pray to God. Rāmakṛṣṇa recommended many practices, but all should be practiced with the sense of surrender to God and with the sincere prayers.

(ii) Chanting a Name of God

It is seen earlier that according to Rāmakṛṣṇa the highest goal of human life is to attain the vision of God. For this he advices his disciples to practice sādhanā in various ways. Among them, the most important and easily practicable is the chanting of God's name. Through chanting one becomes pure. He says, 159 "Chant his name and purify your body and mind. Purify your tongue by singing God's holy name." (GSR: 159) Rāmakṛṣṇa gives the hierarchy of the feelings towards God. In that, to reach the highest, first one needs to chant God's name. he says, "One attains God through japa. By repeating the name of God sincerely and in solitude, one receives Divine grace. Then comes His vision. Higher than worship is japa higher than japa is meditation, higher than meditation is bhāva and higher than bhāva are niṣhāmahābhāva and prema." (GSR: 588)

Rāmakṛṣṇa gave his disciples the following instructions regarding the chanting of God's name:

"Repeat God's name and his glories and keep holy company and now and then visit God's devotes and holy men. the mind can not dwell on God if it is immersed day and night in worldliness, in worldly duties and responsibilities. It is most necessary to go into solitude now and then and think of God. To fix the mind on God is very difficult, in the beginning, unless one practices meditation in solitude." (GSR: 81) "You will attain God, if you sing his name and glories and pray to him with a longing heart." (GSR: 171) "All the sins of the body fly away if one chants the name of God and sing his glories." (GSR: 181)

Rāmakṛṣṇa says very important and subtle element of sādhanā to his devotees that they should be very careful in chanting the name of God. It should be accompanied with the constant remembrance of God. Just mechanically chanting is futile activity. Therefore, he says, "There is no doubt about the sanctity of Gods name. But can a mere name achieve anything? Without the yearning love of the devotee behind it? One should feel great restlessness of soul for the vision of God. Suppose a man repeats the name of God mechanically, while his mind is absorbed in 'woman and gold', can he achieve anything? Therefore, I say, chant the name of God, and with it pray to Him that you may have love for Him. Pray to God that your attachment to such transitory things as wealth, name and creature comforts may becomes less and less every day." (GSR: 190) Rāmakṛṣṇa believes that it the chanting is practices is this way, it has the immense value. Because, as he says, "Repeating the name of Rāma but once, he gets the fruits of ten million sandhyā." (GSR: 658)

(iii) Company of Holy Persons

As it is seen in chapter II that the identification of self with body is beginningless. The body represents man's worldly inclination, which is due to the ignorance of the knowledge of the real self. Therefore, if one wants to actualize the real nature of self, and to achieve its goal of God-vision, one is supposed to divert his inclination of worldly objects towards God. Rāmakṛṣṇa believes that to turn one's mind from worldliness to Godliness, the company of holy people is necessary. "By constantly living in the company of a holy man one verily becomes holy." (GSR: 401) Further, they instruct in such a way that the goal can be achieved. Rāmakṛṣṇa says, "For the seekers of God the constant company of holy men is necessary. The disease of worldly people has become chronic, as it were. They should carry out the instruction of holy men." (GSR: 194, 865) Why the company of holy men is necessary is shown by Rāmakṛṣṇa that, "Prayer and the company of the holy men begets yearning for God. It begets love of God. Nothing whatsoever is achieved in spiritual life one must love God." (GSR: 96)

Rāmakṛṣṇa advices his devotees to keep themselves away from the worldly-minded people. One should protect oneself from them. Further he says that if a person live unmarried life for the cause of realization, and live in a family is also not good. According to he is neither man of world nor a devotee of God. He advices a person to live in solitude so that he can well remember God and thereby realize the ultimate goal. (GSR: 281)

Rāmakṛṣṇa gave so much importance to this that he believes that even the sight of a holy is very spiritually uplifting for a devotee. Therefore he says, "It is good to keep pictures of sannyāsis and holy men in one's room. When you get up in the morning you should see the faces of holy persons rather than the faces of other men. You acquire the nature of the people whose company you keep" (GSR: 431,606)

Thus, Rāmakṛṣṇa says that every external spiritual practices will be stop when one gradually attain the love for God. He says, "At the beginning of spiritual life the devotee should observe such rites as pilgrimage, putting a string of beads around his neck and so forth. But outward ceremonies gradually drop off as he attains the goal, the vision of God. Then his only activity is the repetition of God's name and contemplation and meditation on him." (GSR: 305)

9. Purity and Truthfulness

(i) Purity of Mind

All above stated sādhanā results in the purity of mind. God dwells in the pure mind only. If mind becomes free from all internal limitations then it will become pure. Therefore, Rāmakṛṣṇa says, "God can not be realized without purity of heart. One received the grace of God by subduing the passion – lust, anger and greed. Then one sees God." (GSR: 161) If one becomes pure in this way, the real longing for God will be achieved. "Thirst disappears with the destruction of attachment. Finally comes peace. God is realized as soon as the mind becomes free from attachment. In order to realize God one must go beyond dharma and adharma." (GSR: 178)

(ii) Truthfulness

Rāmakṛṣṇa emphatically says that truth, honesty and integrity are the real means to achieve God in this age of materialism. Looking at the corruption, a universally spreaded disease in the external as well as internal universe, it is apparent that how Rāmakṛṣṇa is relevant in giving this preaching. He says, 177 "Truthfulness alone is the spiritual discipline in the kaḷiyuga." (GSR: 177) Rāmakṛṣṇa believes that in this age, for tapsya one is not supposed to go to Himalaya, but in this world it one practice truth, then, he will certainly get the vision of God.

It is said in this chapter under the title, Love of God is Beyond All Other Virtues, that Rāmakṛṣṇa surrenders everything to God, all virtues and vices, but he could not surrender 'truth and untruth' for the sake of love. He gave this much importance to the practice of Truth in his own life as well as advices his devotees to practice truthfulness in very honest spirit. He says, "Dwell in the truth and you will certainly realize God. (GSR: 261)

Swami Lokeswaranandji says, "Śrī Rāmakṛṣṇa used to say that the Divine Mother never puts false words in the mouth of one who is steadfastly devoted to truth, and She does not permit him to act falsely. In the master's own life we find many examples of this." Swami Lokeswaranandji: 128) Further Swamiji says, "In later years when young devotees came to him, the Master would be very strict with them about truthfulness. One day he said to Rakhal (Swami Brahmananda), 'Why can't I look at your face? Have you done anything wrong?' Rakhal thought to himself: "What wrong could I have committed? I have not robbed anyone or anything like that?' Then it occurred to him that he had joking told a lie. Śrī R.K. knew this because he could read others minds, and he regarded that seemingly innocent lie as a serious moral lapse. Even jokingly one must not tell lie, because if one repeatedly speaks this way, lying will become a habit." (Swami Lokeswarananda, 1997: 130) Thus, it is seen that

Rāmakṛṣṇa is so truly sensitive about the Truth that even in lightly manner also he never approve any type of lie or untruthfulness.

10. Total Abundance of Lust And Greed

First it should be clarified that Rāmakṛṣṇa has uttered the word 'woman and gold' very frequently in his conversations. One should not think that he has some negative bias for woman. Basically, by uttering that, he meant 'lust and greed' only. It was the situation where majority of male disciples were visiting him. Rāmakṛṣṇa has given advices to his female disciples also. Therefore, it is clear that while telling 'woman and gold', Rāmakṛṣṇa does not have degraded woman at all.

Rāmakṛṣṇa believes that a seeker should try to concentrate his mind sparingly on God's thought. If mind is directed towards any worldly things, it will never have the vision of God. If mind is on anything other than God then it cannot dwell deeply on God. One must have only thinking of God's name, God's glories etc. which are related to God only. Other than this will be very harmful for a sādhakas. Not only this, even a person who has renounce everything and live in the mountain, doing tapasyā and other practices, but if his mind is on worldly objects then nothing will help him. Rāmakṛṣṇa says, "A man practices spiritual discipline, but his mind is on woman and gold. It is turned toward enjoyment. Therefore in this case, the spiritual discipline does not produce the right result. A man may live in a mountain cave, smear his body with ashes, observes tasks and practice austerities. But if his mind dwells on worldly objects, on 'woman and gold', I say, 'shame on him', But I Say that a man is blessed indeed who eats, drinks and reams about, but who keeps his mind free from 'woman and gold'." (GSR: 402)

According to Rāmakṛṣṇa the complete detachment form worldly objects, especially from lust and greed is the prime condition for the attainment of God, because it has momentary pleasure. He says, if mind is on worldly objects then how can it dwell on God? One had to choose between the two. One can either take world, or he can worship God. Therefore, Rāmakṛṣṇa believes that without the removal of lust and greed, no one can get realization. He says, "A man cannot acquire the knowledge of Brahman unless he completely rids himself of his attachment to the world." (GSR: 130,343,307,387)

According to Rāmakṛṣṇa man is attached to the worldly object, it is because of the lust and greed in his mind. Therefore, he defines world as the lust and greed. To make it clean he called lust and greed as 'woman and gold'. Thus, according to Rāmakṛṣṇa the woman and gold is the world, and that is the māyā. It is difficult for a mind which is attached to woman and gold, to concentrate on God. When it will be free from that attachment then only it can absorb in the Divine thought. He says, "Come outside the house of māyā, give up woman and gold. And then the sun of knowledge will destroy ignorance. The darkness of the mind is destroyed only when a man stands a little apart from 'woman and gold' and thus standing apart, practices a little austerity and spiritual discipline. Then only does the cloud of his ego and ignorance vanish." (GSR: 584, 670,748,793,817)

Rāmakṛṣṇa teaches his disciples how to discriminate in this respect. It is seen in the following passage uttered by Rāmakṛṣṇa with the remark of Śrī Nikhilanandaji:

"You must practice discrimination. 'Woman and gold' (lust and greed) is impermanent. God is the only eternal substance. What does a man get with money? Food, clothes and a dwelling peace-nothing more. You can not realize God with its help. Therefore money can never be the goal of life. That is the process of discrimination. ... consider what is there in money or in a beautiful body? You will find that even the body of a beautiful woman consists of bones, flesh, fat and other disagreeable things. Why should a man forget God for their sake? He advices women on the other hand, to shun 'man'. By it (kaminīkāñcana) he meant only lust and greed." (GSR: 82)

(i) Remaining Away From Even a Very Good Devotee of The Other Sex

Rāmakṛṣṇa warns his male disciple to keep distance from woman, even if she is a devotee. A seeker should not keep association with her. Here, also it may be said that If he would have occasion to tell anything to a female seeker, then he would have warn her from a man who is a devotee. Thus, the basic point is, if one wants to get the realization, one should keep distance from the opposite sex. However, good and divine qualities, he or she is having, one should not entertain any type of relation with the opposite sex. He says, "An aspirant should not associate with a woman, even though she is very much devoted to God." (GSR: 184,188)

Not only this, Rāmakṛṣṇa is also against the motherly relation with anybody. It is seen sometimes that among sādhakas, that they are associated with the feeling of motherly in the context of male and elderly in the context of female. Rāmakṛṣṇa is against any such relation. Rāmakṛṣṇa is very subtle in the sādhanā, that he never approve even slightest loophole in the sādhanā. He says, "This very maternal feeling leads to a downfall."(GSR: 536) Though this conversation was regarding a certain sect, but this shows Rāmakṛṣṇa's feeling towards the subtleness in sādhanā.

(ii) Lust, Also Inclusive of Any Kind of Worldliness

As Rāmakṛṣṇa says that, lust and greed are the two obstacles in the path of sādhanā. This concept of lust includes any type of intense desires. That is, if a person has intense desire for anything in the world is the obstacle in sādhanā. Therefore, Rāmakṛṣṇa has advised his disciples to renounce all desires. This renunciation includes ultimately to the renunciation of ego. He says, "A man of strong renunciation seeks nothing but God. He regards the world as a deep well and feels as if he were going to be drowned in it. He looks on his relatives as venomous snakes, he wants to fly away from them. And he does go away. He never thinks, 'let me first make some arrangement for my family and then I shall think of God.' He has great inward resolution." (GSR: 165,703,896)

Thus, according to Rāmakṛṣṇa, "God is very far away from the mind tainted with worldliness. (GSR: 814,837) And if one wants the realization of God then, he must have intense dispassion for worldly objects. He says, "If you want to realize God, then you must cultivate intense dispassion. You must renounce immediately what you feel to be standing in your way." (GSR: 750) The main cause of all desires is man's ego. Ego is the main obstacle in the path of realization. Rāmakṛṣṇa shows how lust and greed are associated with the pride. He says, "It is attachment to 'Woman and Gold' that begets pride of learning, pride of money and pride of social position. One can not attain divine knowledge till one gets rid of pride." (GSR: 874)

Further, Rāmakṛṣṇa says that for the realization of God, one should not only free from 'lust and greed', money or possessions, or pride but also from eight fetters. "There are eight fetters with which man is bound: shame, hatred, fear, pride of caste, hesitation, the desire to conceal, and so forth." (GSR: 438,899) According to Rāmakṛṣṇa these are also to be conquered by the seeker so that he may have the vision of God.

11. Occult Power as Obstacles to Realization

Rāmakṛṣṇa never practice any discipline to acquire occult powers. He considers the powers as the greatest obstacles to God-realization. According to him, to demand or desire such powers shows the meanness of a person. He says, "Spiritual practices with a view to winning a lawsuit and earning money, or to helping others win in court and acquire property, shows a very mean understanding." (GSR: 285,518,745,903) Because, he firmly believes that, "By siddhis one may acquire powers, strength, money and such things, but not God." (GSR: 695) According to Rāmakṛṣṇa for the one who wishes to have such supernatural powers, it is hard to have pure love for God.

Rāmakṛṣṇa expresses his views by giving the examples from Indian scriptures as well as from his own experience with a devotee. It is clearly seen through the following passages:

"People practice various Tāntrika disciplines to acquire supernatural powers. How mean such people are! Kṛṣṇa said to Arjuna, 'friend, by acquiring one of the eight siddhis you may add a little to your power, but you will not be able to realize Me. One cannot get rid of māyā as long as one exercises supernatural powers. And māyā begets egotism. Body and wealth are impermanent. Why go to so much trouble for their sake? Just think of the plight of the hathayogis. Their attention is fixed on one ideal only—longevity. They do not aim at the realization of God at all. They practice such exercises as washing out the intestines, drinking milk through a tube and the like with that one aim in view. These are physical things and have nothing to do with God." (GSR: 285,308,547)

"Once a rich man came here and said to me. 'Sir, you must do something so that I may win my lawsuit. I have heard of your reputation and so I have come here. My dear sir, I said to him, 'you have made a mistake. I am not the person you are looking for. A true devotee of God does not care for such things as wealth or health. He thinks 'why should I practice spiritual austerities for creature comforts, money or name and fame? These are all impermanent. They last only a day or two." (GSR: 286)

It is worth noting at the end of this chapter that if one wants to get the realization, one should practice the above mentioned disciplines with total commitment. Simultaneously, the seeker should have the faith in Guru together with the grace of guru. (GSR: 232,243,247)

As Socrates says, 'Unexamined life is not worth living.' In the similar way, Rāmakṛṣṇa says that if sincere sādhanā is not performed then a person's life is not worth living. He says, "Man should possess dignity and a alertness. Only he whose spiritual consciousness is awakened possesses this dignity and alertness and can be called a man. Futile is the human birth without the awakening of spiritual consciousness." (GSR: 844) For this, a person's mind should be as pure as like a child's mind. He believes, "Unless a man is guideless, he cannot so easily have faith in God." (GSR: 699,865)

9

Society and Morals

1. Religion and Morality

It is seen earlier that morality is one of the essential ingredients of religious life. Religion is thus more comprehensive than morality. Hence, Rāmakṛṣṇa has brought out this aspect of morality which can be helpful for the achievement of the culmination of religious life. According to him the basic morality is to cultivate the love for God. Rāmakṛṣṇa has enjoined his followers to act always in accordance with this morality with utmost vigilance and enthusiasm. The obligatoriness of this moral law, thus, occupies a central place in Rāmakṛṣṇa's ethics; and yet it is not vitiated by the defects of the doctrine of the 'duty for the sake of duty.' Unlike Kant, Rāmakṛṣṇa has recognized that man, as a rational being, can not act in blind obedience to the moral laws. Again, the law is after all made for the sake of man, and not man for the sake of law. It is immoral, on Kant's own principle, to treat man not as an end in himself, but as a mere means for the realization of an abstract law. Thus, his concept of morality is not separate form the spiritual way of life.

So the moral laws in Rāmakṛṣṇa are clearly subservient to the realization of self. Thus, the ethics of Rāmakṛṣṇa is, to use Prof. Broad's terms, teleological and not deontological, as far as the question of the rightness of a rule is concerned. From the standpoint of Rāmakṛṣṇa the categorical character of the obligatoriness of the moral laws does not mean absence of all reference to teleology. It rather means that the observance of the moral laws, as defined by him is absolutely necessary for the attainment of self-realization. That is, the violation of the moral laws necessarily results into the frustration of all rational purposes of man.

Rāmakṛṣṇa's unique philosophy of morals is the practical application of his views regarding the fundamental problems of metaphysics, religion and ethics. As one whose life-teaching was to guide people towards the highest level of consciousness, Rāmakṛṣṇa was very much interested in its practical implication. Rāmakṛṣṇa, thus, gives foremost importance to the performance of duties and the cultivation of virtues prescribed by him. Thus, his morality is nothing but the practice of spirituality in life. In the Gospel he has gone to the extent that one is not rightly living the life if he leads a life without practicing spirituality. "One faces (the same) difficulty leading the life of householder. A few succeed in it through the grace of God and as a result of their spiritual practice. But most people fail. Entering the world, they become more and more involved in it, they drown in worldliness and suffer the agonies of death. A few only, like Janaka, have succeeded, through the power of their austerity, in leading the spiritual life as householder. Therefore spiritual practice is extremely necessary; otherwise one cannot rightly live in the world." (GSR: 154) According to Rāmakṛṣṇa to lead a spiritual like in the life of a householder is very difficult. Therefore, the one who succeeds in this life is the rare and chosen one. "A devotee who call on God while living a householder life is a hero indeed. God thinks 'He who has renounce the world for my sake will surely pray to Me...people will cry shame on him if he fails to do so but he is blessed indeed who prays to Me in the midst of his worldly duties...Such a man is a real hero'." (GSR: 471)

"There are four stages of life: brahmācārya, garhasthya, vanaprastha and sanyāsa. During the first three stages a man has to perform his worldly duties. The Sannyāsi carried only his staff, water-pot and begging-bowl. He too may perform certain nityakarma, but his mind is not attached to it, he is not conscious of doing such work. Some Sannyāsis perform nityakarma to set an example to the world. If a householder or a man belonging to the other stages of life performs action without attachment, then he is united with God through such action...In the case of paramahaṃsa, like Shukadeva, all Karmas, all Puja, Japa, Tarpan, Sandhyā and so forth-drop away. In this state a man communes with God through the mind alone. Sometimes he may be pleased to perform outward activities for the welfare of mankind. But his recollection and contemplation of God remain uninterrupted."

(GSR: 388) Thus, Rāmakṛṣṇa mentioned the four āśramas, but put first three adhramas in one category in the reference to sādhanā.

Therefore, instead of accepting the four-fold āśramavyavasthā of the ancient Hindu life, Rāmakṛṣṇa has recognized only two adhramas-Householders (Gruhasthadhrama) and Renunciates (Sannasadhrama). He must have seen that the reinstatement of the ancient system exactly in the same form is neither possible, nor desirable under the changed conditions of life. He has, therefore, accepted only two adhramas, without, however, going against the principle on which the ancient four āśramas were based. It is to be specially noted that unlike the ancient four āśramas, these two ashrams are alternative to each other, and not the continuous stages of the life of the one and the same individual. That is, Rāmakṛṣṇa has not regarded it necessary for each individual to accept the life of a householder for a particular period of his life, and then enter the life of a renunciate. These two āśramas are the paths of pravṛtti and nivṛtti respectively. These two are equal when a person can lead a life like a Janaka, who has complete detachment towards his possessions. But it is not easy to live that type of life. According to Rāmakṛṣṇa the individual is supposed to select any one of these two paths in accordance with his natural inclinations. Because, "Most people don't feel any longing for God unless they have once passed through the experience of wealth, name, fame, creature comforts and the like, that is to say, unless they have seen through these enjoyments." Rāmakṛṣṇa says, "The truth is that a man doesn't feel restless for God unless he is finished with his enjoyments and duties." (GSR: 216) Further, "It is not always best to tell householders about the sorrows of life." (GSR: 224)

Rāmakṛṣṇa has laid more emphasis upon the inner aspect of spiritual life rather than its external garb. "One can realize God in the world, too, if only one is sincere... .I ask people to renounce mentally. I do not ask them to give up the world." (GSR: 561) (To Pandit) "Why should you give up? Give up mentally, live unattached in the world." (GSR: 610) But to lead the life in the world with the feeling of detachment is very difficult. Hence, most people living a life of a householder become worldly-minded ones. As according to Rāmakṛṣṇa "The worldly man's yearning for God is momentary."

(GSR: 220,384,402) And "Worldly people have no stuff in them... Worldly people are salves of three things: they are slaves of their wives, slaves of their money, slaves of their masters. Can they have any inner stuff?" (GSR: 615) and "No matter how much one washes a cup that has contained a solution of garlic, still a trace of the smell will certainly linger...Man who have associated a long time with 'woman and gold' smell of the garlic." (GSR: 709), the path of nivṛtti is superior to the path of pravṛtti. It is important to note here that between these two, Rāmakṛṣṇa put more importance to the path of nivṛtti. Ultimately one has to go upto that level in spiritual life. Once Narendra asked a question: Must one renounce the world? Rāmakṛṣṇa answered, "Renunciation is necessary. If one thing is placed upon another, you must remove the one to get the other. Can you get the second thing without removing the first...When one sees everything filled with God alone, does one see anything else? Does one then see any such thing as the world? I mean mental renunciation." (GSR: 944) However, he has not discouraged the people who lead a life of a householder, but he advice them also to pray for and to practice for the attainment of nivṛtti and thereby the attainment of liberation.

From the point of view of the possibility of the attainment of God, Rāmakṛṣṇa put on equal level the path of a householder and the path of a renunciate. But on the praxis level, those have differences. He showed the basic difference between them. He says, "You may ask, 'Is there any difference between the realization of two Jñānīs, one a householder and the other a monk?' the reply is that the two belong to one class. Both of them are Jñānīs; they have the same experience but a householder Jñānī has reason to fear. He cannot altogether get rid of his fear as long as he is to live in the midst of 'woman and gold'...if a monk who has renounced the world attains divine wisdom, he appears as spotless as the white flower; but who stays in the frying pan of the world after attaining knowledge may get a little blemish!...Through perfect knowledge a man becomes like a child five years old; he does not know the distinction between a man and a woman." (GSR: 857) As Rāmakṛṣṇa emphasis on the praxis part of spirituality in sādhanā, he found difference between the two paths of sādhanā. "There is a great deal of difference between the knowledge of householder and that of an all-renouncing Sannyāsi. The householder's knowledge is like the light of a lamp...But the knowledge of the all-renouncing monk is like the light of the sun." (GSR: 485) "Nivṛtti alone is good and not pravṛtti...In leading the worldly life one has to humour mean-minded people and do many such things." (GSR: 518) Giving the example of bee and fly, he says that the bee will sit only on a flower while a fly may sit at one time on a flower and at another time on dirt. Hence, "There is an ocean of difference between a real all-renouncing devotee of God and a householder devotee." (GSR: 520) Regarding the householders entangled in worldliness, the Master said: "They are like silk-worm. They can come out of the cocoon of their worldly life if they wish. But they can't bear to, for they themselves have build the cocoon with great love and care. So they die there...only one or two make good their escape by running away. They are the liberated souls." (GSR: 155) Similarly, he praised the devotees who do have the affection towards the worldly objects. "Blessed indeed are those young aspirants, who like Sukadeva, practice renunciation from their very boyhood and think of God day and night without being involved in worldly life." (GSR: 348)

Thus, he showed the dangers in leading a life of a householder. In his basic advice for moral practices, Rāmakṛṣṇa has equal thing to say. He put major importance on the love for God, detachment for world and that can be achieved through spending more time in solitude. "Whether man is a monk or a householder, he has to shake off all attachment from his mind." (GSR: 105) Thus, he is not even against the life of a householder. "Once a man realizes God through intense dispassion, he is no longer attached to woman. Even if he must lead the life of a householder, he is free from fear of and attachment to woman." (GSR: 167) To save a householder devotees form the danger of becoming a worldly-minded, he gave certain practices for them to follow.

2. Duties pertaining to the Householder

(1) Rāmakṛṣṇa used the metaphor that to fight in the open field is dangerous because from any side the disturbances may accrue. But to fight from inside the fort is less dangerous. In the same way, to live a life of a householder is like fighting from inside the fort. If mind is little bit satisfied then it will not create disturbances in sādhanā. He did not discouraged the householder devotees, but rather encouraged

them by telling that it is not harmful if one lead a life of a householder. But he gave clear instructions for them to practice for the achievement of the goal, that is, the salvation. He says, "If married people develop love for God, they will not be attached to the world." (GSR: 586) Not only that, he also gave practical advice to his devotees how to behave with the evil minded people. Following are the advices he gave to his householder devotees:

It (To be a householder) rather helps in the practice of spiritual discipline. It is like fighting from inside a fort...the householder should pacify his wife and the other members of his family. He should provide them with food and other necessities. Thus he removes the obstacle to his practice of spiritual discipline...Those, who still have a few worldly experiences to enjoy should lead a householder's life - and pray to God. 648 In the world a man must fight against passion like lust and anger, against many desires, against attachment. It is convenient to fight from inside a fort-from his own home. (GSR: 244)

(To Dr. Sarkar and Dr. Dukari) But renunciation of 'woman and gold' is not meant for you. You may renounce these mentally... For householders, money is a means of getting food, clothes and a dwelling-place, worshipping the Deity and serving holy men and devotees...It is useless to try to hoard money. You (Doctor) should not renounce woman completely. It is not harmful for a householder to live with his wife. But after the birth of one or two children, husband and wife should live as brother and sister...It is attachment to 'woman and gold' that begets pride of learning, pride of money and pride of social position. (GSR: 874)

Whatever may be a householder's profession, it is necessary for him to live in the company of holy men now and then. If a man loves God, he will himself seek the company of holy men. (GSR: 883)

Do all your, duties, but keep your mind on Gods; live with all-with wife and children, father and mother and serve them. Treat them as if they were very dear to you, but know in your heart of hearts that they do not belong to you...If you enter the world without first cultivating love for God, you will be entangled more and more. You will be overwhelmed with its danger, its grief, its sorrow. And the more you think of worldly things, the more you will be attached to them. (GSR: 81)

A wife endowed with spiritual wisdom is a real partner in life. She greatly helps her husband to follow the religious path. After the birth of one or two children they live like brother and sister. Both of them are devotees of God - His servant and his handmaid. Their family is a spiritual family. They are always happy with God and His devotees. They know that God alone is their own, from everlasting to everlasting. (GSR: 402)

The renunciation of 'woman and gold' is meant for the sannyāsi. He must not look even at the picture of a woman... But this renunciation is not meant for householders. You (a householder) may live among women, as far as possible in a spirit of detachment. Now and then you must retire into solitude and think of God. Women must not be allowed there. You can lead an unattached life to a great extent if you have faith in God and love for Him. After the birth of one or two children a married couple should live as brother and sister. They should then constantly pray to God that their minds may not run after sense pleasure any more and that they may not have any more children. (GSR: 866)

You should give her (wife) spiritual advice and support her during lifetime and provide for her livelihood after your death, if she is a chaste wife... But if you are intoxicated with the knowledge of God then you have no more duties to perform... Why shouldn't a man realize God in the world? Certainly he can. (GSR: 628)

When you feed your child, you should feel that you are feeding God. You should look on your father and mother as veritable manifestations of God and the Divine Mother and serve them as such. If a man enters the world after realizing God, he does not generally keep up physical relations with his wife. Both of them are devotees; they love to talk only of God and pass their time in spiritual conversation. They serve other devotees of God for they know that God alone has become all living beings and knowing this they devote their lives to the service of others... In order to lead such a life, both husband and wife must be spiritual...God's special grace is necessary to create such a couple...It is extremely difficult to practice spiritual discipline and at the same time lead a householder's life. There are many handicaps: disease, grief, poverty, misunderstanding with one's wife, and disobedient stupid and stubborn children...But still there is a way out.

One should pray to God, going now and then into solitude and make efforts to realize Him. (Someone asked that should one leave the home, Rāmakṛṣṇa answered,) No, not altogether whenever you have leisure, go into solitude for a day or two. At that time don't have any relations with the outside world and don't hold any conversation with worldly people on worldly affairs. You must live either in solitude or in the company of holy men." (GSR: 326)

There is nothing wrong in your being in the world. But you must direct your mind toward God; otherwise you will not succeed. Do your duty with one hand and with the other hold to God. After the duty is over, you will hold to God with both hands. (GSR: 137)

There is no harm in your leading the life of a householder. But do your duties in an unselfish spirit fixing your mind on the Lotus Feet of God...Live in the world like an immoral woman. Though she performs her household duties, her mind is fixed on her sweet heart. (GSR: 903)

After the birth of one or two children, the husband and wife should live as brother and sister. The other kinds of sexual intercourse do not injure them much...A householder has various debts: debts to the Gods, to the fathers and to the ṛṣis. He also owes a debt to his wife. He should make her the mother of one or two children and support her if she is a chaste woman...Householder do not know who is a good wife and who is a bad wife, who is a Vidyāśakti and who is a Avidyāśakti. A Vidyāśakti, a good wife, has very little lust and anger. She sleeps little. She pushes her husband's head away from her. She is full of affection, kindness, devotion, modestly and other noble qualities. Such a wife serves all, looking on all men as her children. Further, she helps increase her husbands' love of God. She doesn't spend much money lest her husband should have to work hard and thus not get leisure to think of God...Mannish women have different traits. These are bad traits: Squint eyes and hollow eyes, cat like eyes, lantern jaws like a calf's, and pigeon-breast. (GSR: 701)

"You are a goswami. It is your duty of to officiate a priest in the temple. You cannot renounce the world; otherwise, who would look after the temple and its services? You have to renounce mentally... It is God Himself who has kept you in the world to set an example to men. You may resolve in your mind a thousand times to renounce the world, but you will not succeed. God has given you such a nature that you must perform your worldly duties. [Gītā-Kṛṣṇa-Arjun]. (GSR: 255)

You (a householder) must engage in such activities as contemplation, singing His praises and other daily devotions...You can perform them (worldly duties) too, but only as much as you need for your livelihood. At the same time, you must pray to God in solitude, with tears in your eyes, that you may be able to perform those duties in an unselfish manner. You should say to Him: 'O God, make my worldly duties fewer and fewer; otherwise O Lord, I find that I forget Thee when I am involved in too many activities. (GSR: 142)

You cannot go into Samādhi as long as your worldly experiences are not finished, or as long as you have duties to perform. (To Shashadhar) you will have peace when your duties are finished. (GSR: 835)

A man living in society should make a show of Tamas to protect himself from evil minded people. But he should not harm anybody in anticipation of harm likely to be done to him. (GSR: 85)

So you must hiss at wicked people. You must frighten them, lost they should do you him. But never inject your venom into them. One must not injure others. (GSR: 86)

By leading a householder's life a man needlessly dissipates his mental powers. The loss he thus incurs can be made up if he takes to monastic life. The first birth is a gift of the father, then come the second birth, when one is invested with the sacred thread. There is still another birth at the time of being initiated into monastic life...A worldly man should hiss, but he shouldn't pour out his venom. He mustn't actually injure others. But he should make a show of anger to protect himself from enemies. Otherwise they will injure him but a Sannyāsi need not even hiss. (GSR: 247)

(2) Rāmakṛṣṇa observes that all of a sudden a man can not achieve the detachment of the world and achieve the true love for God. So before living in the world, one should be careful in his/her practices. According to Rāmakṛṣṇa the main solution to this problem is to go into

solitude for prayer and meditation. Following are the advices in this regard given to householder devotees:

First secure the oil of divine love and than set your hands to the duties of the world. You must put aside all other duties, sit in a quiet spot and churn the curd. Only then do you get butter. (GSR: 82)

One cannot be King Janaka all of a sudden. Janaka at first practiced such austerity in solitude...Even if one lives in the world, one must go into solitude now and then. It will be of great help to a man if he goes away from his family, lives alone and weeps for God even for three days. Even if he thinks of God for one day in solitude, when he has the leisure, that too will do him good. People shed a whole jug of tears for wife and children. But who cries for the Lord? Now and then one must go into solitude and practice spiritual discipline to realize God. Living in the world and entangled in many of its duties. The aspirant, during the first stage of spiritual life, finds many obstacles in the path of concentration. (GSR: 39)

One should first realize God through spiritual discipline in solitude and then live in the world. Only then can one be a King Janaka. (GSR: 293)

It is difficult to lead the life of householder in a spirit of detachment...can one be like King Janaka by merely wishing it? How many austerities he practiced in order to acquire divine knowledge! He practiced the most intense form of asceticism for many years and only then returned to the life of the world...Is there, then, no hope for householders? Certainly there is. They must practice spiritual discipline in solitude for some days. Thus they will acquire knowledge and devotion. Then it will not hurt them to lead the life of the world. But when you practice discipline in solitude, keep yourself entirely away from your family. You must not allow your wife, son, daughter, mother, father, sister, brother, friends or relatives near you. While thus practicing discipline in solitude, you should think: 'I have no one else in the world. God is my all'. You must also pray to Him, with tears in your eyes, for knowledge and devotion...If you ask me how long you should live in solitude away from your family, I should say that it would be good for you if you could spend even one day in such a manner. Three days at a time are still better. One may live in solitude for twelve days, a month, three months or a year, according to one's convenience and ability. One hasn't much to fear if one leads a life of a householder after attaining knowledge and devotion. (GSR: 313)

The worldly man must constantly live in the company of holy men. It is necessary for all even for Sannyāsis. But it is especially necessary for the householder. (GSR: 344)

For the householder it is very good to look on God as the Master. [attitude towards God-Master and servant] The householder is conscious of doing the duties of life himself. Under such condition how can he say, 'I am He?' To him who say, 'I am He' the world appears to be a dream. His mind, his body, even his ego are dreams to him. Therefore he cannot perform worldly duties. So it is very good for the householder to look on himself as the servant and on God as the Master. (GSR: 369)

A man can realize God even in the world. But at the beginning he must spend a few days in solitude. He must practice spiritual disciplines in a solitary place. (GSR: 626)

Why shouldn't a man be able to realize God in the world? But he must have discrimination and dispassion; he must have the unshakable awareness that God alone is real and all else is unreal and had but a two days' existence. (GSR: 681)

It is extremely difficult to realize God while leading a worldly life...Therefore one should go into solitude now and then to practice spiritual discipline...Keshav-live in the world after being strengthened in spiritual life. (GSR: 434)

Perform your duties in the world and also cultivate love of God. (GSR: 703)

Those who lead a householder's life should practice spiritual discipline; they should pray eagerly to God in solitude. (GSR: 183)

Blessed indeed is the householder who performs his duties in the world, at the same time cherishing love for the lotus feet of God. He is indeed a hero...One cannot lead such a life without great spiritual power...But a man must practice some spiritual discipline in order to be able to lead a detached life in the world. It is necessary for him to spend some time in solitude be it a year, six months, three months or even one month. In that solitude he should fix his mind on God and pray with a longing heart for love of God. He should also say to himself; there is nobody in this world that is my own. Those whom I call my own are here only for two days. God alone is my own. He alone is my, all in all. Atlas, how shall I realize him?'...One can live in the world after acquiring love of God...To live in the world in a detached spirit is very difficult. By merely saying so, you cannot be a kind Janaka. How much austerity Janak practiced! How long he remained in one posture, with head down and feet up! You don't have to practice these extreme disciplines. But you need Sādhanā; you should live in solitude. You may lead the life of a householder after having attained divine knowledge and love, in solitude...On account of his detachment from the world Janaka was also known as the 'Videha', that is, one, free from consciousness of the body, though living in the world. (GSR: 856)

(3) Rāmakṛṣṇa belies that if a person is living a life of a householder, he should not lose in the performing the worldly duties. He should give partial attention to those activities with sincerity, but major attention he should devote to the thinking of God. Rāmakṛṣṇa put much importance to this point of sādhanā, so he gave special advices in this regard also. Following are the advices in this regard:

Do your duty to the world after knowing God with one hand hold to the Lotus feet of the Lord and with the other do your work. (GSR: 325)

To live in the world unattached, like a maidservant in a rich man's house. (GSR: 90)

The world is contains a mixture of truth and untruth...Discard the untruth & take the truth...live in the world like mudfish. (GSR: 472)

Live in the world (householder) like a mudfish. The mudfish lives in the mud but itself remains unstained...one cannot think of God unless one lives in solitude...There is a way. One succeeds if one develops a strong spirit of renunciation. Give up at one, with determination, what you know to be unreal...After realizing God and divine love in solitude, one may live in the world as well. (GSR: 246)

He who leads the life of a house-holder should devote fifteen parts (out of sixteen) of his mind to God; otherwise he will face ruin and fall into the clutches of Death. He should perform the duties of the world with only one part of his mind...A man may lead the life of a householder after obtaining knowledge. But he must attain knowledge first. (GSR: 367)

Do your worldly duties with a part of your mind and direct most of it to God. A Sādhu should think of God with three quarters of his mind and with one quarter should do his other duties. He should be very alert about spiritual things...the life of a Sādhu is affected when his spirituality is touched. (GSR: 440)

Live in the world but in order to realize God, hold fast to His Lotus Feet with one hand and with the other do your duties. When you get respite from your dukes, cling to God's Lotus Feet with both hands - live in solitude and meditate on Him and some Him ceaselessly... Fight from a fort...Sages like Janaka, Vyasa and Vashishtha lived in the world after attaining knowledge. They fenced with two swords, the one of knowledge and the other of action. 336 Live in the world as the mudfish lives in the mud. One develops love of God by going away from the world into solitude, now and then, and meditating on God. After that one can live in the world unattached...such a man can lead the life of a house-holder in the spirit of detachment...One can realize God if one feels intense dispassion for worldly things...If he really feels that kind of dispassion, he renounces home and family. It is not enough for him to live in the world in a spirit of detachment. (GSR: 627)

One may lead a householder's life after realizing God...Janaka fenced with two swords, the one of Jñāna and the other of Karma. The Sannyāsi renounces action, therefore he fences with one sword only that of knowledge. (GSR: 387)

A man cannot realize God unless he renounces everything mentally. A Sādhu cannot lay things up... (To Mahima) you are a householder. Therefore you should hold both to 'this' and to 'that' - both to the world and to God. (GSR. 647)

He moved about as a Jīvanamukta, a free soul living in a body. But for most people freedom from body-consciousness is something very far off. Intense spiritual discipline is necessary...Janaka was a great hero. He fenced with two swords, the one of knowledge and the other of work. (GSR: 857) (to Surendra) The renunciation of 'woman and gold' is for Sannyāsi. It is not for you. Now and then you should go into solitude and call on God with yearning heart. Your renunciation should be mental...Unless a devotee is of the heroic type he cannot pay attention to both God and the world. King Janaka lived a householder's life only after attaining perfection through austerity and prayer. He fenced with two swords, the one of knowledge and the other of action...for you, as Caitanya said, the disciplines to be practiced are kindness to living beings, service to the devotees, and chanting the name of God. (GSR: 695-696)

(4) Rāmakṛṣṇa showed the subtle things to be observed by a devotee who wants the salvation. He showed that how a human psychology can misguide a devotee in sādhanā. Following are the subtle advices in this regard to be taken care:

Why shouldn't one be able to attain spirituality, living the life of a householder? But it is extremely difficult. Sages like Janaka entered the world after attaining knowledge. But still the world is a place of terror. Even a detached householder has to be careful... I have seen householder devotees filled with spiritual emotion while performing their daily worship wearing their silk clothes. They maintain that attitude even until they take their refreshments after the worship. But afterwards they become their old selves again. They display their rajasik and tamasik natures. (GSR: 250)

Give up such a wife if she proves an obstacle in the way of spiritual life. Let her commit suicide or anything else she likes. The wife that hampers her husband's spiritual life is an ungodly wife... If a man has sincere love for God, then all come under his control - the King, wicked person and his wife. Sincere love of God on the husband's part may, eventually help the wife to lead a spiritual life. If the husband is good, then through the grace of God, the wife may also follow his example. (GSR: 126)

Worldly people often think themselves very intelligent, but they are attached to the things of the world. They are the actual players and can not understand their own moves correctly. But holy men, who have renounced everything, are unattached to the world; they are really more intelligent than worldly people. Since they do not take any part in worldly life, their position is that of onlookers, and so they see things more clearly. (GSR: 863)

(5) Rāmakṛṣṇa accepts the Indian traditional views regarding different types of debts to be paid by householders. So he advised his devotees to pay three types of debts. Following are the advices regarding this three debts-daivaṛṇa, pitṛṛṇa and ṛṣiṛṇa:

A householder has his duties to discharge, his debts to pay, his debt to the Gods, his debt to his ancestors, his debt to the ṛṣis and his debt to wife and children. If a wife is chaste, then her husband should support her, he should also bring up their children until they are of age. Only monk must not save. (GSR: 156)

A man is born with several debts..: debts to his father, the devas and the ṛṣis. Besides, there is his debt to his mother. He also has a debt to his wife. She must be supported. If the wife is chaste, the husband must provide for her after his death... I ask people to live in the world and at the same time fix their minds on God. I don't ask them to give up the world. I say, fulfill your worldly duties and also think of God. (GSR: 828)

(6) It is well known that as a Bengali person, the impact of Caitanyadeva on Rāmakṛṣṇa was apparent. Thus, according to Rāmakṛṣṇa, the morality includes the service to the vaiṣṇavas as well as the chanting of God's name too.

Caitanyadeva said that the duties of householders were kindness to living beings, service to the Vaiṣṇavas and the chanting of God's holy name... But the renunciation of the world is needful for those whom God wants to be teachers of men. One who is the ācārya should give up 'woman and gold'; otherwise people will not take his advice. It is not enough for him to renounce only mentally; he should also renounce outwardly. Only then will his teaching bear fruit. 421 But a man cannot act as an ācārya without renouncing the world... Unless a man renounce everything, his teaching cannot be accepted by all...The world is indeed a place of enjoyment. (GSR: 579)

Further, Rāmakṛṣṇa advised his followers in this way:

Truthfulness, submission to God and looking on the wives of other men as one's own mother - there are the means to achieve God. (GSR: 844)

Whether a man should be a householder or a monk depends on the will of Rāma. Surrender everything to God and do your duties in the world. What else can you do?...If a householder become a Jīanamukta, then he can easily live in the world if he likes. A man who has attained knowledge does not differentiate between 'this place' and 'that place'. All places are the same to him. (GSR: 649)

I ask people to live in the world after the awakening of their spiritual consciousness...I ask people to live in the world in a spirit of detachment. (GSR: 827)

A householder should not hold the view that everything is illusory, like a dream. (GSR: 952)

When one grows old one should retire, and devote oneself to the thought of God. (GSR: 392)

When a man is seized with the spirit of intense renunciation he regards the world as a deep well and his relatives as venomous cobras. (GSR: 937)

3. Duties for Sannyāsi

(1) Rāmakṛṣṇa advised the renunciates to remain always cautious in the sādhanā. However a renunciate has achieved dispassion, one should be careful always. Following are the advices in this regard:

So, practice spiritual discipline in solitude and obtain the butter of knowledge and love. Even if you keep that butter in the water of the world the two will not mix. The butter will float...By meditating on God in solitude, the mind acquires knowledge, dispassion and devotion. But the very same mind goes downward if it dwells in the world. In the world there is only one thought 'woman and gold'. (GSR: 82)

(2) Rāmakṛṣṇa says that a renunciate person should lead a life of strict observance. There are two main reasons for this. First, for his personal sādhanā, it is necessary. Secondly, as a saint, he is the example for the rest of the people, therefore it is needed. Thus, a renunciate should observe strict disciplines. Following are the advices in this regard:

The Sannyāsi...If he clings to enjoyment, then he has reason to be afraid. 'woman and gold' is enjoyment...There are different kinds of enjoyment: money, wealth, name, fame and sense pleasure. It is not good for a Sannyāsi to sit in the company of a woman devotee or even to talk to her. This injures him and others as well. Then others cannot learn from him; he cannot set an example to humanity. A Sannyāsi keeps his body in order to teach mankind...To sit with a woman or talk to her a long time has also been described as a kind of sexual intercourse. There are eight kinds. To listen to a woman and enjoy her conversation is one kind; to speak about a woman is another kind; to whisper to her privately is a third kind; to keep something belonging to a woman and enjoy it is a fourth kind; to touch her is a fifth. Therefore a Sannyāsi should not salute his guru's young wife, touching her feet. These are the rules for Sannyāsis. (GSR: 701)

Total renunciation is for Sannyāsis. They must not look even at the picture of a woman. To them a woman is poison. They must keep themselves at least ten cubits away from her; and if that is not possible, at least one cubit. And they must not talk much with a woman, no matter how devout she may be. Further, they should choose their dwelling at a place where they will never, or scarcely ever, see the face of a woman...Money, too, is like poison to a Sannyāsi. If he keeps money with him, he has worries, pride, anger, and the desire for physical comforts. Money inflames his rajas, which brings tamas in its train. Therefore a Sannyāsi must not touch 'gold'. 'Woman and gold' makes him forget God. (GSR: 874)

The Sannyāsi must observe very strict discipline. He must not look even at the picture of a woman. But this rule doesn't apply to householders. An aspirant should not associate with a woman, even though she is very much devoted to God. A Sannyāsi even though he may have subdued his passions, should follow this discipline to set an example to householder...Worldly people learn renunciation by seeing the complete renunciation of a monk; otherwise they sink more and more. A Sannyāsi is a world teacher. (GSR: 184)

Others learn from the Sannyāsi's example. That is why such strict rules are prescribed for him. A Sannyāsi must not look even at the portrait of a woman...A Sannyāsi must not only not have intercourse with woman; he must not even talk to her...But on attaining the state of the Paramahaṃsa one becomes like a child. A child five years old doesn't know the difference between man and a woman. But even a Paramahaṃsa must be careful, so as not to set a bad example to others. (GSR: 442)

He (a Sannyāsi or a renunciate) must not look even at the portrait of a woman...A Sannyāsi must not sit near a woman and talk to her, even if he may have controlled his passion...A Sannyāsi must renounce both 'woman and gold' (money). (Why all these strict rules for a Sannyāsi?) It is for the welfare of mankind as well as for his own good. A Sannyāsi may himself lead an unattached life and may have controlled his passion, but he must renounce 'woman and gold' to set an example to the world. (GSR: 387)

A Sannyāsi must absolutely renounce woman. A Sannyāsi must not look even at the picture of a woman...To lose semen is extremely harmful for a Sannyāsi...A Sannyāsi may have control over his senses, but to set an example to mankind he should out talk with women . . . even if she is a devotee of God. (GSR: 412)

The Sannyāsi must renounce 'woman and gold' for his own welfare. Even if he is unattached, and consequently not in danger, still in order to set an example to others, he must not keep 'woman and gold' near him. The Sannyạsi, the man of renunciation is a world teacher. It is his example that awakens the spiritual consciousness of men. (GSR: 443)

A holy man who has renounced the world will of course chant the name of God. That is only natural. He has no other duties to perform. If he meditates on God it shouldn't surprise anybody. On the other hand, if he fails to think of God or chant His holy name, then people will think ill of Him...But it is a great deal to his credit if a householder utters the name of the Lord. (GSR: 194)

The rules for a Sannyāsi are extremely heard. He cannot have the slightest contact with 'woman and gold'. He must not accept money with his own hands, and he must not even allow to be left near him. (GSR: 584)

I had forbidden him (Naran) to tie a knot, to sew his clothes, to lock a box, to pull up a curtain and similar things,...He who would renounce the world must practice all these disciplines. They are meant for Sannyāsis. (Narayan) – Don't let yourself touch the air near a woman's body. Cover yourself with a heavy sheet lest the air should touch your body. And keep yourself eight cubits, two cubits or at least one cubits away from all women except your mother. [initially as black cobra, but after realization as Blissful Mother] (GSR: 595)

(3) Rāmakṛṣṇa believes that mere the change of cloths and put on the geruā cloths will not sufficient to reach the destination. It alone can not bring detachment which is helpful for salvation. One must have the feeling of detachment and renunciation mentally.

Merely taking the vow of monastic life will not help a man if he is attached to the world. 487 It is not good to renounce anything before the proper time arrives. (GSR: 224)

There are many kinds of renunciation. One of them may be called markaṭavairāgya monkey renunciation. It is a false renunciation stimulated by the afflictions of the world. That renunciation doesn't last long. Then there is real renunciation. A man with everything in the world, lacking nothing, feels all to be unreal It is not possible to acquire renunciation all at once. By constantly hearing about renunciation one's desire for worldly objects gradually wears away. (GSR: 502)

Those who regretfully, renounce the world belong to an inferior class. (GSR: 956) Why this gerrua? Should one put on such a thing for a mere fancy?...There are three or four varieties of renunciation. Afflicted with miseries at home, one may put on the ochre cloth of a monk; but that renunciation doesn't last long. Again, a man out of work puts on an ochre wearing-cloth and goes off to Benares. After three months he writes home: I have a job here. I shall come home in a few days. Don't worry about me again. A man may have everything he wants. He lacks nothing, yet he does not enjoy his possessions. He weeps for God alone. That is real renunciation. Far better is the white cloth of a householder. Attachment to worldliness, occasional lapses from the ideal and an outer garb of gerrua how dreadful. 244 But it is quiet different with genuine Sannyāsi. A real Sannyāsi will not enjoy and kind of bliss except the Bliss of God. (GSR: 196)

One cannot realize God without renouncing woman and gold. (GSR: 349)

The renunciation of Woman and gold is the true renunciations. (GSR: 22)

The real Sannyāsi lives away from Woman and gold therefore through the practice of spiritual discipline he can always fix his mind on God. (GSR: 210)

The one thing needful is the renunciation of woman and gold. That renunciation is the real and supreme renunciation. Householder should go into solitude now and then, practice spiritual discipline in order to cultivate devotion to God; they should renounce mentally but the Sannyāsi should renounce both mentally and physically. (GSR: 291)

Mental renunciation is the essential thing. That too, makes one a Sannyāsi. But one must set fire to one's desires. Then alone can one succeed. (GSR: 938)

They can enjoy the Bliss of God alone. A man of true renunciation cannot enjoy anything but God. He leaves any place where people talk of worldly things; he listens only to spiritual talk. A man of true renunciation never speak about anything but God. (GSR: 957)

Thus, according to Rāmakṛṣṇa, the practice of renunciation is not only in negative sense, the dispassion for the worldly objects, but positively it has the element of the love for God. Once Mahendranath asked that Renunciation does not mean simply dispassion for the world. It means dispassion for the world and also longing for God. Rāmakṛṣṇa said he is right. (GSR: 506)

Rāmakṛṣṇa also emphasis the duty to serve humanity to both, householders as well as Sannyāsi and the spirit and the method of this has been described by Swami Prabhananda by saying, Śrī Rāmakṛṣṇa urged the spiritual aspirants to serve man, the highest temple of God. To him God resided in every being, jīva is śīva. The body is a mere covering like a lantern with a light burning inside. (GSR: 312) this juva-śīva concept clearly shows how to reshape human relationship and conduct man's dealing with his fellow beings. Contrary to secular humanism preached by the Brahmos, Śrī Rāmakṛṣṇa's spiritual humanism offered a dynamic religion in place of static piety. This viewpoint gives man tremendous strength, love and humanistic impulses, and a sense of dedication. Appreciation this unique spirit of Śrī Rāmakṛṣṇa's life's mission, Will Durant remarked, He (Rāmakṛṣṇa) tolerated sympathetically the polytheism of the people, and accepted humbly the monism of the philosophers; but in his own living faith God was a spirit incarnated in all men, and the only true worship of God was the loving service of mankind. (Will Durant: The Story of Civilization, Vol. I, 617 (Studies on Rāmakṛṣṇa, Swami Prabhananda, The Brahmo Movement and Śrī Rāmakṛṣṇa p140-141)

10
Social Problems

In Rāmakṛṣṇa's philosophy, to spend much of one's life time in solitude, an away form person is the central point of sādhanā. This does not mean that he was not concerned for the people who are needy in any way. Further, he himself had never claimed to be a social reformer. Despite his apparent indifference to social reform, political activities, and things like that, Śrī Rāmakṛṣṇa's teachings have turned out to be the most dynamic social philosophy of the age and this has created for him a position among the greatest remarkers of mankind. (Swami Prabhananda, 1988: 138) Rāmakṛṣṇa was very much concerned for poor and deprived persons. As earlier it is shown that according to Rāmakṛṣṇa Daya (compassion) springs form sattva and sattva is helpful for a person to the attainment of salvation. In the life of Rāmakṛṣṇa, there are many occasions in which his social concern was seen. Among these, only two are mentioned here. These two occasions are nicely put by Swami Nikhilananda in the introduction of The Gospel.

Rāmakṛṣṇa was on a pilgrimage to the sacred places of northern India. At Vaidyanath in Behar, when the Master saw the inhabitants of a village reduced by poverty and starvation to mere skeletons, he requested his rich patron (Mathur) to feed the people and give each a piece of cloth. Mathur demurred at the added expense. The Master declared bitterly that he would not go on to Benares, but would live with the poor and share their miseries. He actually left Mathur and sat down with the villagers. Where upon Mathur had to yield. On another occasion, two years later, Śrī Rāmakṛṣṇa showed a similar sentiment for the poor and needy. He accompanied Mathur on a tour to one of the latter's estates at the time of the collection of rents. For two years the harvest had failed and the tenants were in a state of extreme poverty. The Master asked Mathur to remit their rents, distribute help to them, and in addition give the hungry people a sumptuous feast. When Mathur grumbled, the Master said: You are only the steward of the Divine Mother. They are the Mother's tenants. You must spend the Mother's money. When they are suffering, how can you refuse to help them? You must help them. Again Mathur had to give in. ((Introduction to (GSR: 35-36)

These two occasions are examples of his teachings. However, as like all his thinking, his social concern has also a different basis form the people who make propaganda of social services. Rāmakṛṣṇa's sympathy for the poor sprang from his perception of God in all created beings. His sentiment was not that of the humanist or philanthropist. To him the service of man was the same as the worship of God. (Introduction to (GSR: 36)

1. Caste System

Rāmakṛṣṇa showed that rituals, pilgrimages, and caste rules were non-essentials and would wear off with the growth of real knowledge. The person who has realized God has no feeling of high and low in regard to other persons. So he doesn't discriminate about caste. (GSR: 171) This perfected soul will go beyond any type of choices. He has no feeling of high or low. Rāmakṛṣṇa says that The Gītā describes such a devotee as content with what comes to him without effort. A good Brahmin, without any personal motive, can accept food even from the house of an untouchable. (GSR: 336) it is the fact that a realized soul becomes as innocent as a child. Though, he is aware of the knowledge, he is child-like person. Rāmakṛṣṇa says that as a child does not have any pride of high cast or a feeling of low cast, like that, a true saint, a true jñānī will never believe in the high and low casts. A child has no pride of caste or family. A child is beyond all ideas of purity and impurity. He is not bound by social conventions. A characteristics of tamas is pride. Pride and delusion come from tamas. (GSR. 861)

He firmly believes that the cast system can be removed by one means only, and that is the love of God. Lovers of God do not belong to any cast. The mind, body, and soul of a man become purified through divine love. Caitanya and Nityananda scattered the name of Hari to everyone, including the pariah, and embraced them all. A Brahmin without this love is no longer a Brahmin. And a pariah with the love of God is no longer pariah. Through bhakti an untouchable become pure and elevated. (GSR: 155, 157)

It is believed in Indian tradition that Janmanā jāyate śudra saṃskārāt dvija ucyate, that is, a person called Brahmin not by the fact that he has taken birth in the family of Brahmin, but through the tendencies, he is known as a Brahmin. Rāmakṛṣṇa put the touch of spirituality in it, and said that it is not that by birth in a certain family, a person is to be known, but through the love of God one becomes pure and otherwise everyone is a śudra. The master asked Mani Mallik to quote the words of Tulsidas to the effect that one who had developed love of God could not observe caste distinction even the butcher and the untouchable, become pure by repeating Hari's name. Without Hari's name the people of the four castes are but butchers. Man becomes pure by repeating the name of God. (GSR: 309) Not only that many realized soul born in low family. Even through an eternal perfect soul is born in a low family, still he retains his innate perfection. He can not do anything else. (GSR: 249)

Rāmakṛṣṇa gave the example in tune with his views that Caitanyadeva distributed bhakti to all, including the outcaste. (GSR, 379) Another example he gave of a devotee named Kṛṣṇakishor, who was true Hindu and still, as a disciple of Rāmakṛṣṇa, did not believe in the cast system and believed that simply by the utterance of Hari's name makes a man pure. Rāmakṛṣṇa says, What tremendous faith Kṛṣṇakishor had. Once, while at Vrindavan, he felt thirsty and went to a well. Near it he saw a man standing. One being asked to draw a little water for him, the man said, I belong to a low caste, sir. You are a Brahmin. How can I draw water for you? Kṛṣṇakishor said: Take the name of śīva. By repeating His holy name you will make yourself pure. The low caste man did as he was told, and Kṛṣṇakishor, orthodox Brahmin that he was, drank that water. What tremendous faith! (GSR, 117,310) Rāmakṛṣṇa's another disciple, Padmalochan, also express his liberal attitude towards cast system of India. Padmalochana said: What does it matter if I accompany you to a meeting at the house of a fisherman? With you I can dine even at the house of a pariah. (GSR: 376)

Thus, not only Rāmakṛṣṇa but his disciples were also having broad attitude towards all casts. Once a brahmin asked him that is it that only Brahmins can achieve liberation? Rāmakṛṣṇa clearly answered that it is not only brahmin who can get perfection. Anyone, person from any cast can achieve that state if he earnestly pray and cultivate the love for God. He mentions the names of great saints who were born in the low family and still they were on the highest state of consciousness. It is said that in the Kaḷiyuga the śudras achieve love of God. There are the instance of Shavari, Ruhidas, the untouchable Guhaka and others. (GSR: 703)

2. Status of Woman

Rāmakṛṣṇa used the word 'woman and gold' frequently in his conversations. That may leads one to the misunderstanding that Rāmakṛṣṇa thought low for the woman. Swami Nikhilananda clarified it nicely. The term 'women and gold', which has been used throughout in a collective sense, occurs again and again in the teachings of Rāmakṛṣṇa to designate the chief impediments to spiritual progress. This favourite expression of the Master, 'kaminīkāñcana', has often been misconstrued. By it he meant only 'lust and greed', the baneful influence of which retards the aspirant's spiritual growth. He used the word 'kaminī' or 'woman', as a concrete term for the sex instinct when addressing his man devotees. He advised women, on the other hand, to shun 'man'. 'kāñcana', or 'gold', symbolizes greed, which is the other obstacle to spiritual life.

Rāmakṛṣṇa never taught his disciple to hate any women, or womankind in general. This can be seen clearly by going through all his teachings under this head and judging them collectively. Rāmakṛṣṇa looked on all women as so many images of the Divine Mother of the Universe. He paid the highest homage to womankind by accepting a woman as his guide while practicing the very profound spiritual disciplines of Tantra. No other saviour or spiritual leader has ever given such an honour to womanhood in the annals of religious history. (Swami Abhedananda, 1988: 14-15) His wife known and revered as the Holy Mother was his constant companion and first disciple. At the end of his spiritual practices he literally worshipped his wife as the embodiment of the Goddess Kālī, the Divine Mother. After his passing away the Holy Mother became the spiritual guide not only of a large number of householders, but also of many monastic members of the Rāmakṛṣṇa Order. (GSR: 82) Therefore, The Indian Mirror observed that the place which Rāmakṛṣṇa assigned to women was 'far higher than which the passions of men might reach.' (The Indian Mirror, 15 June, 1879 quoted Cakravarty , 1988: 175)

Rāmakṛṣṇa had a great sympathy and concern for women. That can be possible if a person had high level of Emotional Intelligence. In the modern terms of EIQ, it can be said that Rāmakṛṣṇa was having highest level of that which can be seen throughout in his life. One of the instances is that he asked Mahendranath to bring his grief-stricken wife to the garden house, where she could have her meal. Rāmakṛṣṇa said to him: Ask her to come. Let her stay here a couple of days. She may bring the baby...Grief pushes out devotion. And he was such a big boy! (GSR: 959) Thus, he fully understands all of the mother's emotions, which shows his high EIQ. There is another instance where he showed his compassion for women. He has Sympathy for a crazy woman. Shashi, one of his devotees said: 'If she comes again, I shall shove her out of the place.' Rāmakṛṣṇa tenderly but strongly responded: 'No, no! Let her come and go away.' (GSR: 952) At still another place he said about one of his closest devotees, Niranjan's earning for his mother. He said: He (Niranjan) is earning money for his mother. There is no harm in that. (GSR: 458) Not only this, he believes to the extent that even one's mother is not a good lady, still, one should not leave her. How worthy of worship one's parents are!... You must not renounce your mother even if she commits adultery. (GSR: 424) Thus, there are so many instances where he very naturally shoed his concern for women.

It is to be noted that in Indian family in general, women are generally not being asked whether or not they have taken their meal. Rāmakṛṣṇa was as tender as mother that he took care of ladies who had not eaten food. There occurs an instance when his caring nature was seen. It is shown in the Gospel that two ladies, devotees of Rāmakṛṣṇa, entered the room and saluted the Master, they had been fasting in preparation for this visit. Both of them had their faces covered with veils. Rāmakṛṣṇa gave them some spiritual instructions to be followed for the attainment of God realization. Mahatma Gandhi said that for the status of women, women should not do mimicry of men. Here, Rāmakṛṣṇa also give instructions to women which are suitable to them. This way, Rāmakṛṣṇa followed the right spirit of feminism. Showing concern, he asked: 'Why have you fasted? You should take your meal before you come here. Women are but so many forms of my Divine Mother. I cannot bear to see them suffer. You are all images of the Mother of the Universe. Come here after you have eaten, and you will feel happy.' Saying this, Rāmakṛṣṇa asked Ramlal to give the ladies some food. They were given fruits, sweets, drinks and other offerings from the temple. Rāmakṛṣṇa said: 'You have eaten something. Now my mind is at peace. I cannot bear to see women fast.' (GSR: 431-432)

It is seen earlier that lust and greed are two main obstacles for the realization of God. To consider the other sex as an obstacle is required at the initial stage of sādhanā. But after reaching a certain level in sādhanā, one will see all things as the manifestations of the Divine Being. Therefore, Rāmakṛṣṇa said that while practicing sādhanā a man should regard a woman as raging forest fire or a black cobra. But in the state of perfection, after the realization of God, she appears as the Blissful Mother. Then you will look on her as a form of the Divine mother. (GSR: 595) Rāmakṛṣṇa's own perception towards all the women, even towards prostitutes is nicely told by him in the Gospel. He says, She alone assumed all female forms. Therefore I look on all women as mother. (GSR: 701) he talked of his approach towards women in the high state of consciousness, where he found all as the embodiment of the Divine Mother. His experience in his own words are this: At that time I used to invite maidens here and worship them. I found them to be embodiments of the Divine Mother Herself. One day I saw a woman in blue standing near the bakul tree. She was a prostitute. But she instantly kindled in me the vision of Sītā. (GSR, 231) I saw two prostitutes standing on a verandah. They appeared to me to be embodiments of the divine mother. Herself, I saluted them. (GSR: 776) I shall look upon them (public woman - playing part in the play) as the blissful mother herself. (GSR: 546)

Thus, Rāmakṛṣṇa's perception of the Divine is so wide that he regarded all women, even prostitutes, as manifestations of the Divine mother. He addressed them all as 'Mother'. He said: I look on all women as my mother...To me every woman is mother. (GSR: 284) It is his firm belief that there is nothing but the God who manifest Himself in different forms. He believed that all women are the embodiments of Śakti. It is the Primal Power that has become women and appears to us in the form of women. (GSR: 336) Therefore, according to him, it one has realized God, then he will never hate anybody, because all are nothing but the embodiment of that Reality only. Therefore, initially, to conquer lust, women should be looked by men and vice-versa, as 'cobra' which can do harm. But after realization there is not need to fear. He said, Shall we hate women then? He who has realized God does not look upon a woman with the eye of lust, so he is not afraid of her. He perceives clearly that women are but so many aspects of the Divine Mother. He worships them all as the Mother Herself. (GSR: 168) Once, Rāmakṛṣṇa told about a woman who had a Madhurabhāva towards him, that is, she considered Rāmakṛṣṇa as her beloved. But Rāmakṛṣṇa said regarding that: 'But I look on all women as manifestations of the Divine Mother. All women are mothers to me.' (GSR: 958)

Thus, initially the seekers are advised to be aware of the power of māyā. Just see the bewitching power of woman. I mean the women who are the embodiment of avidyā, the power of delusion. They fool men as it were. They take away their inner substance. Rāmakṛṣṇa quoted the hymn of Narada that "all men are parts of Thee. All women are parts of Sītā, the personification of Thy māyā." (GSR: 748) This appears as if Rāmakṛṣṇa thought low of woman as the obstacle to sādhanā of man. But looking at his own cosmology and the concept of self, it becomes clear that all the empirical selves, whether men or women, are the embodiment of māyā. Then, here, he forgets to say the reverse thing, that for women, men are the objects by which women are dragged down. Rāmakṛṣṇa would completely agree to this with reference to his views on sādhanā. Because he believed that to conquer lust and greed are essential for the attainment of God.

Here it is important to note that Rāmakṛṣṇa's sympathy towards even prostitutes. This does not mean that he accepts the profession of sex-workers, as some modern intellectuals do. From spiritual standpoint a person with realization will see all beings as the spirit. But from social and ethical standpoint, Rāmakṛṣṇa believed that if a person has repentance for his certain deed and if he does not wish to prolong it any more, then he will certainly be saved. They (prostitutes) too will be saved, if only they cry to God with a yearning heart and promise not to repeat their sins. (GSR: 740) Thus, unlike general trends in the Indian society not to accept that type of woman who wants to come out of that situation, Rāmakṛṣṇa is very open-minded in that respect and he can whole heartedly accepts the fallen souls, who want to fly high.

Again, in all religious literature, it is difficult to find the instructions sparingly given to women. The doctrine of liberation theology deals with this problem. In the Gospel, all throughout one can see that there is not a consciousness of the sex distinction in his conversation. He instructed women also whenever the situation came. Not only that, in just utterances also it is seen that he count all devotees, males or females, as equal beings. He mentions the names of perfected souls as examples, in which one finds no distinction of sexes at all. He says, "One attains liberation through bhakti alone. Savitri was the daughter of a hunter, she, Rohidas and others belonged to the śudra caste, they were liberated through bhakti alone." (GSR: 549) and "Rani Bhāvani, so much knowledge and devotion in a woman." (GSR: 605) Thus, like any truly perfected person, Rāmakṛṣṇa gave women equal status with men, there is no distinction and no discrimination in his thinking as well as in his behaviour.

3. Compassion for poor and deprived

There was a conversation between Rāmakṛṣṇa and Vivekananda regarding doing service to others. That conversation is the example which shows how Rāmakṛṣṇa felt concern for the welfare of others. Swami Vivekananda at first wanted liberation for himself but Śrī Rāmakṛṣṇa scolded him. He said, 'What! You are so low? I thought you would be like a huge tree in the shade of which travelers going along the road could take refuge from the heat of the sun. And now I see that you want only your own liberation!' Afterwards what a great change came about in Swamiji! He said, as long as there is one starving, dog in this country, it is my religion to feed it. He told a disciple, if you seek liberation for yourself, you with go to hell. You must seek liberation for others. If you work for yourself, you will go to hell; if you work for the liberation for others, that is better than going to heaven. (Swami Lokeswarananda, 1997: 85) Vivekananda also said that simply to perform rituals to the stone image of God is not worthy but to serve the image of God in the form of men is the only duty of a true seeker of Truth. Swami Vivekananda said, leaving this living God, will you worship a stone image? Sitting on the bank of the Ganga, you want to dig a well? (Swami Lokeswarananda, 1997: 188)

Rāmakṛṣṇa believes that those souls are the great souls who themselves are liberated and who can lead others to that destination. He says, "the great souls who retain their bodies after Samādhi, feel compassion for the suffering of others. They are not so selfish as to be satisfied with their own illumination." (GSR: 152) After attaining Samādhi, Narad, Sukadava and other came down a few steps, as it were, to the plane of normal consciousness and broke their silence, out of compassion for the suffering of others and to help them. (GSR, 276) They (Paramahaṃsas) do this (preaching & teaching) only to teach others and to help them in spiritual life. (GSR, 500)

Thus, Rāmakṛṣṇa had taught his disciples in such a way that his disciples founded an institution which is known for its missionary activities all over the globe. This shows how Rāmakṛṣṇa was compassionate towards the poor and deprived that his disciples feel to follow his teachings with the missionary spirit. In all institutions, mathas or missions related to Rāmakṛṣṇa order are doing the activities for the welfare of human beings. Because, Rāmakṛṣṇa believes that, 'If God can be worshiped through a clay image, then why not in man?' (GSR: 409) So, he forcefully asserted that service to man is the highest form of worship. He said, "Isn't feeding people a kind of service to God? God exists in all beings as fire. To feed people is to offer oblations to that indwelling spirit." (GSR: 450) Thus, for Rāmakṛṣṇa service to men is service to God. Ultimately anything done with the spirit of the service to God will certainly leads a man to the realization of God, which is the highest goal of all human beings.

This God-centric humanism was unique, being different from the Christian charity, or Vaiṣṇava kindness or Buddhist compassion. (Vedānta kesarī, June 1935, Vol. XXII, No.2, 'What We Stand for', 49) It is different because, in all other ways there underlay the something doing for others, while, in Rāmakṛṣṇa, though he believes that 'he who has no compassion is no man.' (GSR: 628), but the theory underlay here is that it is service to God, because, God dwells in all beings. He says, 'It is said that man is greater than the śāligrāma. Man is Nārāyaṇa himself. If God can manifest himself through an image, then why not through man also?' (GSR, 405) Swami Lokeswarananda has mentioned Swami Vivekananda's thought regarding 'service to human is service to God', in this way, Swamiji (Vivekananda) said, 'My God the afflicted, my God the ignorant, my God the poor.' This is the mantra for the new age: 'Not man, but God'. Those who are not monastics, who live in the world, should also work with this attitude. Whatever they do, they should think they are serving God through that medium. In his poem 'To A Friend' Swamiji says, "These are His manifold forms before thee, Rejecting them, where seekest Thou for God? Who loves all beings, without distinction, He indeed is worshiping best his God." (Swami Lokeswarananda, 1997: 318)

Thus, Despite his apparent indifference to social reform, political activities, and things like that, Rāmakṛṣṇa's teachings have turned out to be the most dynamic social philosophy of the age and this has created for him a position among the greatest remarkers of mankind. [Benoy Kumar Sarkar: The Might of Man in the Social Philosophy of Rāmakṛṣṇa and Vivekananda, (Śrī Rāmakṛṣṇa Math, Madras, 1963: 2] (Cakravarty, 1988: 169-170)

Rāmakṛṣṇa instructed his householder devotees to provide help to the needy people as much as possible. Once he told Manilal, his devotee that, People in his (Rakhal) native village have been suffering from a scarcity of water. Why don't you build a reservoir there? That will do the people good. (GSR: 202) Rāmakṛṣṇa likes the person, who helps people who are in need of the things. He appreciated them before others may be to inspire others. He considers such actions as good and right gestures which create good tendencies in man. He says, "What a nice disposition he has now! No one that goes to him for help comes away empty handed." (GSR, 449) This shows that Rāmakṛṣṇa considered 'help to people' as a necessary condition to create good disposition which helps one to achieve the highest goal. But he also believes that a person who is not good and neither repenting for that not trying to improve that is not deserve any service or help He says, one should not feed the wicked, I mean people who are entangled in gross worldliness or who have committed heinous crimes like adultery. Even the ground where such people sit becomes impure to a depth of seven cubits. (GSR: 450) He strongly and assertively avoid the wicked persons and said that a persons who have habit of bad deeds do not deserve any service from others.

Rāmakṛṣṇa's thinking about money is similar to that of Mahatma Gandhi's principle of Trusteeship Principle of Trusteeship teaches that whatever amount of money one earns, one is not the owner of that property but one is only trustee of it. That trustee can use the money which is necessary for the fulfillment of his minimum basic needs of food, clothing and shelter. The remaining money should be used for the welfare of the poor and needy people. Rāmakṛṣṇa said the similar thing that those who have money should give it to the poor and needy. (GSR, 398) Because he believes that one should use the money only for the fulfillment of one's basic needs as food, clothing and shelter. But rest of the money is meant for the help of people who need it. Money is not meant for the fulfillment of any selfish motive. He says, Money enables a man to get food and drink, build a house, worship the deity, serves devotees and holy men, and helps the poor when he happens to meet them. These are good use of money. Money is not meant for luxuries or creature comforts or for buying a position in society. (GSR: 285) Thus, it is seen that Rāmakṛṣṇa's thought is highly effective to create the balance in the contemporary economic system. In the modern age, the consumerism and globalization has created the great humanistic crisis in which the right balance is lost. If all behave in the way Rāmakṛṣṇa or Gandhi have told, then only the true balance will occur. He showed his disliking for the person who spends everything for his own self. He says: a worldly man spends thousands of rupees for his daughter's marriage. Yet all the while his neighbors are dying of starvation, and he finds it hard to give them two morsels of rice. (GSR: 757) according to him the true use of money is this, They alone make good use of their money who spend it for the worship of God or the service of holy men and devotees. Their money bears fruit. (GSR: 958)

Rāmakṛṣṇa not only preached to work for the welfare of people, but he also practiced it in a genuine way. Though he was suffering from the pain of cancer, he did not left serving people through his conversations which help people to achieve the highest goal. Swami Lokeswarananda said, Śrī Rāmakṛṣṇa's life also exemplifies this. He felt the suffering of others as his own and longed to help them. He said: Even if I fall sick and live only on sago, I shall continue to do good to others... Even after his body had become emaciated from cancer of the throat, he continued to speak, it was very painful for him yet he went on talking about God, even when death was imminent. He wanted to remind everyone of their ultimate goal in life, God realization. He knew that only God-realization would permanently remove people's suffering. (Swami Lokeswarananda, 1997: 86)

The function what Rāmakṛṣṇa performed was taken over by Hardeman, the Holy Mother after him. She also felt great concern for the people. After the Master's passing, Holy mother prayed with tears in her eyes: Taker, you came and left. Is that the end of everything? Then What need was there for you to take so much trouble in coming? It is my wish that all those who follow your teachings will live together, and worldly people coming to them will hear their words and get peace. (Swami Lokeswarananda, 1997: 190) Her approach is well being understood by the expression of Swami Lokeswarananda with Holy Mother's own words. It is said thus, that perhaps the most prominent trait of holy mother was her never seeing anyone's faults or sins, and her acceptance of all the virtuous and the unvirtuous. She said, 'Did the Master come only to eat rasagollas? No, he came just for this to raise the fallen.' A woman once said to her, I have done so many bad things that I am not worthy to enter your room. Holy mother embraced and said, what if you have done something wrong? Come, I will give you a mantra. And she gave the woman a mantra and showered her blessing on her...On another occasion, Holy Mother said, as Sarat (Swami Saradanandji) is my son so also is Amjad (a Muslim dacoit). In mother's eyes they were the same. It was not that she was unaware of Amjad's misdeeds. She knew all about him, but she would say, 'I am the mother of the virtuous and I am also the mother of the wicked.' Further, 'anyone can destroy. Who is able to build? Everyone can criticize bad people, but how can you make them good? Who can tell us how?' She also said, 'if my child becomes smeared with dirt, is it not my duty to wash him? Our coming is just for that.' To make the world better, to put the wicked on the path to good, to make the sinner free from sin - for this Śrī Rāmakṛṣṇa and holy mother took birth. (Swami Lokeswarananda, 1997: 104) This shows how both of them felt concern for the upliftment of the people, good or bad. For them, like God, all men are equal in the question of service to them is concerned.

Here, it is very important to note that Rāmakṛṣṇa is very much aware of the fact that each phenomenon of the world is transitory and not permanent. So, one should not forget the basic thing, that is, the realization of God, is behind all his instruction regarding social services. In the beginning of this chapter it is said that according to Rāmakṛṣṇa, the service to men is the service to God. So when one realizes God, he will act as per the God's Will. Rāmakṛṣṇa asked in the reference of Shambhu, who was a true devotee of God and wished to build hospitals and dispensaries, that will you ask God for hospitals and dispensaries when you see him? (GSR: 613) This shows that according to Rāmakṛṣṇa, first of all, one should attain certain level of consciousness, then only one can do anything for the welfare of men. Because, it is his firm belief, that without the command from God, not one will hear you.

Besides, sometime people believe that they are dong charity while doing arbitration. Some times seekers can be victim of self-deception. People may think that they are doing something for others, while in the subtlest level of consciousness, one may have some other motive like prestige etc. To become aware of that he advice devotees first to cultivate love for God and then, after the command from inside, one can act accordingly. Further, it is his belief that when one's love for God increases, his activities will be less than previous. So, social services are not desirable for all types of devotees. He believes that they are of different class, because he accepts the path of pravṛtti as well as the path of nivṛtti. So, he advised Ishan, his devotee, that, Arbitration and leadership? How trifling these are! Charity and doing good to others? You have had enough of these. Those who are to devote themselves to such things belong to a different class. Now the time is ripe for you to devote your mind to the lotus feet of God. First God then charity, doing good to others, doing good to the world, and redeeming people. (GSR, 615)

4. Towards the Violence of animals

Rāmakṛṣṇa was a Bengali, to whom the non-vegetarian food is natural. So, many believe that he was not against non-vegetarian food. But just before three years of his leaving the body, his views regarding sacrifice, were different than that of commonly believed. Being a Bengali and devotee of Goddess Kālī, he did not disregard the sacrifice as a prasāda, but he himself was unable to see and eat that. He says, the śāstra prescribes sacrifice on social occasion. Such sacrifice is not harmful... I am now in such a state of mind that I cannot watch a sacrifice. Also I can not eat meat offered to the Divine Mother. (GSR: 185-186) It is goes without saying that his compassion was not limited to only human beings, but it was extended up to the whole living beings.

Aurobindo gave a genuine tribute to Rāmakṛṣṇa's social concern in this words, The characteristic of this new Movement has been, according to Śrī Aurobindo, 'a very wide synthesis of past religious motives and spiritual experiences topped by a reaffirmation of the old asceticism and monasticism, but with new living strands in it and combined with a strong humanitarianism and zeal of missionary expansion.' [Śrī Aurobindo: The Renaissance if India, (1973), 31-32] (Swami Prabhananda, 1988: 138)

11

Psychoanalysis of Rāmakṛṣṇa's Behaviour

Rāmakṛṣṇa is a mystic in its real sense of the term. Any mystic is considered by psychoanalysts, as having a certain kind of mental disorder. Therefore, here it is attempted to do some analysis of the psychology of religion and mystic with the help of the great thinker and American psychologist William James and a distinguished psychoanalyst Sudhir Kakar.

Rāmakṛṣṇa can be said to be a "mystic" in its true sense of the term. The mystical consciousness or mystical behaviour is so much away and above the normal state of consciousness that the psychologists in general and psychoanalysts in particular, tend to consider mystical behaviour to be "abnormal" behaviour. It is important to clarify here what the word "abnormal" means in psychology. Etymologically, the word abnormal=ab+normal. 'ab' means 'away' and 'normal' means 'according to norms'. Thus, abnormal means "away from normal." Normal behaviour in psychology means the average behaviour of the 68% of the population. Thus, normal behaviour in psychology does not mean the "Ideal behaviour as per the norm", but 'normal' in psychology means the behaviour that 68% of the people would perform in a particular situation. The word 'normal' has been defined in psychology through 'Normal Probability Curve' as under:

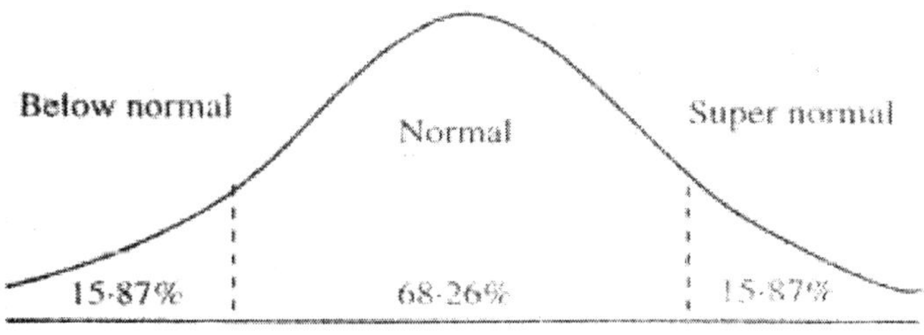

The behaviour that comes within this 68% area of the curve is said to be 'normal' and below (16%) and above (16%) the average behaviour is said to be 'abnormal'. Thus, because the mystical behaviour does not constitute the behaviour of the 68% of the population, it is normally considered to be 'abnormal' behaviour in the empirical science of psychology. However, with the advent of humanistic psychology of Abraham Maslow and Carl Rogers, the above-normal behaviour is being recognized as the 'self-actualization' state of personality development. Abraham Maslow has described the characteristics of self-actualized people which are not considered as the pathological behaviour of 'below-normal' category. And Rāmakṛṣṇa's behaviour is the behaviour of a self-realized person, which is still above than even the behaviour of a self-actualized persons.

However, especially, Rāmakṛṣṇa's behaviour being of a unique mystical pattern, a number of psychoanalysts, unaware of the psychology of religion in general and of Eastern religion in particular, have been tempted to interpret his behaviour as pathological or schizophrenic. This being so, an attempt is made here to analyze Rāmakṛṣṇa's mystical behaviour in the light of the three eminent psychologists, namely, William James, Sudhir Kakar and Jeffery Kripal.

1. William James

Eminent American psychologist William James says that, to the psychologist the religious propensities of man must be at least as interesting as any other of the facts pertaining to his mental constitution. From the logical point of view, there are the two entirely different orders of questions which shout be considered by psychologists who want to study the psychology of religion. They are as under:

(1) What are the religious propensities?

(2) What is their philosophical significance?

William James said that in the recent books on logic, the distinction is made between the two orders of inquiry concerning anything. Among these two, the first question deals with the nature, constitution, origin, history of the subject of inquiry, while the second question deals with the importance, meaning, significance of the subject of inquiry. Here, the important point to be noted that the answer to the first question will be of the nature of an existential judgment. But the answer to the second question, which is related to the problem of understanding the meaning of religion and religious behaviour, will be of a proposition of value. Thus, the religious behaviour is not of the type of existential judgment in the above mentioned term. However, as Spinoza says, "I will analyze the actions and appetites of men as if it were a question of lines, of planes, and of solids", one should not ignore to study these so-called pathological behaviour. While not ignoring the study of this type of behaviour, one should remember that all the religious behaviour should be studied considering them as natural as any other above normal or genius behaviour. James says that, a more fully developed example of the same kind of reasoning is the fashion, quite common nowadays among certain writers, of criticizing the religious emotions by showing a connection between them and the sexual life. James has defined the religious 'genius' and suggested to study them. He says, "We must make search rather for the original experiences which were the pattern-setters to all this mass of suggested feeling and imitated conduct. These experiences we can only find in individuals for whom religion exists not as a dull habit, but as an acute fever rather. But such individuals are 'geniuses' in the religious line; and like many other geniuses who have brought forth fruits effective enough for commemoration in the pages of biography."

James says that following are the characteristics observed in religious 'geniuses'.

1. Religious geniuses are found to be exceptional and eccentric.

2. They have shown symptoms of nervous instability.

3. Religious leaders have been subject to abnormal psychical visitations.

4. They have been the subject of exalted emotional sensibility.

5. Often they have led a discordant inner life.

6. Often they had melancholy during a part of their career.

7. They have known no measure, been liable to obsessions and fixed ideas.

8. Frequently they have fallen into trances, heard voices, seen visions.

9. Often, these pathological features in their career have helped to give them their religious authority and influence.

Thus, James says that the religious geniuses presented all sorts of peculiarities which are ordinarily classed as pathological. Regarding Rāmakṛṣṇa's somewhat this type of behaviour, as a rational being even, Swami Vivekananda also formerly believes such visions as hallucinations. Rāmakṛṣṇa says, Narendra said to me, 'The forms of God that you see are the fiction of your mind'. You (Narendra) used to say, at first, that 'these were all hallucinations'. On that Swami Vivekananda says, "How was I to know? Now I see that you are always right." (Gospel: 511,772)

Thus, according to William James, religious experiences of even great masters have shown above stated features which are termed in psychology as "pathological".

(i) Answer to the Pathological Diagnosis of Religious Behaviour

It is true that the above stated features of religious experiences are of course, not "normal" phenomena. They cannot be classified as "normal" behaviour because, they are not observed in 68% of the normal population as per the Normal Probability Curve. However, as discussed earlier, anything that is not normal, cannot be necessarily classified as abnormal or pathological. All the above-normal behaviour of the "geniuses", scientists, mystics or artists are not at all normal behaviour. But they cannot be called pathological. Creativity, originality and geniuses also demonstrate above-normal personality traits and behaviour.

(ii) William James gives the answer to the problem as under:

Psychologists will say that there are two main phenomena of religion, namely, melancholy and conversion, are essentially phenomena of adolescence, and therefore synchronous with the development of sexual life.

To which he answer that even were the asserted synchrony unrestrictedly true as a fact (which it is not), it is not only the sexual life, but the entire higher mental life which awakens during adolescence. One might then as well set up the thesis that the interest in mechanics, physics, chemistry, logic, philosophy, and sociology, which springs up during adolescent years along with that in poetry and religion, is also a perversion of the sexual instinct:- but that would be too absurd.

Further, giving another argument, he says, if the synchrony is to decide, what is to be done with the fact that the religious age par excellence would seem to be old age, when the uproar of the sexual life is past? (James: Lecture-1)

(iii) Rāmakṛṣṇa's Answer to This Problem

Rāmakṛṣṇa did not give much importance to the worldly-minded people, who simply cannot understand this states of consciousness. According to him, not mystics, but rather, those who tell mystics mad, are themselves mad after worldly objects. They (worldly people) are in the state of madness, intoxicated with 'woman and gold'. (Gospel: 780) They (entangled in worldliness) laugh at those who think of God and meditate on him, and call them lunatics. Let people say, 'This man has lost his head for God'. (Gospel: 631,646) Rāmakṛṣṇa says, Some people may say about the devotees: 'Day and night these people speak about God. They are crazy; they have lost their heads. But how clever we are! How we, enjoy pleasure-money, honour, the senses!' But Rāmakṛṣṇa considers them as a crow that first in the morning eat dirt. What is the meaning of this 'cleverness'? (Gospel: 669) Thus, Rāmakṛṣṇa was very clear about the meaninglessness of that worldly wisdom and he gave much importance to the 'spiritual madness'. He says, "Was Rādhā's madness the madness that comes from brooding over worldly objects and makes one unconscious? One attains that madness by meditating on God. Haven't you heard of love-madness, and knowledge-madness?" (Gospel: 220,548)

Rāmakṛṣṇa gave the example of a devotee Kṛṣṇakishor, in this way. [About Kṛṣṇakishor] He too passed through a God-intoxicated state, when he would repeat only the word 'Om' and shut himself up alone in his room. His relatives thought he was actually mad, and called in a physician. Ram Kaviraj of Natagoro came to see him. Kṛṣṇakishor said to the physician. 'Cure me, sir, of my malady, if you please, but not of my Om.' (Gospel: 118)

Rāmakṛṣṇa put it on logical ground that logically how it is possible that one becomes unconscious by constantly thinking of the Consciousness. Mad! That is the thing! Shivnath once said that 'one loses one's head' by thinking too much of God. What said I. 'Can anyone ever become unconscious by thinking of consciousness? God is of the nature of Eternity, Purity and Consciousness. Through his consciousness one becomes conscious of everything; through his intelligence the whole world appears intelligent. Shivanath said that some Europeans had gone insane, that they had 'lost their head', by thinking too much about God. In their case it may be true; for they think of worldly things. There is a line in a song: 'Divine fervour fills my body and robs me of consciousness'. The consciousness referred to here is the consciousness of the outer world.' (Gospel: 615) Too much thinking of material things may be harmful, but the Divinity Itself is the Nectar, then, thinking of that never become harmful, rather, it is helpful to regain out real consciousness. Rāmakṛṣṇa called the Consciousness the 'Nectar Lake'. He says, the 'Nectar Lake' is the lake of Immortality. A man sinking in it does not die, but becomes immortal. Some people believe that by thinking of God too much the mind becomes deranged; but that is not true. God is the lake of Nectar, the ocean of Immortality. Sinking in it, one does not die, but verily transcends death. (Gospel: 115,108,674-75)

The psychoanalysts may have wrongly diagnosed Rāmakṛṣṇa as a insane person, but in his own time, many people believe that he was not a normal. His above normal personality was misinterpreted as abnormal. He says, "Some say that this state of mine is a disease. I say to them, how can one become unconscious by thinking of him whose consciousness has made the whole world conscious?" (Gospel: 256) Therefore, he advices that Never for a moment harbour the idea that by thinking too much of God one becomes insane. Man does not lose his consciousness by being mad about God. (Gospel: 456) Because, only ignorant people say that one should not have an excess of devotion and divine love. Can there be any excess of divine love? (Gospel: 467)

Logically, Rāmakṛṣṇa explained his views in this way. He says, Shivnath said that one lost one's head by too much thinking of God. In other words, one becomes unconscious by meditating on the

Universal Consciousness. Think of it! Becoming unconscious by contemplating Him who is of the very nature of Consciousness and whose Consciousness endows the world with consciousness! And what does your 'Science' say? This combined with this produces that, that combined with this produces this. One is more likely to lose consciousness by contemplating those things-by handling material things too much. Losing consciousness by contemplating God-through whose Consciousness even inert matter appears to be conscious, and hands, feet and body move. People say that the body moves of itself; but they do not know that it is God who moves it. They say that water scalds the hand. But water can by no means scald the hand; it is the heat in the water, the fire in the water that scalds. In the same way, man says that the sense-organs do their work of themselves; but he does not know that inside dwells He whose very nature is Consciousness. (Gospel: 915-16)

(iv) Characteristics of Self-realized Soul According to Rāmakṛṣṇa

Knowing fully well and aware of the so-called pathological signs of the mystic, Rāmakṛṣṇa himself had described these signs and clearly and logically argued how they are not really pathological. As he says, "It is said in the Bhāgavatama that a man who has seen God behaves sometimes like a child, sometimes like a ghoul, sometimes like an inert thing and sometimes like a madman. For he maintains the same attitude toward things holy and unholy. Therefore he seems to be a lunatic." (Gospel: 451-452,493,791) Further he says, "He (Vijñānī) is sometimes like an inert thing, sometimes, like a ghoul, sometimes like a child and sometimes like a mad man. People noticed his ways and actions and think of his as insane or sometimes he is like a child-no bondage, no shame, no hatred, no hesitation, or the like. One reaches this state of mind after having the vision of God. Lust, anger, and the other passions cannot exist after the vision of God." (Gospel: 405,476,678)

Thus, the most important criterion or proof of the above-normal aspect of the mystic is that he becomes free from the shackles of the passions like lust, anger etc. In this way, Rāmakṛṣṇa has defined logically and experientially the so-called insanity of the realized religious geniuses.

2. Sudhir Kakar on Rāmakṛṣṇa's Mystical Behaviour

Sudhir Kakar, an eminent Indian psychoanalyst had nicely discussed the psychoanalysis of Rāmakṛṣṇa's behaviour in his book, "The Analyst and the Mystic: Psychoanalytic Reflections on Religion and Mysticism." Kakar's analysis of Rāmakṛṣṇa's behaviour is described briefly in the following sub-titles:

(i) Mysticism and Its Types:

The mystical path is one of the most ancient and universal path in religion.

(1) Nathan Soderblom's classification of mystical experiences:

(1) First, 'Mysticism of the infinite.' This concept consists of the idea of 'an elevation of awareness' where the unifying experience with the superhuman eliminates perception of the concrete and abstract element from the sensate world. And

(2) 'Mysticism of personal life' where the experience is not rooted in ecstatic rapture, but in a meeting with God in the midst of life's problems and struggles, a meeting experienced at a deep level of faith within normal waking consciousness.

(2) William James' classification of mystical experiences:

Kakar says that, yet another distinction is the one made by William James between Sporadic and Cultivated mysticism, which corresponds to Arthur Deikman's separation between untrained-sensate and trained-sensate mystical experience. (William James, The Varieties of Religious Experience, (New York: Longmans, Green, 1902) (Kakar, 1991:1)

(3) Indian traditional classification of mystical experiences:

Sudhir Kakar explained the classification of the Indian tradition of mysticism into two-upanishadic mysticism and yogic mysticism. He mentioned the differences between the two and narrate how Rāmakṛṣṇa's mysticism is different.

(1) Upanishadic Mysticism

Upanishadic mysticism is a quest for spiritual illumination wherein a person's deepest essence is discovered to be identical with the common source of all other animate and inanimate beings.

(2) Yogic Mysticism

Yogic mysticism strives to realize the immortality of the human soul outside time, space and matter.

Kakar says that, of course such distinctions are more sign posts rather than sharp dividers, since shades of both 'infinity' and 'personality' will exist in every mystic. Regarding Rāmakṛṣṇa's mysticism he says that Rāmakṛṣṇa was a career mystic, and though his initial forays into mysticism may have been sporadic and untrained, the latter half of his life was marked by regular and frequent mystical experiences of the cultivated and trained-sensate kind. Regarding Indian mystical classification with reference to Rāmakṛṣṇa, Kakar believes that, in both upanishadic and yogic mysticism, there is no trace of love of or yearning for communion with God, which is considered the highest manifestation of the mystical mood, without which no "unio mystica" is conceivable.

It is only in bhakti or devotional mysticism-Rāmakṛṣṇa's preferred form-where love for the Deity creeps in, where the mystic's soul of 'self' is finally united with God (or Goddess) in an ecstatic surrender, that Hindu mysticism exhibits a strong family resemblance to the mysticism of monotheistic faiths. (Kakar, 1991:3)

Thus, according to Kakar, Rāmakṛṣṇa's mysticism is different from the above mentioned classifications mysticism. His was the 'Devotional Mysticism' where deep love and yearning for God is at its basis.

(ii) Kakar's Argument Against the Pathology of Rāmakṛṣṇa's Behaviour

Sudhir Kakar, being a psychoanalyst prefers Rāmakṛṣṇa for analysis because according to him Rāmakṛṣṇa most aptly represents Hindu mysticism and the "Oceanic Feeling" as described by Freud. As Kakar says, "The individual I have selected for my own explorations is the nineteenth-century Bengali mystic Śrī Rāmakṛṣṇa. Together with Ramaṇa, Rāmakṛṣṇa is widely regarded as the preeminent figure of Hindu mysticism of the last three hundred years, whatever preeminence may mean in the mystical context. He is a particularly apt choice for a psychoanalytic study of ecstatic mysticism since Freud's observations on the mystical experience, on what he called the 'oceanic feeling', an omnibus label for all forms of extreme mystical experience, were indirectly occasioned by Rāmakṛṣṇa's ecstasies." (Kakar, 1991: 6)

When Romain Rolland was writing a biography of Rāmakṛṣṇa, he has wrote to Freud in 1927 that though his analysis of religion in his book "The Future of an Illusion" was 'Juste' (apt), he would ideally have liked Freud to make an analysis of spontaneous religious feeling, or more exactly, religious sensations which are entirely different from religion proper and much more enduring. [Harrison I. B., 1979: 409] (Kakar, 1991: 7) Romain Rolland went to call this sensation oceanic, without perceptible limits. And added that Romain Rolland himself had all his life found the oceanic feeling to be a source of vital revival. Freud's response to Rolland, his analysis of the "oceanic feeling" was then spelled out in "civilization of its Discontents". It is highly probable that the term "oceanic feeling" itself is taken from Rāmakṛṣṇa's (salt-doll) imagery to describe the ineffable." (Kakar, 1991: 7)

Kakar says that "ocean as a symbol for boundless oneness and unity in which multiplicities dissolve and opposites fuse not only goes back to the Upanishads in the Hindu tradition, but is one of the preferred metaphors of devotional mystics for the melting of ego boundaries in the Buddhist, Christian and Muslim traditions as well." [Dushan, 1989: manuscript] Christian mystics, for instance, have been greatly fond of the metaphor. "I live in the ocean of God as a fish in the sea." (Kakar, 1991: 7)

Thus, the frequently used term and analyzed by Freud is the "oceanic feeling" representing the mystical experience in general and Hindu mysticism in particular. This oceanic feeling was the basic characteristic of Rāmakṛṣṇa's mystical experiences and its narrations. This being so, Kakar has deeply analyzed Rāmakṛṣṇa's mystical experiences within psychoanalytic framework in his above mentioned book.

Kakar gave argument against the people who consider mystical behaviour as pathological. His views are as under:

(1) Kakar says, many analysts interested in the phenomenon would

now agree that in spite of superficial resemblances, the mystical retreat is neither as complete nor as compelling and obligatory as psychotic regression. Moreover, in contrast to the psychotic, the mystic's ability to maintain affectionate ties remains unimpaired when it does not actually get enhanced.

(2) Secondly, to the psychoanalysts whose contention that mystical experiences are nothing but the outcome of psychological disorder, we can say that given the analyst's commitment to Freud's dictum that the capacity "to love and work" is perhaps the best outer criterion for mental health, then the mystic's performance on both counts is impressive-that is, if one can succeed in emancipating one's self from a circumscription of the notions of love and work dictated by convention.

(3) Thirdly, some of the more recent work in psychoanalysis recognizes that mystical states lead to more rather than less integration of the person. (Horton C., 1974: 364-80) David Aberbach D., 1987: 509-26)

(4) Further, giving Romain Rolland's testimony, Kakar says, "in the time of Rāmakṛṣṇa and till today, many believe Rāmakṛṣṇa as an insane on the ground of psychoanalysis of Freud." Sudhir Kakar has shown what Freud himself say about the experiences of Rāmakṛṣṇa, when Freud was asked by Romain Rolland in this context. Sudhir Kakar says that in fact, what I would like to do here is address the question Romain Rolland, in writing of Rāmakṛṣṇa's initial trances, posed for 'physicians both of the body and of the mind', namely, "There is no difficulty in proving the apparent destruction of his whole mantle structure, and the disintegration of its elements. But how were they reassembled into a synthetic entity of the highest order?" (Rolland R., 1986: 38) To put it differently, how does the mystic become master of his madness and of his reason alike whereas the schizophrenic remains their slave?

Sudhir Kakar tries to answer this question by saying that "Today, psychoanalysis is in a relatively better position of adequatio (adequateness) in relation to mystical phenomena as well as other states of altered consciousness, such as the possession trance. The adequatio principle, of course, states that the same phenomenon may hold entirely different sets of meaning for different observers. [Walsh R. N. et al., 1980: 36-52]" (Kakar S. 1991: 5)

Explaining the position of mystical phenomena within the psychoanalytic framework, Kakar further says that "The increase in the level of analytical "adequatio" has not become about because of any analyst's personal experience of training in the mystical disciplines (as far as I know). In part, this higher adequtio is due to the increased availability of analytically relevant information which is no longer limited to the writings or biographical and autobiographical accounts of a few Western mystic such as Teresa of Avila and John of Cross. In the last fifteen years, we have had access to psychodynamically informed interviews with members of mystical path and have experienced various states of altered consciousness, including ecstatic trance." [Buckley & Galanter M., 1979: 281-89] (Kakar, 1991: 5)

Further Kakar says, "More than the availability of additional information, the greater adequatio of psychoanalysis in relation to mysticism stems from the work of many writers-Erik Erikson, Donald Winnicott, Wilfred Bion, and Jacques Lacan come immediately to my mind-who, in spite of their very different theoretical concerns, pursued a common antireductionist agenda. The cumulative effect of their writings had been to allow the adoption of what Winnicott, in talking of transitional phenomena, called "a particular quality in attitude", with which I believe mystical states should also be observed. In other words, my own enhanced feeling of adequatio reflects the presence of an unstated project in contemporary psychoanalysis in which the copresence of different orders of experience is tolerated and no attempts are undertaken to explain one in terms of the other without reciprocity." (Kakar, 1991: 5-6)

Thus, Sudhir Kakar as an eminent Indian psychoanalyst propounds that modern psychoanalysis does give a room to mystical experiences as an altered state of consciousness without reducing it to pathology.

3. Different between Visions and Hallucinations

The most prevalent feature of Rāmakṛṣṇa's mystical behaviour was the various types of visions as experienced by him. It is because of these visions that the people in general and psychoanalysts in particular were led to consider them as hallucinations and delusions and thereby to diagnose Rāmakṛṣṇa as schizophrenic or psychotic.

This being so, a detailed analysis of Rāmakṛṣṇa's visions and Kakar's comments on them are discussed here in detail.

Showing the difference between mystical visions and hallucinations, Sudhir Kakar says, that in my own explorations, I prefer to use the religious term vision rather than its psychiatric counterpart hallucination for the same reason that I have talked of mystical ecstasy rather than of euphoria, namely the connotations of psychopathology associated with psychiatric categories. The distinction between the two, though, is not very hard and fast, their boundaries constantly shifting. Both can be produced by severe depression or manic excitement, toxic psychosis due to exhaustion or starvation or sensory deprivation or simply a febrile illness. What is important in distinguishing them is their meaning and content and not their origin.

Visions are like hallucinations in that they too are images, such as flashes of light, which are visually perceived without the external stimulation of the organ of sight. They are, however, not hallucination in that they occur during the course of intense religious experience rather than during a psychotic episode. They are thus less bizarre and less disorganized. Visions belong more to the realm of perceptions that take place, say, during a dream, while falling asleep (hypnagogic) or when awakening (hypnopompic). None of these can be called a consequence of psychic impairment. Visions are, then, special kinds of dreams which find their way into waking life. Visions can be the production of mental disorder as well as of real events being drawn across the barrier of sleep into the formation of dreams.

Freud recognized the special nature of visions. As he remarked, "It is easy to imagine, too, that certain mystics may succeed in upsetting the normal relations between the different regions of the mind, so that, for instance, perception may be able to grasp happenings in the depths of the ego and in the id which were otherwise inaccessible to it. [Freud S., 1933: 79-80]" (Kakar, 1991:23)

In short, visions of mystics may have some reality basis and hence, they are not necessarily signs of mental disorder like hallucinations.

Rāmakṛṣṇa's visions, as perhaps those of other mystics, do not constitute a unitary phenomenon. They span the whole range from what can be described as hallucination in the psychiatric sense, through more or less conscious visions, to what I would call "unconscious visions" (or "visions of the unconsciousness?") which can not be described since the observing ego is absent. There are the ineffable "salt doll" visions which comprise a small, though perhaps the most striking part of the total mystical repertoire. (Kakar, 1991:24)

(i) Bodily signs

The effects of mystical experience are also manifested in the body, and Ramskṛṣṇa's visions had certain well-defined physical correlates. At times, he would shudder while tears of joy streamed unchecked down his cheeks. At other times, his eyes would become half-closed and unfocused, a faint smile playing around the mouth while his body became completely rigid and had to be supported by a disciple lest he fall and hurt himself. The accompaniment to certain other trance states was a fly shed chest or a strong burning sensation all over the body. Then there is the feeling of being famished-one wonders spiritual receptivity with a bodily analogue or there are the bouts of gluttony in which he consumed enormous quantity of food, generally sweets. The craving for a particular dish or a sweet would come upon Rāmakṛṣṇa unexpectedly, at any time of night or day. At these moments, Rāmakṛṣṇa would be like a pregnant woman who is dominated by her obsession and cannot rest till the craving is satisfied.

Kakar says that from inside the tradition, all these manifestations are some of the nineteen bodily signs of the mystical experience. (Kakar, 1991:24) Thus, in mystical tradition, the bodily sighs are also described. This clearly suggests that visions and other bodily sighs, though resemble the pathological state, actually they are totally different experiences of altered states of consciousness, underlying normal if not higher level of personality formation.

(ii) Nightmares

Rāmakṛṣṇa once says, "I would spit on the ground when I saw them. But they would follow me and obsess me like ghosts. On the day after such a vision I would have a severe attack of diaorrhea, and all these ecstasies would pass out through my bowels." (Gupta, Vacanāmṛta, vol.3, 238-89) (Kakar, 1991:25)

Such hallucinations, or better, nightmarish visions, are not alien but perhaps as much a part of Rāmakṛṣṇa's personality as are his artistic sensibility or his more elevated, mystical visions as observed in Ernest Hartmann's work on nightmares. (Hartmann E., 1984) (Kakar, 1991:25)

In his study of non-psychiatric volunteers who suffered from nightmares since childhood, Hartmann found that these subjects were usually sensitive people with a strong artistic bent and creative potential. More important, they demonstrate what he calls "thin boundaries of the mind," a permeability between self and object, waking/sleeping, fantasy/reality, adult/child, human/animal and other such boundaries, which are relatively fixed for most people. Rāmakṛṣṇa, and perhaps most other mystics, have a genetic biological predisposition, reinforced by some early experiences of thin boundaries, also between nightmarish and ecstatic visions. (Kakar, 1991:25) Thus, Rāmakṛṣṇa had the visions what psychology termed as nightmarish as well as he has ecstatic visions. The visions of Rāmakṛṣṇa, which can be defined in the terms of psychology as nightmarish, also suggest creative potential rather than personality disintegration.

(iii) Conscious visions

The other class of visions is the conscious ones. Welcomed by a prepared mind, they fall on a receptive ground. Conscious visions may be symbolic representations of an ongoing psychic process, the symbols taken from the mystic's religious and cultural tradition. This is true, for instance, of Rāmakṛṣṇa's vision of his "enlightenment," which he 'saw' in the traditional Yogic imagery of Kuṇḍalini, the coiled serpent energy rising through the different centers (charkas) of his body and opening up the 'lotuses' associated with these centers, a specifically Hindu metaphor for mental transformation and the opening up of the psyche to hitherto inaccessible psychic experience. "I saw a twenty-two, twenty-three-year-old, exactly resembling me, enter the Suṣumnā nerve and with his tongue 'sport' (ramaṇa) with the vulva (yoni) shaped lotuses. He began with the center at the anus, through the centers of the penis, navel, and so on. The respective four-petaled, and six-petaled lotuses which had been drooping, rose high and blossomed. I distinctly remember that when he came to the heart and sport with it with his tongue, a twelve-petaled lotus which had been drooping rose high and opened its petals. Then he came to the sixteen-petaled lotus in the throat and the two-petaled one in the forehead. And last of all, the thousand-petaled lotus in the head blossomed." (Gupta, Vacanāmṛta, vol.3, 89) (Kakar, 1991:26)

This particular vision, in which self-representation is split into observing and participating aspects can also be seen through psychiatric glasses as a heutroscopic depersonalization which occurs particularly among individuals with tendencies toward self-contemplation and introspection. Yet in the absence of any associated painful or anxious affect and the fact that this king of vision was only one among Rāmakṛṣṇa's vast repertoire of visions with very different structures and qualities, I would tend to see its ground in a creativity, akin to the heightened fantasy of an artist or a writer, rather than in pathology. Goethe and Maupassant are two instances of creative writers who also experienced the phenomenon of their doubles. (J.M.R. Damas Mora et.al., "On Heutroscopy or the Phenomenon of the Double", British Journal of Medical Psychology 53 (1980): 75-83) (Kakar, 1991:26)

(iv) Universal Visions

Other conscious visions are visual insights, images full of conviction and sudden clarity, couched either in a universal mystical or in a particular, cultural-historical idiom.

Some examples of the universal visions would be seeing the universe filled with sparks of fire, or glittering like a lake of quicksilver, or all its quarters illuminated with the light of myriad candles. Such visions of light have been reported by mystics throughout the ages, and indeed, seeing the divine light has been a central feature of many mystical cults. Another visual insight of the universal variety is seeing everything throbbing with consciousness: "Sometimes I see the world soaked with consciousness in the same way as the earth is soaked with water during the rains." (Gupta, Vacanāmṛta, vol.1, 388) (Kakar, 1991:26-7) Thus, universal visions are found universally among mystics and hence, they cannot be termed as pathological hallucinations.

(v) Culturally constituted visions

The full import of the more culturally constituted visions can only be appreciated if we keep in mind that Rāmakṛṣṇa was a Hindu Brahmin living at a time, the nineteenth century, and place-rural Bengal-in which the ideas of pollution and polluting substances were string, caste taboos strict. Visions dissolving religious distinctions and caste taboos, such as the ones on touching forbidden substances or taking foods from forbidden persons, were thus primarily expressed in a cultural imagery relevant to Rāmakṛṣṇa's community. For instance, "Then I was shown a Muslim with a long beard who came to me with rice in an earthen plate. He fed other Muslims and also gave me some grains to eat. Mother showed me there exists only one and not two." (Gupta, Vacanāmṛta, vol.3, 109) (Kakar, 1991:27) "Another day I saw excrement, urine, rice, vegetables, and other foods. Suddenly the soul came out of my body and, like a flame, touched everything: excrement, urine, everything was tasted. It was revealed that everything is one, that there is no difference." (Gupta, Vacanāmṛta, vol.1, 431) (Kakar, 1991:27) Or, when on the repeated egging on by his nephew, he asked the Goddess for occult powers and saw a middle-aged prostitute come up, squat on her haunches with her back to him, and proceed to evacuate. The vision revealed that occult powers were the shit of that whore. (Kakar, 1991:27) Thus, cultural taboos and Rāmakṛṣṇa's revolt or resistance against those cultural taboos, which were either inhuman or inconsistent with the ultimate unity of all things are reflected in hi visions. Rāmakṛṣṇa's strongly internalized conviction of the Oneness is reflected here clearly.

(vi) Visions of transmutation of stimuli

There is another class of visions, or strictly speaking, mystical illusions, since, these, rest on a transmutation of external stimuli into creations which are nearer to those of the artist. Thus the way an English boy leans against a tree is transformed into a vision of Kṛṣṇa; a prostitute walking toward him is changed into a vision of the Mother Goddess-both images irradiate his body and mind with beneficence. In Blake's words, these illusions are "auguries of innocence" enabling the mystic "to see a world in a grain of sand, and a heaven in a wild flower." (Kakar, 1991:27-8) Thus, real mystical visions which are called illusions in the terms of psychology also do not reflect pathological, according to Kakar.

(vii) Unconscious visions

There are the indescribable, unconscious visions. Rāmakṛṣṇa once said to his disciples, "you see, something goes up creeping from the feet to the head. Consciousness continues to exist as long as this power does not reach the head; but as soon as it reaches the head, all consciousness is completely lost. There is no seeing or hearing anymore, much less speaking. Who can speak? The very idea of 'I' and 'You' vanishes. While it (the serpent power) goes up, I feel a desire to tell you everything-how many visions I experience, of their nature, etc. Until it comes to this place (showing the heart) or at most this place (showing the throat) speaking is possible, and I do speak. But the moment it goes up beyond this place (showing the throat) someone forcibly presses the mouth, as it were, and I lose all consciousness. I cannot control it. Suppose I try to describe what kind of visions I experience when it goes beyond this place (showing the throat). As soon as I begin to think of them for the purpose of description, the mind rushes immediately up, and speaking becomes impossible." (Saradananda, Śrī Rāmakṛṣṇa, vol.1, 417) (Kakar, 1991:28) Thus, ineffability which is the basic characteristic of mystical phenomena, is, when applied to mystical visions, then they are termed as "unconscious visions."

(viii) Keeping the trace of ego Visions: A sign of Mental Health

Rāmakṛṣṇa deliberately used to maintain a trace of observing ego even during absorbing vision. This capacity of maintaining "Doubling Consciousness", one experiencing the mystical vision and the other observing it-itself is the greatest sigh of highest mental integration. Expressing his feelings through metaphors, Rāmakṛṣṇa says, "I feel like a fish released from a pot into the water of the Ganges." Rāmakṛṣṇa, however, does not seem to have been overly enamored of these states which have been so often held as the apex of the mystical experience. He consciously tried to keep a trace of the observing ego- a little spark of the big fire-so as not to completely disappear, or disappear for a long time, into the "unio mystica" with its non differentiation of 'I' and the 'Other.' As Rāmakṛṣṇa says, "In samādhi, I lose outer consciousness completely, but God generally keeps a little trace of the ego in me for the enjoyment. Enjoyment is possible when 'I' and 'You' remain." Elsewhere, he also says, "I want to taste sugar, not become sugar." Thus, Rāmakṛṣṇa shows highest maturity of personality development in his capacity to maintain a trace of ego even in his mystical experience. However, as Kakar says, Yet, in spite of himself, he was often the salt doll that went into the ocean. (Kakar, 1991:28)

4. Yearning or mystical motivation (or the feeling of loss as psychologists define)

Kakar says, "The vicissitude of separation have been, of course, at the heart of psychoanalytic theorizing on mysticism. The yearning to be reunited with a perfect, omnipotent being, the longing for the blissful soothing and nursing associated with the mother of earliest infancy has been consensually deemed the core of mystical motivation. What has been controversial is the way this longing has been viewed and the value placed on it by different analysts." (Kakar, 1991:29)

The traditional view, initiated by Freud, sees this yearning as reactive, a defense against the hatred directed toward the Oedipal father. Analyzing this in case of Rāmakṛṣṇa, Sudhir Kakar says, "Given the limitation that Rāmakṛṣṇa did not spend any time on the couch, I can only say that there is no evidence in the voluminous record of his conversations, reminiscences, and accounts of his visions which remotely suggestive of any strong hostility toward the Oedipal father. The evidence for the denial of the dreaded aspects of the mother is slightly greater, namely through a plausible interpretation of some elements of his vision in the Kālī temple when he had taken up a sword to kill himself. However, seen in the total context of a large number of visions of the Mother Goddess, the ambiguous evidence of one particular vision is not enough to compel an acceptance of the Kleinian notions on mystical motivation." (Kakar, 1991:29)

Poul Horton has advanced a more adaptive view of mystical yearning and mystical states, especially during adolescence. ((Kakar, 1991:29) He sees them as a consequence of the pangs of separation in which the felt reality of being utterly and agonizingly alone is "transiently" denied. The mystical experience is then a transitional phenomenon which soothes and reassures much as a baby is soothed by a blanket, a child by a stuffed toy or fairy tale am adult by a particular piece of music-all these various creations, material and nonmaterial, providing opportunities for the controlled illusion that heals.

Thus, Kakar believes that the mystical yearning and resultant mystical states heal the adolescent feeling of less, separation and loneliness. He derive a hypothesis that experiences of separation and loss spurred Rāmakṛṣṇa onto the mystical path. We know that Rāmakṛṣṇa's first quasi-mystical ecstasy when he became unconscious at the sight of white cranes flying against a background of dark clouds took place in the last year of his father's final illness (according to one place in Rāmakṛṣṇa's reminiscences, two years after his father's death), that is, at a time of an impending loss. And "I have described", as Kakar further says, "the marked change that came over Rāmakṛṣṇa-his heightened mystical yearnings with all the outward sighs of a full-scale depression-at the death of his brother, at a time in his life cycle, during adolescence, when the developing ego is particularly vulnerable to stress.

Kakar believes that the mystical path is then also a way of lessening the agony of separation, mitigating the grief at loss, reducing the sadness of bereavement. In my interviews with members of a mystical cult in India, loss was the single most important factor in their decision to seek its membership. The very embarkation on the mystical path had a therapeutic effect by itself, while any experience of a mystical state had a further marked effect in altering the person's dysphoric state of mind." (S. Kakar, Shamans, Mystics and Doctors (New York: Knopf, 1982), (Buckley and Galanter, "Mystical Experience", 285; C.Horton, "The Mystical Experience as a Suicide Preventive", American Journal of Psychiatry 130 (1973), 294-96) (Kakar, 1991:30-31) In contrast to the person's previous feelings of apathy and depression, the turn to mysticism had the consequence of his dealing with grief in a more orderly and more detached, though in a more transcendent, manner. Perhaps, T.S.Eliot is correct in observing that "A man does not join himself with the universe so long as he has anything else to join himself with. (Cited in Aberback, 'Grief and Mysticism', 509)" (Kakar, 1991:31)

5. Difference between the Concept of Self-actualization of Maslow and the Concept of Self-realization in Rāmakṛṣṇa

From this, one may derive, as Kakar says, that Rāmakṛṣṇa's spiritual yearning, though seems to begin with loss and separation in adolescence, his spiritual quest and yearning for the Love of God throughout his life underlies the highest 'Divine' motivation of self-realization. It can be compared with Maslow's concept of "self-actualized" person. In Malsow's words one can that Rāmakṛṣṇa's spiritual or mystical journey begins with "Deficiency Motivation" but it gradually culminates into "Growth Motivation" of self-actualization. But, it is very much important to note that the concept of self-actualized and the concept of self-realized are all together different concepts. The former may have been achieved by the starting feeling of "Deficiency Motivation", in the second state of consciousness can be achieved through the concept in mind the highest Ideal of human being. In Maslow's concept of self-actualization. Thus, this is the basic difference between the two.

(1) Maslow believes that there are basic five needs, and after the fulfillment of first four needs, one can have the need for self-actualization. While, in Rāmakṛṣṇa, the ultimate goal of human life is to realize the Ultimate Reality. Hence, in Maslow, in self-actualization, there is the actualization of self, while, in Rāmakṛṣṇa, there is the realization of the Ultimate Reality.

(2) In Maslow, called the 'being need' to the need of self-actualization and this 'being' means the actualization of one's potentials. While, in Rāmakṛṣṇa, realization is not the actualization of one's potentials, but to know the real nature of man, which is different from the worldly human potential. Though, that potentials are there in the mystics, but the mystical phenomena is all together different from that of actualizing worldly potentials.

(3) To further clarify his concept of self-actualization by examples, Maslow gave the name of persons, to whom he considers as self-actualized persons. He began by picking out a group of people, some historical figures, some people he knew, whom he felt clearly met the standard of self-actualization. Included in this august group were Abraham Lincoln, Thomas Jefferson, Albert Einstein, Eleanor

Roosevelt, Jane Adams, William James, Albert Schweitzer, Benedict Spinoza, and Alduous Huxley, plus 12 unnamed people who were alive at the time Maslow did his research. It is to be noted that these esteemed persons may be called by Maslow the self-actualized persons, but by no means are they considered as the self-realized persons, who have got the realization of the Ultimate Reality.

(4) Lastly, the most basic difference between the two can be explained in this way. As it is said that to become a self-actualized is a need of man, though very few. According to Maslow, these types of persons have the need of the higher level and that need should be fulfilled by them, in order to be happy. To differentiate the need of self-actualization from the 'instinctive needs', Maslow called it 'Metaneeds' and simultaneously says that if that needs are not fulfilled, then the person will suffer "Matapathologies". Dr. C. George Boeree has nicely explained this in the following way:

6. Metaneeds and metapathologies

Another way in which Maslow has approached the problem of what is self-actualization is to talk about the special, driving needs of the self-actualizers. They need the following in their lives in order to be happy:

Truth, rather than dishonesty.

Goodness, rather than evil.

Beauty, not ugliness or vulgarity.

Unity, wholeness, and transcendence of opposites, not arbitrariness or forced choices.

Aliveness, not deadness or the mechanization of life.

Uniqueness, not bland uniformity.

Perfection and necessity, not sloppiness, inconsistency, or accident.

Completion, rather than incompleteness.

Justice and order, not injustice and lawlessness.

Simplicity, not unnecessary complexity.

Richness, not environmental impoverishment.

Effortlessness, not strain.

Playfulness, not grim, humorless, drudgery.

Self-sufficiency, not dependency.

Meaningfulness, rather than senselessness.

G. Boeree says that according to Maslow, when a self-actualizer doesn't get these needs fulfilled, they respond with 'metapathologies' -- a list of problems as long as the list of 'metaneeds'! He says, "Let me summarize it by saying that, when forced to live without these values, the self-actualizer develops depression, despair, disgust, alienation, and a degree of cynicism." With reference to these needs of self-actualized person, it should be noted that these qualities are very much present in the life of a realized person or mystic, but these behaviour are very natural to him and they are not as need to be fulfilled.

In fact, after some time, Maslow has devoted his attention not to his own theory, but to the humanistic psychology and human potentials movement. Narrating Maslow's last thinking, Boereen says that toward the end of his life, he inaugurated what he called the **fourth force** in psychology: Freudian and other 'depth' psychologies constituted the first force; Behaviorism was the second force; His own humanism, including the European existentialists, were the third force. The fourth force was the "transpersonal psychologies" which, taking their cue from Eastern philosophies, investigated such things as meditation, higher levels of consciousness, and even parapsychological phenomena. It is important to note that as it is seen earlier that Rāmakṛṣṇa do not believe in any occult powers which are considered sometimes as a parapsychological phenomena. Then, we can say that Rāmakṛṣṇa's mysticism is even beyond the "forth force" mentioned by Maslow.

The following views of Kakar and Lacan are somewhat near to this philosophical thinking regarding Rāmakṛṣṇa's yearning and it is shown that the yearning of a mystic is very much different from the other's desire for the worldly things. Not only this, the concept of Deficiency or loss, is not sufficient to understand a mystical phenomena, as Kakar says.

7. Answer to What Psychologists define as Feeling of Loss

Kakar rightly says that Rāmakṛṣṇa's two actual experience of loss are not sufficient to explain the totality of his mysticism, the intensity of his yearning throughout life to end the state of separation from the Divine and the acuteness of his distress at the absence of the Mother. (Kakar-30-1)

Lacan, for instant, had postulated that man's psychic life constantly seeks to deal with a primordial state of affairs which he calls The Real. The Real itself is unknowable, though we constantly create myths as its markers. Perhaps the principal myth involves the rupture of a basic union, the separation from the mother's body, leaving us with a fundamental feeling of incompletion. The fantasies around this insufficiency are universal, governing the psyche of both patients and analysts alike. In the psyche, this lack is translated as desire, and the human venture is a history of desire as it ceaselessly loses and discovers itself in (what Lacan calls) The Imaginary. And with the advent of language, the Symbolic order. The mystic, unlike most others, does not mistake his hunger for its fulfillment. If we are all fundamentally perverse in the play of our desire, then the mystic is the only one who seeks to go beyond the illusion of The Imaginary and, yes, also the māyā of The Symbolic register. (Kakar, 1991:32)

8. Mystical Experience and Creativity

As Michael Eigen has pointed out, "Ideal Experiencing", that is the state of beatific perfection, in which mystical states can be included, usually involved something in disguise-mother, father, sex, aggression etc. (Eigen, 1979: 278-98) But as Kakar says, Lacan, Winnicott, Bion and implicitly, Erickson on the other hand, look at ideal experiencing in its own right, as a spontaneously unfolding capacity for creative experiencing. Describing this Creative aptitude with reference to Rāmakṛṣṇa's aptitude, Margaret Bedrosian says that "Describing the essential nature of creative aptitude, the American psychologist James Vargiu states that one of its basic characteristic is its orientation towards universality, The over coming of successive boundaries towards ever-growing expansion, inclusion and identification. Other, such as the psychologist Abraham Maslow have referred to the creative insight as 'an isomorphism', wherein the creative agent and the world come together in a complementary manner, each molding itself to the other until perfect fusion occurs. Indeed, thinkers as diverse as Teilhard de Chardin, Śrī Aurobindo, and Henri Bergson have agreed that behind the diversifying evolutionary thrust of nature, 'there must be an underlying unifying impulse of the creative field explains why the greatest artists, scientists, and religious teachers have described their highest insights in the most coherent terms: discovering the thread of unity which graces any system of thought or creative work with coherence and wholeness.'

Turning from these general observations to their specific manifestation in Rāmakṛṣṇa's life, we see that the source of his spiritual power was a meticulous and creative discipline in which nothing was left to chance and each theory was tested to the end. Given his comprehensive orientation, it is no wonder that his teaching impress us with their crystalline beauty, projecting the timeless wisdom of the Absolute through the medium of language and imagery exactly suited to his time and place." (Bedrosian M., 1988: 62)

All these authors emphasize the positive, regenerative aspects of this experiencing not as idealists but as empirical analysts who chart out its developmental vicissitudes from early infancy onward. The experiencing itself, they maintain, should not be confused with the introjections of the mother and father images or functions. These only foster or hamper this capacity. "If one reads these authors carefully, one discovers that the primary object of creative experiencing is not mother or father but the unknowable ground of creativeness as such. Winnicott, for example, emphasizes that what is at stake in transitional experiencing is not mainly a self or object (mother) substitute, but the creation of a symbol, of symbolizing experiencing itself. The subject lives through and toward creative immersion (including phases of chaos, unintegration, waiting)." (Eigen, 1979: 431) (Kakar, 1991:33-4)

Mystical experience is one and the preeminent way of uncovering the vein of creativity that runs deep in all of us. Albert Einstein writes of his own motivations for the scientific enterprise, "The most beautiful, the most profound emotion we can experience is the sensation of the mystical. It is the fundamental emotion that stands at the cradle of true art and science." Einstein goes on to say that there is a need "to escape from everyday life with its painful crudity and hopeless dreariness, from fetters of one's own shifting desires." Instead the scientist and the artist creates his own reality, substituting it for the world of experience and thus overcoming it: "Each makes his own cosmos and its construction the pivot of his emotional life, in order to find in this way peace and security which he cannot find in the narrow whirlpool of personal experience." (Einstein A., 1954: 75) Kakar says that here it seems to me that Einstein is not talking as someone who is depressed but with a creative individual's clear-sighted and inevitable response to the world as it is. When Buddha, as the young Siddhartha confronted with illness, old-age, and death proclaims "Sabbam dukham" (All is suffering), he too is not depressed but in perfect attunement with the reality principle. To see the world with a creative eye but a sober perspective is perhaps our greatest adaptation to reality-a state where Buddha, Freud and Rāmakṛṣṇa come together.

In short, the mystical experiences in general and Rāmakṛṣṇa in particular represent more than the unfoldment of creative potentials.

9. Androgyny

The word Androgyny comes from the two words, 'Andro' and 'Gene'. 'Andro' means Male and 'Gene' means Female. Thus, the word "Androgyny" implies the realization of the masculine and the feminine, both the potentials within the same individual. The concept of Androgyny says that every human being has both the potentials within one's own personality, irrespective of one's biological structure. A great psychologist Carl Jung has termed this as 'Anima' and 'Animus'. In China, it has been represented by 'Yin' and 'Yang'. In Hindu tradition also, the concept of Lord Śīva as 'Ardhanārīnaeśvara' represents the ideal of "Androgyny" only, in which half male and half female, implying total integration and realization of both potentials which should be achieved within one's own personality.

In an empirical study by Dr. Yajnik Achinta on the androgyny among saints and artists, it was found that though saints were found to have more androgynous sex-role orientation as compared to controls (normals), within the higher androgyny of saints also, femininity was found to be more prevalent among the saints of Christianity, Hinduism, Jainism and Buddhism. (Yajnik A. J., 2007)

Kakar also says that the renunciation of adult masculinity is not only a feature of Hindu devotional mysticism but it is also a feature of Christian emotional mysticism. Femininity pervades both. In the case of medieval Europe, most of the practicing mystics were women. But even the outstanding male mystic-St. John of the Cross, Francois de Sales, Fenelon-show string feminine identifications and produced their most important ideas under the direct influence of women. [Moller H., 1965: 259-67 and McDonnel E. W., 1954: 320-32] (Kakar, 1991:36) The psychological stance of Christian ecstatics toward Divinity, paralleling that of the Vaiṣṇava mystics, is either that of the infant towards a loving maternal parent, or of a woman toward a youthful lover. The message of the European emotional mystics seems to be the same as that of Rāmakṛṣṇa: the actual gender of the mystic is not important for his practice. It is, however, vital that the mystic accept and cultivate his or her femininity to the point that the female-self part becomes dominant in his or her inner psychic reality. (Kakar, 1991:36)

We have already seen how Rāmakṛṣṇa's enduring wish to be a woman, expressed variously in dressing and moving his limbs like one, his fantasy of being a girl widow who secretly trysts with Kṛṣṇa every evening, fitted in well with a tenet of Vaiṣṇava mysticism that all mankind is female while God alone is male. (Kakar, 1991:38)

Kakar believes that it would not be difficult to diagnose Rāmakṛṣṇa in traditional Freudian terms as a secondary transsexual. He would seamlessly fit in with Robert Stoller's description of the secondary transsexual as being someone who differs from his primary counterpart in that he does not appear feminine from the start of any behaviour that may be classed in gender terms. [Robert Stoller R., 1979: 109-38] (Kakar, 1991:38-39) Under the surface of masculinity, however, there is the persistent impulse toward being feminine, a usage which generally manifests itself in adolescence. The most obvious manifestation of these urges is the wish or the actual wearing of women's clothes. (Kakar, 1991:39) This urge to be feminine itself reflects the urge for perfection, the urge for androgyny, for unfoldment of total potentialities of feminine and masculine, both.

He further says that the male-self part of Rāmakṛṣṇa's personality was split off in early childhood and tended to grow, if at all, rather slowly. In contrast, the female-self part of his personality dominated his inner psychic reality. Rāmakṛṣṇa's girl-self was neither repressed nor disassociated. (Kakar, 1991:39) It is this feminine growth of the male, which suggests the androgyny of Rāmakṛṣṇa. However, his fully developed femininity as found in his Gopī-bhāva or Rādhā-bhāva is of divine category of above-normal level of consciousness.

What is perhaps essential in mysticism is not the presence of secondary but of 'primary' femininity-the 'pure female element' (not the female person) in Winnicott's sense of the term. In his theory of the life of male and female elements in a person, the purely male element, in both man and woman, presupposes separateness and traffics in terms of active relating, of being passively related to, and is backed by the whole apparatus of instinctual drives. (D.W. Winnicott, 'Creativity and its Origins', in Playing and Reality (London: Tavistock, 1971), 72-85) (Kakar, 1991:40) The feminine element, on the other hand, relates to the other in the sense of an identity between the two. When this element finds the other, it is the self that had been found. It is female element that establishes the simplest, the most primary of experiences, the experience of *being*.

To summarize, in the words of Kakar, the pure female element, in both men and women, continues to testify to the category of mystery as a basic dimension in which we all, and especially the mystic, live. As analysts, however, we cannot look at mystery as something eternally beyond human comprehension, but as a phenomenon to which we repeatedly return to increase our understanding. As our perspectives change, our earlier views do not get replaced but are subsumed in an ever-widening set of meaning. (Kakar, 1991:40)

Thus, we have seen that unlike some psychoanalysts, the eminent psychoanalyst Sudhir Kakar has tried to justify the so called pathological behaviour of Rāmakṛṣṇa as the above-normal behaviour.

10. Jeffery J. Kripal's Critical Considerations from Psychoanalytic Point-of-view and It's Answers

Jeffery J. Kripal, in his most controversial book, "Kālī's Child: The Mystical and the Erotic in the Life and Teachings of Rāmakṛṣṇa" has made very critical remarks about Rāmakṛṣṇa's mystical behaviour.

His comments are found to be so much baseless and meaningless. Because, it seems that many remarks reflected through ignorance of mysticism, spirituality and Eastern culture in general and Indian culture in particular. It is believed that many Bengali words are literally non-sensibly interpreted which the word actually does not mean at all. Here, some of the criticisms by Kripal are stated and discussed in the light of answers given by Somnath Bhattacharya, a professor and scholar in Psychology. The whole discussion is made in the following titles which are taken from Prof. Bhattacharya's writing. They are as under:

(i) Sexual Abuse

Kripal insists that village people must have abused Rāmakṛṣṇa presumably because he had states of absorption right from his childhood. But Rāmakṛṣṇa's own descriptions of his childhood suggests quite the contrary, e.g. "During my younger days the men and women of Kāmārpukur were equally fond of me. No one distrusted me. Everybody took me in as one of the family." (GSR 239-240; KA 5.45)

He cites a bedroom scene with Mathur and his wife to suggest Rāmakṛṣṇa's abuse by Mathur. Rāmakṛṣṇa's memory of this is far from being anything suggestive of abuse. "I used to sleep in the same room with Mathur and his wife. They took care of me as if I were their own child." (GSR 390; KA 4.72) Moreover his recollections about Mathur's devoted service for fourteen years, with unfailing eagerness to meet his necessities and demands, are all very positive and happy. Having been taken to a brothel against one's will can be termed as abusive; but Rāmakṛṣṇa was an adult -- with an independent and often willful thinking -- who was taken to the brothel only without his knowledge and not by force.

Moreover, even if his samādhi in this situation is taken to be a dissociative trance it in no way explains his going into samādhi, scores of times every day, under happy and non-threatening conditions, and emergence there from with profound insights.

(ii) Feminine Identity

It is easy to talk loosely with Masson about Rāmakṛṣṇa's transvestite activities, but dressing up in a feminine dress as a part of a legitimate and culturally accepted sādhanā for a short period of time does not amount to transvestism. Rāmakṛṣṇa after all also dressed like a śākta and a Vaiṣṇava during his Śakti and Vaiṣṇava sādhanā days and like a Muslim during his Islam sādhanā -- and these were male attires -- only to try and make his identification with these cults complete (GM 299). Moreover, contrary to Kripal's thesis, most transvestites are heterosexual (DSM-IV).

(iii) Trans-sexuality

Further, suggestions about his secondary trans-sexuality (KC xxi) are also all too facile. The American Psychiatric Association (Diagnostic and Statistical Manual IV) defines trans-sexuality as strong and persistent cross-gender identification, and not merely a desire for any perceived cultural advantages of being the other sex. It is a disorder always involving distress to the person, with a feeling of estrangement from the body and a felt need to alter the appearance of the body. If Rāmakṛṣṇa sometimes talked about his femininity he was also clear about what he meant by it - "Formerly I too used to see many visions, but now in my ecstatic state I don't see so many. I am gradually getting over my feminine nature; I feel nowadays more like a man. Therefore I control my emotions; I don't manifest it outwardly so much. The younger Naren has the nature of a man. Therefore in meditation his mind completely merges in the Ideal. He does not show emotion. Nityagopal has a feminine nature. Therefore while he is in a spiritual mood his body becomes distorted and twisted; it becomes flushed."(GSR 798; KA 4.214)

In the Kathāmṛta when M. finds Rāmakṛṣṇa pacing like a lion (KA 1.36, GSR 92), when we find him displaying "leonine strength" at dance (GM 801), or engaging in persuasive conversation with well known intellectuals, scholars, and social leaders of his days like Keshab Sen, Bankim Chandra Chatterjee, Kṛṣṇadas Pal and Iswarachandra Vidyasagar, asserting his will vis-a-vis his teachers (like the Bhairavi and Tota Puri), preaching to varied audiences and closely guiding his disciples, we are actually witnessing what would be classified as a masculine role not only in the then Bengal, but also in the present day USA. In the Kathāmṛta and related texts, in fact, we also find Rāmakṛṣṇa playing multiple roles across genders and ages with Ḥlan. Women could evidently relate to him as one of their own group (GM 394-98) as much as young boys and elderly men. This is especially significant at a time when social identities were largely compartmentalized. Psychologically speaking, all humans have the potential for dual gender identification (social influences play a major role in defining our gender stereotypes), and Rāmakṛṣṇa clearly had both these aspects well developed and harmonized. Unfortunately, to carry through this thesis of feminine identification Kripal resorts to erroneous documentation. Thus a whole section is devoted to bhāgavatamir tanu or goddess body that Rāmakṛṣṇa is supposed to have possessed.

The actual Kathāmṛta term however is bhāgavati tanu which simply means divine body, and has no engendered connotation. (The term is actually a Sanskrit term, and grammatical and physiological genders don't always go together in Sanskrit. E.g., the term 'dārā', meaning wife, is masculine). Bhāgavatamir and Bhāgavati are two different words, and a person who reads the one for the other only reveals his lack of knowledge for that language. It is this typical ignorance of Kripal which disqualifies him totally to comment a single word on mystical experiences, mystical traditions and especially on the greatest mystic of modern age like, Rāmakṛṣṇa.

Besides, Rāmakṛṣṇa specifically identifies this bhāgavati tanu with the causal body, "by means of which one enjoys the bliss of God and holds communion with him", and notes its distinction from the gross physical body and the subtle body (or the mental complex) [GSR 902; KA 1.250]. To assign a physical or even psychological sex to this category then is a reductive strategy, which robs the analyst of the possibility of deeper insight into human nature and its possibilities. Similarly, Rāmakṛṣṇa's wearing silken clothes (garader kapar) during pūjā (GSR 544; KA 4.175) is taken to mean feminine dress (KC 92, 103-4) simply because Kripal doesn't know that male priests in Bengal routinely wear silken clothes.

(iv) Homoeroticism and Misogyny

To take Rāmakṛṣṇa's talk about his care, eager concern, and longing for his young male disciples or his affectionately feeding and touching them as evidence of homosexuality or even homoeroticism again suggests a misconceived line of thinking. For that matter, every father's touching and caressing his son is homoerotic at a dynamic interpretative level, but psychoanalysts know better than that. Moreover, the fact that an Indian guru should be concerned and caring toward his disciples and devotees is the norm rather than exception, and no conflict is known to accompany such behaviour (see also Roland, 1997). It is worth remembering that the Kathāmṛta is a male dominated record simply because its recorder was a male and the social segregation of men and women in nineteenth century Bengal made it nearly impossible for him to be present during Rāmakṛṣṇa's meetings with the women devotees. We thus often find Rāmakṛṣṇa being taken to the inner quarters of the devotees' houses but no record of the conversations that transpire there. But what do we notice about Rāmakṛṣṇa's behaviour on the few occasions that women actually appear on the Kathāmṛta scene -- we find him playing with a small girl and singing for her (GSR 490; KA 4.105), tenderly asking ladies to refrain from fasting while visiting him and offering them food (GSR 432; KA 5.122), making anxious enquiries about and arranging to console a bereaved mother (GSR 973-4; KA 2.243) and visiting a bereaved widow's house -- also to console her (GSR 822-4;KA 3.206-8). He even tenderly asks his disciples to refrain from driving out the mad woman with a lover's attitude towards him (an attitude which Kripal is confident Rāmakṛṣṇa hated) (GSR 952; KA 3.263).

Numerous other records of his interactions with his women disciples of all ages and classes (which are studiously ignored by Kripal) reveal his dealings with them to be as affectionate and close as were his dealings with his male disciples. It is all too easy to play around with the word kaminī and say that Rāmakṛṣṇa hated women (or for that matter women as lovers) and that when he spoke of sexual abstinence he only had heterosexuality in mind. Here also Kripal's utter ignorance of spiritual path is revealed. In all the world religions, be it Christianity or Jainism or Hinduism, it is universally accepted fact that the seekers are advices for sexual abstinence very strictly. This point simply cannot be criticized even from the repressive nature as Freud did, as it is not repressive, but here it is all sublimation. Then, there is no question of its criticism from homo or heterosexuality point-of-view.

As a matter of fact, in the Kathāmṛta we find Rāmakṛṣṇa repeatedly talking about indriya sukha (sense pleasures), dehasukha (bodily pleasures), viṣayasukha (object gratification), kāma (lust in general), and bhoga (enjoyment) as impediments to spiritual growth. All these terms stand for the pleasure principle and are indicative of the erotic in a much broader (Freudian) sense than just heterosexuality. Of course, we don't have any specific comment from Rāmakṛṣṇa about homosexuality simply because homosexuality as a construct was not current in Bengal of Rāmakṛṣṇa's times. Rāmakṛṣṇa's lifelong love and devotion for the Goddess Kālī also clearly does not fit into Kripal's homoerotic thesis. So, he must somehow include a castration story to get over this problem (and that would make things appear more 'psychoanalytical' too!). His attempt to do so by trying to prove that the banana offered during a goat sacrifice is actually the goat's penis is ludicrous. Kripal would also do well to remember that the female is not a castrated male. Equally comical are his attempts to weave in some anal themes. Unfortunately, he claims to be a historian of religion, and not a novelist -- and if he got angry responses he surely has invited them.

(v) Some Empirical Evidence Against Kripal

The available empirical evidence also does not support Kripal's agenda.

(1) Andrew Greely

In Kripal's own backyard, sociologist Andrew Greely of University of Chicago's National Opinions Research Council (NORC) tested people who had profoundly mystical experiences, such as being bathed in white light. When these persons were subjected to standard tests measuring psychological well being, the mystics scored at the top University of Chicago psychologist Norman Bradburn, who developed the test, said that no other factor had ever been found to correlate so highly with psychological balance as did mystical experience. (Greely 7-9)

(2) Greely and William McReady

In a landmark US national poll reported in the New York Times Magazine of Jan 16, 1975, Greely and William McReady found that people with mystical experiences had happy and positive recollections of their childhood. Also, even the small group of subjects who reported mystical events occasioned by orgasm (the sample was from the general population and did not specifically study celibates or people with formal spiritual persuasions) found the spiritual experience to be categorically different from orgasmic pleasure and much more powerful.

(3) Walsh and Vaudhan

In an important study on the psychological effects of meditation, using subjects at various stages of Buddhist enlightenment the following results were reported:

Interestingly, the initially enlightened subjects displayed evidence of normal conflicts around issues such as dependency, sexuality, and aggression. However, they showed remarkably little defensiveness and reactivity to these conflicts. In other words, they accepted and were unperturbed by their neuroses. Those few meditators at the third stage of enlightenment gave reports that were unique... they showed no evidence of drive conflicts and appeared free of psychological conflicts usually considered an inescapable part of human existence. This finding is consistent with classic claims that psychological suffering can be dramatically reduced in advanced stages of meditation. (Walsh and Vaughan 61-62). Incidentally, Rāmakṛṣṇa's samādhi states were accompanied by very profound inward withdrawal of consciousness, and remarkable physiological changes, consistent with the highest stages of meditative absorption as documented in Hindu Tantra and Yoga as well as Buddhist literature. Thus the famous physician Mahendarlal Sarkar himself examined and found Rāmakṛṣṇa without heartbeat and corneal reflexes during samādhi. (GM-801) These physiological changes (clinically taken as signs of death) ...and these were not metaphorical changes...are not known to occur in a dissociative trance.

(4) Medard Boss

Medard Boss, the influential Swiss existential psychotherapist, who was analyzed by Sigmund Freud and had trained with such prominent psychoanalysts as Bleuler, Ernest Jones, Karen Horney, Otto Fenichel, Hans Sachs and Wilhelm Reich, had this to say about the holy men he met on his lecture-visit to India: there were the exalted figures of the sages and holy men themselves, each one of them a living example of the possibility of human growth and maturity and of the attainment of an imperturbable inner peace, a joyous freedom from guilt, and a purified, selfless goodness and calmness.... No matter how carefully I observe the waking lives of the holy men, no matter how ready they were to tell me about their dreams, I could not detect in the best of them a trace of a selfish action or any kind of a repressed or consciously concealed shadow life. (Boss 187-88)

(5) Katchadourian and Lunde

It is worth noting that although we commonly speak of a sex drive, sex does not fit the usual conception of drive as a felt need that gets stronger and stronger until it is satisfied. Indeed sexual abstinence probably decreases sexual motivation over the long run (Masters and Johnson). Also there is no evidence that, despite myths to the contrary, abstinence from sexual activity is detrimental to a person's health (Katchadourian and Lunde) Kripal translates the term mātṛbhāva as attitude of the mother and (as we see next) quickly advances to draw sexual connotations. In actual fact Rāmakṛṣṇa himself defines mātṛ-bhāva as "the attitude of the Child toward God" on the part of the aspirant "O God, Thou art my Mother and I am thy child" (GSR 701; KA 5.141).

Kripal is convinced that this passage has a "same sex-structure" and talks about "a human male taking on a feminine identity in order to erotically engage a male deity or disciple". He conveniently forgets that the basic structure of the metaphor is heterosexual; Rāmakṛṣṇa never says that this practice is applicable only to men [in fact the Kathāmṛta records in detail how Rāmakṛṣṇa advises two young ladies in the worship of Siva (GSR 431-432; KA 5.121-2), and the 'state of the Child' in Rāmakṛṣṇa's discourse lacks engendered connotations. Moreover, the entire metaphor is to illustrate the abstract love for Satcidānanda, a neuter entity. Kripal feels that the passage is 'hyper-sexualized and demands a sexual reading', what with hair pores becoming 'great vaginas'! To such a simplistic reading Rāmakṛṣṇa would probably have said (as he did to the celebrated writer Bankim Chandra Chatterjee) – "Analogy is one sided. You are a pundit, haven't you read logic? Suppose you say that a man is as terrible as a tiger. That doesn't mean that he has a fearful tail or a tiger's pot face" (GSR 669; KA 5.199).

Predictably, snug in this viewpoint, Kripal can now assert that the Self is 'male' and 'penetrating' and ramaṇa can mean nothing but sexual intercourse ('logistic difficulties' notwithstanding) even when the text is clear that it is ātmar sahit ramaṇa...sport with one's own Self. [Incidentally, ramaṇa is derived from the root ram which means (interpersonal) interaction and can denote pleasure, not invariably (and not necessarily) orgasmic pleasure. It also is a common Indian name, e.g., the great monastic sage, Ramaṇa Maharṣi] He can also be certain that yoni cannot mean family lineage even when the context is about Sītā -- a proud queen who was forced to live in humble and trying conditions. Also Puruṣa and Prakṛti must be simply 'man' and 'woman' even in a metaphorical reference to the Absolute and to God.

(vi) On Intertextuality:

Inter-textuality also calls for giving adequate weightage to intertextual evidence. For example: take the common trope sarva-yoni mātṛyoni of looking upon all women as Mother. Kripal is convinced that this needs to be translated as 'all vaginas are mother's vagina', and that a fully sexualized reading is in order because Nikhilananda omits this phrase in his translation. Let's consider the three other sentences where Rāmakṛṣṇa used the term mātṛyoni. Firstly, he talks about his ritual worship of a sixteen year old maiden as Mother (mātṛbhāva), 'with the attitude of the child' and adds – "I saw (her) breasts (as) Mother's breasts (mātṛstana), womb (as) mother's womb (mātṛyoni)" (KA 5.141). Of course, the breast and the womb are universally acknowledged symbols of motherhood. In another passage Rāmakṛṣṇa himself glosses the meaning Mine is mātṛyoni. I look upon all women as Mother (KA 2.228, GSR 958, also see KA 4.284, GSR 934). Compare this with Rāmakṛṣṇa"s Mine is mātṛbhāva (KA 4.80, GSR 408). Mātṛyoni and mātṛbhāva are clearly synonymous. Now, this śākta worship of women as Mother aims at helping the aspirants transcend their sexual impulses and reducing transcendence to sexuality or even eroticism denies the very significance of this ritual. Moreover, talk of the breast and the womb immediately brings up associations of infantile states of symbiotic fusion. But this is misinformed thinking. As

Meissner points out: it is clear that the sense of fusion with the object in mystical states is not the same as the regressive fusion to primary narcissistic union that might occur in states of psychotic regression. Rather, authentic mystical experience (as distinguished from pseudo-mystical or psychotic experience) not only does not undermine or destroy identity, but in fact has a powerful capacity to stabilize, sustain and enrich identity. This can be clearly verified if one watches the two individuals (the mystic and the pseudo-mystic or psychotic) in a longitudinal study. Kripal is troubled by Rāmakṛṣṇa's use of the terms yoni and lingam. Certainly, when Rāmakṛṣṇa speaks about worshipping his own lingam nobody, including Nikhilananda, has any doubt about the meaning of the term. But, then, Rāmakṛṣṇa explicitly uses it as a symbol (and this is the core lexical meaning of the term lingam) of Siva (GSR 491; KA 4.106), and he is categorical about the meaning of the Siva puja as worship of the symbol of fatherhood and motherhood so that one may not be born into the world again (GSR 603-4; KA 2.155) Again his ritual worship of the lingams of small boys cannot be taken to suggest a homoerotic proclivity for the Kathāmṛta tells us of his ritual worship of young girls (GSR 231;KA 2.49) as symbols of the divine Mother and his worship of the female genital tract (Kulagara) as a part of a legitimate and public tāntric ritual is recorded by his biographer (LP-206;GM- 227). If Kripal is bothered about the moral implications of such worship then he clearly needs to associate with the traditions that place a high moral value on this ritual. Rāmakṛṣṇa's visions about the rising of Kuṇḍalini Śakti (GSR 830;KA 4.238; GSR 934; KA 4.282 etc.) is almost a textbook description of the same as described in Woodroffe's translation of the Shat-cakra bheda (235) -- the Jīatman identified with Kuṇḍalini rising and penetrating drooping lotuses representing the different cakras. That these lotuses have their own devatās and devīs symbolized by lingams and yonis is a well-known fact. Similarly the ovoid or accurate shape (yonirupa) is a standard symbol of Śakti -- and each cakra is a specific centre of Power with its own energies. Moreover, Rāmakṛṣṇa specifically calls this vision as "sport of the Self" (GSR 744; KA 3.138). Passing this vision off as cunnilingus (simply because the terms jihva, yoni-rupa and ramaṇa happen to be together), besides confusing the sign for the significate, provides no explanation to the richness, the textbook nature and the deep transforming power of the vision.

Again, to suggest that terms like brahmayoni (cosmic source) have physiologically sexual correlates is absurd.

(vii) Consider two more translations that Kripal again tries to justify:

Tribhaṅga...Kripal is convinced that this posture is erotic because Rāmakṛṣṇa ascribed it to prema of Rādhā, and the relationship between Rādhā and Kṛṣṇa is nothing but erotic in Vaiṣṇava poetry! But, as he himself notes subsequently, for orthodox Vaiṣṇavas prema (the transcendent love) and kāma (sexual desire) are qualitatively different realities (the former being a gift of Kṛṣṇa's grace and the latter a mere instinct). Rāmakṛṣṇa is also very categorical... "As the tiger devours other animals, so does the 'tiger of zeal for the Lord' eat up lust, anger and the other passions. The gopīs of Vrindavan had that state of mind because of their zeal for Kṛṣṇa," (GSR 206; KA 2.32) 'The gopīs were free from lust' (GSR 244;KA5.52). Even the sahajiya position calls for 'transforming' kāma to prema and reducing the latter to the former is only as easy as regaining milk from curd. Rāmakṛṣṇa himself was unequivocally critical of sects, which enjoyed sensuous pleasures in the name of religion (GSR 571; KA 2.142 etc.). In fact, his repeated reminders to male audiences about the strict moral code for spiritual aspirants, which are cited as evidences of misogyny, are nothing but warnings against the "both-and" reading that Kripal wishes to employ. This 'state of the Child' (mātṛbhāva, santanabhāva) is the very psychological state that Kripal studiously avoids or distorts (as seen in his sample hermeneutical passage) into amorphous or polymorphous sexuality. This is especially ironical because this book bears the title Kālī's Child! Kripal also wishes to read a conflicted regression in Rāmakṛṣṇa's 'state of the Child' ostensibly because Rāmakṛṣṇa, on occasions, spoke about the fear of fall of the male spiritual aspirant (particularly a monk) who associated closely with women (KC 130-43). This deduction is faulty. Continence of various degrees, in Rāmakṛṣṇa's discourse, is a prerequisite for spiritual growth and fulfillment. If an aspirant is circumspect about a situation that could (by arousal of passion) act as a hindrance to his or her self chosen goal, then that fear is correctly classified as a 'rational fear' and rational fear cannot be taken as evidence of conflict. Further, a conflicted homosexual, by the very nature of conflict, will at times indulge in heterosexual behaviour, something that even Kripal accepts Rāmakṛṣṇa didn't do. Moreover, such apparent regression has been described by ego-psychologists as 'adaptive regression in service of the ego' which is not only found in healthy people but is considered a sine qua non of psychological health.

(viii) Śakti as conflicted Energy

Kripal also posits a mystico-erotic energy ("the conflicted energies of the saint's homosexual desire") called Śakti whose "awakening" signaled the onset of his mystical experiences (KC322-25). Now, "awakening", at best, is an ambiguous term, but one thing can be said with certainty -- a conflicted state, by its very definition opposes the release of psychic energies. To quote Fenichel, "The (neurotic) conflict results in the blocking of necessary discharges, and in this way creates a state of being dammed u"(129) Philosophically speaking, a unified ontological ground does not exclude the existence of polar opposites in the empirical world. Thus the Tāntric conception of Śakti as the Mother, Creatrix, or Power does not mean that in the empirical world the nature and direction of spiritual and sexual "energies" is the same. Quite the contrary; and this is recognized by the Tantras as much as by monistic Vedānta. (http://prof-somnath-bhattacharyya.sulekha.com/blog/post/2002/12/i-kali-s-child-i-psychological-and-hermeneutical.htm)

We have already shown with reference to the views of William James, Sudhir Kakar and Somnath Bhattacharya that no rational person can ever agree to the view that Rāmakṛṣṇa was affected by any kind of pathological phenomena. Rāmakṛṣṇa was not in any sense abnormal person; his consciousness was above normal and thoroughly mystical. In order to give few conformation of the position taken by us, we give following passages from William James: lecture I, included in his book "The Variety of Religious experiences":

The plain truth is that to interpret religion one must in the end look at the immediate content of the religious consciousness. The moment one does this, one sees how wholly disconnected it is in the main from the content of the sexual consciousness. Everything about the two things differs, objects, moods, faculties concerned, and acts impelled to. Any general assimilation is simply impossible: what we find most often is complete hostility and contrast. If now the defenders of the sex-theory say that this makes no difference to their thesis; that without the chemical contributions which the sex-organs make to the blood, the brain would not be nourished so as to carry on religious activities, this final proposition may be true or not true; but at any rate it has become profoundly uninstructive: we can deduce no consequences from it which help us to interpret religion's meaning or value. In this sense the religious life depends just as much upon the spleen, the pancreas, and the kidneys as on the sexual apparatus, and the whole theory has lost its point in evaporating into a vague, general assertion of the dependence, somehow, of the mind upon the body. (James: Lecture-1)

In the natural sciences and industrial arts it never occurs to any one to try to refute opinions by showing up their author's neurotic constitution. Opinions here are invariably tested by logic and by experiment, no matter what may be their author's neurological type. It should be no otherwise with religious opinions. Their value can only be ascertained by spiritual judgments directly passed upon them, judgments based on our own immediate feeling primarily; and secondarily on what we can ascertain of their experiential relations to our moral needs and to the rest of what we hold as true.

In the end it had to come to our empiricist criterion: By their fruits ye shall know them, not by their roots. Jonathan Edwards's Treatise on Religious Affections is an elaborate working out of this thesis. The roots of a man's virtue are inaccessible to us. (James, 1902: Lecture-1)

12

Conclusion and the Philosophical Position of Rāmakṛṣṇa

In this chapter we have taken a bird's eye view of Rāmakṛṣṇa's philosophy propounded in the chapter 1-11 and then tried to determined the philosophical position of Rāmakṛṣṇa.

Chapter 1

In first chapter we have shown the contemporary relevance of understanding the philosophy of Rāmakṛṣṇa and given the brief biography of Rāmakṛṣṇa together with the observation of eminent contemporary persons regarding life and importance of Rāmakṛṣṇa. Besides, in this chapter we have given introduction to "The Gospel of Śrī Rāmakṛṣṇa" and indicated a long-felt need of making in-depth study of "The Gospel of Śrī Rāmakṛṣṇa". And shown our justification for selection of the topic for research, namely 'The Philosophy of Rāmakṛṣṇa Paramahaṃsa with Special Reference to His Gospel'.

Chapter 2

As Rāmakṛṣṇa has the mystical experience of the Ultimate Reality or God, we have explained his concept of Ultimate Reality with the help of the nature and characteristics of mystics. Rāmakṛṣṇa has clear conviction that the Reality is formless as well as with form. He believes that if one of these two is accepted, then that this will bo limiting the Ultimate Reality which is limitless and infinite.

Rāmakṛṣṇa has shown the fundamental unity of all religions by his own practice of different world religions and different sects of Hinduism. Besides this, in metaphysics also, we find that his philosophical position accommodates important philosophical truths of different and apparently opposite philosophical positions, together with maintaining complete consistency in the different aspects of his philosophical position.

The most important point to be noted here is that he believes in both, Brahman and Kālī. It may appear that he is accepting a contradictory position, but the apparent contradiction is not really there because, he has repeatedly clarify that these two are the two aspects of the same Ultimate Reality. When Ultimate Reality is inactive, it is called Brahman and when it is active in the creation, preservation and destruction of the world, it is called Śakti the Power of God, and which is also called Kālī.

The concept of God in Rāmakṛṣṇa is that God or the Ultimate Reality is infinite, because, as we have seen, the attributes of existence, knowledge, and bliss, possessed by Him are not limited anyway. Similarly, the limitations of space, time and causality are not applicable to God, because he is omnipresent and eternally self-existing being. Again, God in Rāmakṛṣṇa is beyond the limitation of change and mutability because, as we saw, Rāmakṛṣṇa has emphasized the imperishability and eternal perfectness of God. It is clearly seen earlier through the views of Mādhvācarya as well as of Anselm. He also accepts the theory of incarnation and the concept of Vibhūti, special manifestation of the Ultimate Reality in some people.

To summarize his views in his own words, "That Brahman, of the nature of Reality, is eternal. It exists in past, present and future. It is without beginning or end. It cannot be described in words. The utmost that can be said of Brahman is that It is of the very nature of Intelligence and Bliss." (GSR: 585) And again, "Brahman is beyond both knowledge and ignorance... God is both formless and endowed with form. He is many things more. The Absolute and the Relative belong to one and the same Reality. What is beyond speech and mind is born in flesh, assuming various forms and engaging in various activities." (GSR: 366)

The identity of the formless Reality (Brahman) and the Reality having form (Kālī or Śakti) has been described by Rāmakṛṣṇa as under:

"O Mother, Thou art verily Brahman, and thou art verily Śakti. Thou art Puruṣa and Thou art Prakṛti. Thou art Virat. Thou art Absolute, and Thou dost manifest thyself as the Relative. Thou art verily the twenty-four cosmic principles." (GSR: 123)

We have discussed the above mentioned views of Rāmakṛṣṇa with reference to important Indian philosophies and some Western philosophers in the chapter one.

Chapter 3

Rāmakṛṣṇa believes that the self is eternal and beyond attributes. He also believes that It is not created element and ignorance or the association with body is beginnigless. But the ascent up to the liberation is possible by strict dispassion towards the worldly objects together with intense love for God. Rāmakṛṣṇa has very subtly classified the different types of people in different ways which are described in detail in chapter III. Further, Rāmakṛṣṇa accepts the plurality of selves and metaphysical dependence of the self upon God. Rāmakṛṣṇa accepts the law of karma and believes in the freedom of will of the self in performing any actions. Freely performed action of the self will result in certain type of situation in the world which will give either pleasure of pain to the self, according to law of karma. Rāmakṛṣṇa also accepts the role redemptive grace of God (Kṛpā), without disturbing the law of karma. While explaining the law of karma and redemptive grace of God, we have critically examined Nicole Macnicol's argument against Indian Theism, which is wrongly considered as a giving a system of legalism, leaving no place of the grace of God. Further, Rāmakṛṣṇa believes prārabdh karmas and in the resulting rebirth. Rāmakṛṣṇa differentiate the suicide from the voluntary death and whole heartedly approve the voluntary death after attaining certain level of consciousness. Rāmakṛṣṇa explains the nature of bound soul, who is entangled in worldly objects. He accepts the two types of a liberated soul, known as Jñānī and Vijñānī. He says that the state of Jñānī, which is a state where one has the experience of the one-ness of the formless Reality. Higher than the state of a jñānī is, according to Rāmakṛṣṇa, that of a Vijñānī. Because, a Vijñānī can have both the experiences. That is, the experience of the Reality without form as well as the experience of the Reality with form. According to Rāmakṛṣṇa a vijñānī can easily move from relative plane to the Absolute plane and from Absolute plane to the relative plane. Rāmakṛṣṇa has also accepted the possibility of a sādhaka becoming a Jīanamukta. The jnvanmukta are living in the world for the welfare of others.

Chapter 4

We have seen in the chapter IV what Rāmakṛṣṇa says, "God is doing all the activities of creation etc. with the help of His Power. The process of creation, preservation and destruction that is going on day and night is due to Śakti, the power of God. This primal power and Brahman are one and the same... As long as god keeps us in his relative world, so long we feel that there are two." (GSR: 365)

Unlike Indian Illusionists and Western Idealists, Rāmakṛṣṇa accepts the reality of the created world. According to Rāmakṛṣṇa the three-fold activities of creation, preservation and destruction of the real world is perform by God. Though, Rāmakṛṣṇa, being a mystic, having the direct vision of God, was not interested in giving the argument for the existent of God as the Creator of the world. In spite of this, some of his observations contain arguments which are comparable to the Cosmological argument for the existence of God and Udayanācārya's one of the arguments, named, Dhṛtyādeḥ. There are sufficient material available in Rāmakṛṣṇa's observations for giving Ontological argument and Teleological argument. The purpose of the creation of the world has reference to worldly people and those interested in getting the liberation or mokṣa. The process of the destruction of the world is the part of ongoing process of creation, preservation and the destruction of the world.

Chapter 5

The human beings leading a religious life is advised to follow any one of the three paths accepted in one form or the other, in all religions. They are the path of knowledge, path of devotion and path of action, which are called Jñāna yoga, bhakti yoga and karma yoga respectively. Rāmakṛṣṇa has fully explained these three path.

In the chapter V, Rāmakṛṣṇa's views on the nature of jñāna yoga, the importance of the study of scriptures and the limitation of mere scholarship is shown. Ultimately, according to Rāmakṛṣṇa one should go beyond knowledge and ignorance. That is the state what Rāmakṛṣṇa defines as a state of a vijñānī.

In describing the concept of bhakti yoga, Rāmakṛṣṇa clearly says that the path of devotion is the most effective and necessary path to be followed. He gave special emphasis on the following the path of devotion for all the seekers. In that he professed the single-minded devotion to God. Further, he also gave the concept of prema-bhakti, which is the highest level of devotion, according to Rāmakṛṣṇa.

With regard to the path of action, Rāmakṛṣṇa believes that basically this path is meant for the householder devotees. And that also upto the attainment of true love of God. According to Rāmakṛṣṇa, after the attainment of the love of God, the actions automatically drop away and one will spend whole of one's life in devotion only. After that even the performance of rituals also become difficult. Further, he believes that without the command from God, one cannot perform social services also.

Among all the three paths, Rāmakṛṣṇa put the path of devotion at the highest level. He believes that initially, the path of devotion is helpful and at the end, after reaching the level of a Vijñānī, which is the highest state of consciousness, according to Rāmakṛṣṇa, one attains the prema-bhakti, that is the highest form of the path of devotion. Thus, Rāmakṛṣṇa had very much emphasized bhakti or love of God at any stage of sādhanā, including the highest stage.

Chapter 6

Rāmakṛṣṇa describes the nature of guru as the Satcidānanda Himself. Still, when a person had a guru in a human form, he should consider him as an embodiment of Satcidānanda only. Further, he says that without the command from inside, one is not eligible to become a guru and one should be careful in making disciples also. Using a metaphor, he describes the types of guru and clarifies the nature of the true and genuine guru.

Chapter 7

Basically, Rāmakṛṣṇa is very well known for his views and practice of different religions. He shows that there cannot be any one religion which can claim as the only path leading to liberation. As the Ultimate Reality is Infinite, the paths to reach It also infinite. Rāmakṛṣṇa accepts the fundamental unity in all religions together with the explanation of the multiplicity of different religions. He advices a person to have single-minded devotion to one's own religion, with equal respect for all other religions. In this chapter we have quoted several eminent scholars like Swami Vivekananada, Swami Ranaganathananda and others with reference to Rāmakṛṣṇa's views and practice of different religions.

Chapter 8

The attainment of the love for God is the basic concern of Rāmakṛṣṇa. Therefore, he gave in detailed the way of disciplines to be followed by a seeker for the fulfillment of the purpose. The following topics are discussed in detail in chapter VIII:

(1) Practice of Disciplines: Vigilance in disciplines, necessity of disciplines, remaining away from the delusion of māyā, negation and affirmation and ingredients of disciplines.

(2) Meditation: meditation on the form of God, control of senses, mind progressing reaching the seventh plane of consciousness, rules of meditation, uninterrupted meditation, ideal time and importance of consistency, final stage of meditation.

(3) Yearning: nature of yearning means to have the vision of God, exclusiveness of yearning.

(4) Importance of Solitude.

(5) Discrimination and Dispassion: to direct inner allegories towards God, discrimination between real and unreal, process of attaining dispassion, egolessness, dispassion leads to renunciation, result of discrimination and dispassion.

(6) Love For God: different types of attitudes, importance of the path of devotion, all other sādhanā are for the cultivation of love for God, love to God is beyond all virtues, pure mind is required, all passions should be directed to God.

(7) Need of firm faith.

(8) Prayer, Chanting the name of God, Company of holy men.

(9) Purity and Truthfulness.

(10) Total abundance of lust and greed.

(11) Occult powers are obstacles to realization.

Chapter 9

In this chapter we have given the list of duties to be performed by householders as well as by sannyāsis. The most important duty for the householder is to maintain the attitude of 'a maid servant' and for sannyāsi, the complete abundance of 'woman and gold' (lust and greed). Rāmakṛṣṇa has also recommended service to humanity as service to God, to both the householders as well as sannyāsis.

Chapter 10

It had been shown in this chapter that regarding cast system, Rāmakṛṣṇa was very liberal and believed that once, a man utter a word of God, he will be the purest among all. With regard to the concern for women, Rāmakṛṣṇa has not talked much. Though he was a married, he was leading a life of a renunciation and he was very strict about even little of the male-female association for seekers. Therefore, it may appear that he was not concern about female devotees. But it is shown in this chapter how he was concerned about the sādhanā of females also. In addition to this, as he had repeatedly advised his devotees to go into solitude, it appears that he was not concerned for people. It is shown in chapter X his compassion for poor and deprived. And lastly, as a Bengali, he was eating non-vegetarian food, but during his last period of life, in spite of being Bengali, he renounces that food. In this chapter, his compassion for animals is also indicated.

Chapter 11

In the time of Rāmakṛṣṇa as well as in recent times, Rāmakṛṣṇa was considered by some people as an insane person. We have tried to show the difference between the pathological phenomena and the mystical phenomena with the help of three scholars, namely, William James, Sudhir Kakar and Somnath Bhattacharya. We have also taken into consideration the views of Swami Tyagananda also. We have elaborately discussed Jeffery J. Kripal's criticism of Rāmakṛṣṇa's behaviour and which had been very effectively refuted by Somnath Bhattacharya. By concluding this chapter we have referred to William James' Lecture 1, in his book, "The Varieties of Religious Experiences". Because, in this lecture William James has very effectively indicated the undesirability of linking mysticism with pathological phenomena.

1. The Philosophical Position of Rāmakṛṣṇa

We shall try to show the philosophical position of Rāmakṛṣṇa with reference to both Indian and Western philosophy. From Indian philosophy, to explain the philosophical position of Rāmakṛṣṇa, we are considering the views of two great ācārya of Vedanta, Śaṅkarācārya and Rāmānujācārya and with reference to western philosophy, we shall consider the important theological doctrines for determining the philosophical position of Rāmakṛṣṇa.

2. Metaphysical Position of Śaṅkarācārya, Rāmānujācārya and Rāmakṛṣṇa:

(1) Śaṅkarācārya has propounded Absolute Monism by emphasizing the Ultimate Reality of Brahman and only Brahman. He makes a distinction between three kings of existence: Prātibhāsik, Vyāvahārik and Pārmārthik. From the pārmārthik point-of-views only, Brahman exists. The realized soul becomes completely identical with Brahman. This kind of realization is acceptable to Rāmakṛṣṇa but unlike Śaṅkarācārya, he does not regard this king of realization as the highest. Rāmakṛṣṇa makes the difference between the state of a jñānī and the state of a vijñānī. The realized soul of Śaṅkarācārya is acceptable to Rāmakṛṣṇa in the state of a jñānī. But this state is lower than the state of a vijñānī, according to Rāmakṛṣṇa. jñānī remains simply merged in Brahman, whereas vijñānī realizes Brahman or God and remains in loving communion with God. This is the highest state where one attains prema-bhakti.

(2) Śaṅkarācārya has regarded the world as mere appearance of Brahman, whereas, according to Rāmakṛṣṇa, the world is mot the 'appearance but it is the reality, which is not different from God. Thus,

Rāmakṛṣṇa accepts the reality of the world and at the same time he emphasizes its identity with God, and regards it as the 'mansion of mirth'.

(3) Śaṅkarācārya and Rāmakṛṣṇa both accept the concept of 'jīvanmukta'. The jīvanmukta, according to Śaṅkarācārya, looks at the world as an illusion, whereas the jīvanmukta, according to Rāmakṛṣṇa serves the world, seeing God himself present in the world. While serving God in this way, he considers himself as a machine, operated by God himself. This kind of attitude is simply impossible for Śaṅkarācārya's concept of jīvanmukta, because, he consider even this attitude as illusory.

(4) Rāmakṛṣṇa refers to Rāmānujācārya and explains his theory in a way consistent with his own vision of the identity of God with everything. But he does not accept the view that God is a Soul (śarīrī) of the world. According to him God and world are one, there is not fundamental difference in their metaphysical position. Thus, while accepting śarīra-śarīrī relation, Rāmānujācārya advocates Qualified Monism, Rāmakṛṣṇa believes in Absolute Monism. And it is already shown with reference to Śaṅkarācārya's philosophical position that Rāmakṛṣṇa's is Absolute Monism is different from Śaṅkarācārya's theory. Because, Rāmakṛṣṇa's Absolute Monism is inclusive of and higher that Śaṅkarācārya's Absolute Monism. Therefore, in order to indicate this specific quality of Rāmakṛṣṇa's Absolute Monism, it should be named as "Comprehensive Absolute Monism."

3. Western Theological Doctrines and Rāmakṛṣṇa

As Rāmakṛṣṇa's philosophy is a philosophy of religion, it seems desirable to make its standpoint clear in the light of the metaphysically important Western theological doctrines, such as, Deism, Pantheism and Theism.

Rāmakṛṣṇa agrees with Deism in so far as the latter lays stress upon the purity, perfection, personality, and transcendence of God. It, however, differs from Deism in conceiving the universe as constantly depending on God. Thus, the immanence of God which is conspicuously absent in Deism finds a very important place in Rāmakṛṣṇa's thoughts.

Like Pantheism, Rāmakṛṣṇa appreciates the idea of immanence of God, but, as we have seen, its conception of God's immanence differs from that of Pantheism. The Pantheistic idea of the unity and divinity of the universe is acceptable to Rāmakṛṣṇa, but it is not prepared to adhere only to this idea at the cost of real multiplicity and difference that is clearly given in out experience. Pantheistic God is a whole of totality of things, which, being His constitutive elements, can never be transcended by Him. God in Rāmakṛṣṇa thought, on the contrary, is wholly present in everything, and yet wholly transcends the whole universe, which is not conceived as integral to Him.

From the standpoint of Rāmakṛṣṇa the inherent difficulty of Pantheism is that although it is put forward as a philosophy of religion and sometimes assumes genuinely religious colouring to the extent that the well known Pantheist, Spinoza, has been described as 'God-intoxicated man', the logical consequences of its premises make the practice and intelligibility of religion and morality impossible. N. Srinivasachari has rightly observed that, "Its fatal defect is the denial of the evilness of evil and the reality of the moral consciousness. The all-God theory destroys God and the self that seeks God, and gives man a logical and moral holiday." (Shrinivasachari N., 1943: 77-78)

Rāmakṛṣṇa stands with Theism in transforming the Pantheistic incorrect assertion, "All is God" into the correct proposition, "All depends on God." It also agrees with Theism in holding, against the one-sided positions of Deism and Pantheism, that both the immanence and transcendence of God are equally important. Again, Rāmakṛṣṇa fully supports Theism in the latter's emphasis upon the personality and the religious availability of God. Rāmakṛṣṇa, thus, firmly believes with Theism that although God is distinct from the world, He is in living and loving relations with it.

Rāmakṛṣṇa's stand, however, differs from Theism in conceiving the universe not as a 'de novo' created thing, but as having a beginningless existence. Unlike Theism, Rāmakṛṣṇa is thus, not open to the criticism leveled against the crude theories of 'ex nihilo' and 'de novo' creation of the world. In Theism, as Vergilius ferm has pointed out, "God is here usually conceived of as creator, as having brought into existence realities 'other than' himself which, though he is not completely (although for certain purposes, partly) dependent upon them, nevertheless are dependent upon him." (Runes and others: 316) This description of Theism also brings out another difference between Rāmakṛṣṇa's thought and Theism. Rāmakṛṣṇa is not prepared to accept any kind of dependence upon man who has the freedom of will. This, however, is regarded as self-limitation of God. Rāmakṛṣṇa believes in the freedom of human action but conceives it is such a way that the sovereignty and independence of God are in no way affected. Rāmakṛṣṇa has, therefore, to say against Theism, that the limited or finite God is no God deserving to be either the guide or the goal of man's ethical and spiritual endeavours.

We, thus, see that Rāmakṛṣṇa has accepted the truth contained in Deism, Pantheism and Theism and avoided the misunderstanding involved in them. Rāmakṛṣṇa thus, represents here also, a synthesis of Western theological thought. As Rāmakṛṣṇa's thought is a reconciliation of Deism, Pantheism and Theism, it cannot itself be said to be deistic, pantheistic or theistic. It however, seems proper to call it Panentheistic. The term Panentheism has been defined by Vergilius Ferm as follows:

"Panentheism: (Gr. Pan=all; en=in; theos;God): The term for the view that God interpenetrated everything without canceling the relative independent existence of the world of entities; moreover, while God is immanent, this immanence is not absolute (as in pantheism); God is more than the world, transcendent in the sense that though the created is dependent upon the Creator, the Creator is not dependent upon the created. God thus, is held to be the highest type of Unity, viz. Unity in Multiplicity. The term is employed to cover a mediating position between pantheism with its extreme immanence and theism of the type which tends to extreme transcendence." (Runes and others: 316)

It will be seen that the above description of Panentheism fully applies to the position held by Rāmakṛṣṇa. It, therefore, seems that we are justified in describing the philosophical position of Rāmakṛṣṇa as Panentheism. (Yajnik J. A. 1972: 133-134)

Thus, in our attempt to describe the philosophical position of Rāmakṛṣṇa we have shown that with reference to Metaphysics, his philosophical position is "Comprehensive Absolute Monism" and with reference to Philosophy of Religion, his philosophical position is "Panentheism."

Bibliography

1 *A Bridge to Eternity: Sri Ramakrishna and His Monastic Order.* (1986). Calcutta: Advaita Ashrama.

2. Aberbach, D. (1987). Grief and Mysticism. *International Review of Psychoanalysis*, 14: 509-26.

3. Bedrosian, M. (1988). Sri Ramakrishna: The Universal Man. In *Studies on Sri Ramakrishna* (pp. 61-74). Calcutta: The Ramakrishna Mission Institute of Culture.

Bhattacharya, S. (2002). http://prof-somnath-bhattacharyya.sulekha.com/blog/post/2002/12/i-kali-s-child-i-psychological-and-hermeneutical.htm

Borirakkucharoen, C. (2003) *The Nature of Religious Experience in the Philosophy of William James.*http:/www.journal.au.edu/abac_journal/2003/may,03/articleo4.pdf

4. Bose, S. C. (1965). quoted from An Indian Pilgrim, cited in Swami Lokeswarnanda. (Ed.), *World Thinkers on Ramakrishna-Vivekananda.* p.29

5. Brown, E. C. (1923). quoted from Sri Ramakrishna: Divine Incarnation of this Age, *Prabuddha Bharata*, May, cited in Swami Lokeswarnanda. (Ed.), *World Thinkers on Ramakrishna-Vivekananda (p.12).* Calcutta: The Ramakrishna Mission.

6. Buckley P. & Galanter M. (1979). Mystical Experience, Spiritual Knowledge, and a Contemporary Ecstatic Experience. *British Journal of Medical Psychology,* 52. (pp.281-89)

7. Campbell, J. (1941). quoted from Sri Ramakrishna, *Prabuddha Bharata*, November, cited in Swami Lokeswarnanda. (Ed.), *World*

Thinkers on Ramakrishna-Vivekananda (p.12). Calcutta: The Ramakrishna Mission.

8. Chakravarty, P. (1988) Role of Sri Ramakrishna in the Nineteenth Century Awakening. In *Studies on Sri Ramakrishna. (pp.163-182)* Calcutta: The Ramakrishna Mission Institute of Culture.

9. D.W. Winnicott, D. W. (1971). Creativity and its Origins. In *Playing and Reality.* London: Tavistock.

10. Damas Mora M. R. et.al., (1980). On Heutroscopy or the Phenomenon of the Double. *British Journal of Medical Psychology.* 53: 75-83.

11. Dasgupta, R. K. (2001). *Sri Ramakrishna's Religion.* Calcutta: The Ramakrishna Mission Institute of Culture.

12. Digby, W. (1901). quoted from Prosperous British India, cited in Swami Lokeswarnanda. (Ed.), *World Thinkers on Ramakrishna-Vivekananda.* p.29

13. Dushan, P. (1989): *The Oceanic Feelin: A Reevaluation.* Manuscript. Belgrade.

14. Eigen, (1979). Area of Faith; Ideal Images, Creativity and the Freudian Drama, *Psychocultural Review*, 3: 278-98.

15. Eigen, (1981). Creativity, Instinctual Fantasy and Ideal Images. *Psychoanalytic Review*, 68.

16. Einstein, A. (1954). *Ideas and Opinions.* New York: Crown Publishers.

17. Ernest Hartmann, E. (1984). *The Nightmare: The Psychology and Biology of Terrifying Dreams.* New York: Basic.

Festinger, L. http://en.wikipedia.org/wiki/Cognitive_dissonance

18. Frazer, A. C. (1894-96). *Philosophy of Theism.* Edinburgh: William Blackwood & Sons.

19. Freud, S. (1933). *New Introductory Lectures.* Standard Edition, vol.22.

20. Freud, S. (1960) *ed.* The Letter of Sigmund Freud. New York: Basic Books.

21. Gandhi, M. K. (1977). quoted from the *Forward* of Life of Sri Ramakrishna, cited in Swami Lokeswarnanda. (Ed.), *World Thinkers on Ramakrishna-Vivekananda (p.9)*. Calcutta: The Ramakrishna Mission.

22. Gibaldi, J. (2004). *MLA Handbook for Writers of Research Papers.* (6th edition) New Delhi: Affiliated East-West Press.

23. Greenley, A. M. (1975). *The Sociology of the Paranormal: A Reconnaissance*. Beverly Hills: Sage Publications.

24. Gupta, M. (1942). *The Gospel of Sri Ramakrishna.* Trans. Swami Nikhilananda. Chennai: Sri Ramakrishna Math.

25. Harrison, I. B. (1979). On Freud's View of the Infant-Mother Relationship and of the Oceanic Feeling-Some Subjective Influences. *Journal of the American Psychoanalytic Association,* 27: 409.

26. Hartmann, E. (1984). *The Nightmare: The Psychology and Biology of Terrifying Dreams.* New York: Basic.

27. Hoffding, H. (1906) *Philosophy of Religion.* London: Macmillan.

28. Hutchison, J. (1956). *Faith, Reason and Existence.* New York: Oxford University Press.

29. James, W. (1902). *The Varieties of Religious Experience.* New York: Longmans, Green.

James, W. *The Varieties of Religious Experiences.* Electronic Text Center, University of Virginia Library. http://historyofideas.org/toc/modeng/public/JamVari.html

30. Kakar, S. (1982) *Shamans, Mystics and Doctors.* New York: Knopf.

31. Kakar, S. (1991). *The Analyst and the Mystic: Psychoanalytic Reflections on Religion and Mysticism.* New Delhi: Penguin Books India.

32. Kierkegaard, S. (1940). *Concluding Unscientific Postscript* (E.T. by D.Swenson and W. Lowrie). Princeton: Princeton University Press.

33. Kripal, J. J. (1995). Kali's Child: *The Mystical and The Erotic in the Life and Teachings of Ramakrishna.* Chicago: The University of Chicago Press.

34. Macnicol, N. (1915). *Indian Theism.* London: Oxford University Press.

35. Mahadevan, T. M. P. (1990). *Ten Saints of India.* Bombay: Bharatiya Vidya Bhavan.

36. Majumdar, R. C. (1962). quoted from History of the Freedom Movement in India, cited in Swami Lokeswarnanda. (Ed.), *World Thinkers on Ramakrishna-Vivekananda.* p.30

Maslow, A. http://webspace.ship.edu/cgboer/maslow.html

37. Max Muller, F. (1896). A Real Mahatman: the Nineteen Century, cited in Swami Lokeswarnanda. (Ed.), *World Thinkers on Ramakrishna-Vivekananda (pp.1-5).* Calcutta: The Ramakrishna Mission.

38. McDonnel, E. W. (1954). The Beguines and Beghards in Medieval Culture. New Brunswick: Rutgers University Press.

39. Mctaggart, J. M. E. (1901). *Studies in Hegelian Cosmology.* Cambridge: Oxford University Press.

40. McTaggart, J. M. E. (1906). *Some Dogmas of Religion.* London: Edward Arnold.

41. Mill, J. S. (1855). *Three Essays on Religion.*

42. Moller, H. (1965). Affective Mysticism in Western Civilization. *Psychoanalytic Review*, 52: 259-67.

43. Nehru, J. (1960). quoted from Sri Ramakrishna and Swami Vivekananda, cited in Swami Lokeswarnanda. (Ed.), *World Thinkers on Ramakrishna-Vivekananda (p.28-29).* Calcutta: The Ramakrishna Mission.

44. Octavio, P. (1981). *The Money Grammarian.* Trans. Helen Lane. New York: Seaver Books.

45. P.C.Horton, P. C. (1973) The Mystical Experience as a Suicide Preventive. *American Journal of Psychiatry*, 130: 294-96.

46. Parekh, M. C. (1936). *Sri Swami Narayana.* Rajkot: Sri Bhagawat-Dharma Mission House.

47. Paul C. Horton P. C. (1974). The Mystical Experience: Substance of an Illusion. *Journal of the American Psychoanalytic Association*, 22: 364-80.

48. Plato: Laws, 886A.

49. Pringle-Pattison, A. S. (1917). *The Idea of God in the Light of Recent Philosophy.* Oxford: Clarendon Press.

50. Radhakrishnan, S. (1948). *The Bhagavadgita.* London: Allen & Unwin.

51. Radhakrishnan, S. (1951). *An Idealist View of Life.* London: Allen & Unwin.

52. Radhakrishnan, S. (1970). quoted from Cultural Heritage of India, Vol. I, cited in Swami Lokeswarnanda. (Ed.), *World Thinkers on Ramakrishna-Vivekananda.* p.29

53. Ranade, R. D. (1959). *The Bhagavadgita as a Philosophy of God Realization.* Nagpur: Nagpur University.

54. Rolland, R. (1979). The Life of Ramakrishna, cited in Swami Lokeswarnanda. (Ed.), *World Thinkers on Ramakrishna-Vivekananda (pp.5-6).* Calcutta: The Ramakrishna Mission.

55. Rolland, R. (2000). *The Life of Ramakrishna.* Calcutta: Advaita Ashram.

56. Royce, J. (1902). *The Conception of God.* New York: Macmillan.

57. Runes and others, (1961). *Dictionary of Philosophy.*

58. Sarkar, B. K. (1963). *The Might of Man in the Social Philosophy of Ramakrishna and Vivekananda.* Madras: Sri Ramakrishna Math.

59. Sarkar, J. (1936). quoted from *Prabuddha Bharata*, February, cited in Swami Lokeswarnanda. (Ed.), *World Thinkers on Ramakrishna-Vivekananda (p.28).* Calcutta: The Ramakrishna Mission.

60. Schiffman, R. (2003). *Sri Ramakrishna: A Prophet for the New Age.* Calcutta: The Ramakrishna Mission Institute of Culture.

61. Seal, B. N. (1988). Shri Ramakrishna: Above Time, Above Space. In *Studies on Sri Ramakrishna. (pp.3-10)* Calcutta: The Ramakrishna Mission Institute of Culture.

62. Shapley, H. (1956). quoted from Mankind in a World of Stars, *Prabuddha Bharata*, January, cited in Swami Lokeswarnanda. (Ed.),

World Thinkers on Ramakrishna-Vivekananda (p.12). Calcutta: The Ramakrishna Mission.

63. Sharma, B. N. K. (1962). *Philosophy of Madhvacharya*. Bombay: Bharatiya Vidya Bhavan.

64. Shifman, A. (1969). Tolstoy and India, cited in Swami Lokeswarnanda. (Ed.), *World Thinkers on Ramakrishna-Vivekananda (p.15)*. Calcutta: The Ramakrishna Mission.

65. Shri Aurobindo, (1950). *Essays of the Gita*. New York: Sri Aurobindo Ligrary.

66. Shrinivasachari, P. N. (1943). *Philosophy of Vishishtadvaita*. quoted in The Philosophy of Sri svaminarayana. (pp. 133-134) Ahmedabad: L. D. Institute of Indology.

67. Sivaramakrishna, M. & Roy, S. (1997). *eds. Perspectives on Ramakrishna-Vivekananda Vedanta Tradition*. New Delhi: A Sterling Paperback.

68. Sivaramakrishna, M. (1996). *Radiant Eternity: Reflection on Sri Ramakrishna*. New Delhi: A Sterling Paperback.

69. Sri Ramakrishna: The Great Prophet of Harmony: A Compilation of Articles on Sri Ramakrishna. (2000). Calcutta: Advaita Ashrama.

70. Stace W. T. Mysticism and Philosophy

71. Stace, W. T. (1960). http:/www.bodysoulspirit.net/mystical_experience/learn/experts_define/stace.shtml

72. Stace, W. T. (1960). *The Teaching of Mystics*.

73. Stoller, R. (1979). The Gender Disorders. In I. Rosen, ed., *Sexual Deviation*. Oxford: Oxford University Press.

74. Swami Abhedananda, (1985). *Spiritual Sayings of Ramakrishna*. Calcutta: Ramakrishna Vedanta Math.

75. Swami Abhedananda, (1988). Sri Ramakrishna: The Greatest Saint of Modern India. In *Studies on Sri Ramakrishna. (pp.11-16)* Calcutta: The Ramakrishna Mission Institute of Culture.

76. Swami Atmasthananda, (2002). *Sri Ramakrishna: God of All*. Calcutta: Advaita Ashrama.

77. Swami Chetanananda, (1993). *They Lived With God.* Calcutta: Advaita Ashrama.

78. Swami Chetanananda, (1999). *Ramakrishna As We Saw Him.* Calcutta: Advaita Ashrama.

79. Swami Chetanananda, (2001). *God Lived With Them.* Kolkata: Advaita Ashrama.

80. Swami Ghanananda, (1987). *Sri Ramakrishna and His Unique Message.* Calcutta: Advaita Ashrama.

81. Swami Lokeswarananda, (1983). *World Thinkers on Ramakrishna-Vivekananda.* Calcutta: The Ramakrishna Mission.

82. Swami Lokeswarananda, (1997). *The Way to God as Taught by Sri Ramakrishna.* Calcutta: The Ramakrishna Mission Institute of Culture.

83. Swami Nirvedananda, (1978). *Sri Ramakrishna and Spiritual Renaissance.* Calcutta: The Ramakrishna Mission Institute of Culture.

84. Swami Paramananda, (1988). Sri Ramakrishna: The Messiah of Spiritual Democracy. In *Studies on Sri Ramakrishna. (pp.17-21)* Calcutta: The Ramakrishna Mission Institute of Culture.

85. Swami Prabhananda, (1988). The Brahmo Movement and Sri Ramakrishna. In *Studies on Sri Ramakrishna. (pp.117-145)* Calcutta: The Ramakrishna Mission Institute of Culture.

86. Swami Ramakrishnananda, (2004). *The Universe And Man.* Madras: Sri Ramakrishna Math.

87. Swami Ranganathananda, (1988). Shi Ramakrishna and Universal Relgion. In *Studies on Sri Ramakrishna. (pp.53-60)* Calcutta: The Ramakrishna Mission Institute of Culture.

88. Swami Saradananda, *Sri Ramakrishna: The Great Master. Vol. I & II.* Trans. Swami Jagadananda. Chennai: Sri Ramakrishna Math.

89. Swami Swahananda, (2003). *Vedanta and Ramakrishna.* Kolkata: The Ramakrishna Mission Institute of Culture.

90. Swami Tapasyananda (1993). *Sri Ramakrishna's Thoughts on Man, World and God.* Chennai: Sri Ramakrishna Math.

91. Swami Tejasananda, (1988). Sri Ramakrishna and The Unity of Religion. In *Studies on Sri Ramakrishna. (pp.75-88)* Calcutta: The Ramakrishna Mission Institute of Culture.

Swami Tyagananda, http://home.earthlink.net/~tyag/Home.htm

92. Swami Vivekanand and Sri Ramkrishna in Sri Aurobindo's writings. Reprint from All India Magazine, September 1993.

93. Swami Vivekananda, (1998). *Ramakrishna And His Message.* Calcutta: Advaita Ashrama.

94. Swami Vivekananda, (2005). *State, Society and Socialism.* Kolkata: Advaita Ashrama.

95. Swami Vivekananda, (2005). The Science And Philosophy of Religion. (12th edition) Kolkata: Advaita Ashrama.

96. Swami Yogeshananda. (1989). *The Visions of Sri Ramakrishna.* Madras: Sri Ramakrishna Math.

97. Tagore, R. (1936). To The Paramahansa Ramakrishna Deva. *Prabuddha Bharata*, February, cited in Swami Lokeswarnanda. (Ed.), *World Thinkers on Ramakrishna-Vivekananda (p.10).* Calcutta: The Ramakrishna Mission.

98. Teachings of Sri Ramakrishna. (2001). Calcutta: Advaita Ashrama.

99. Torwesten, H. (1999). *Ramakrishna and Christ or The Paradox of The Incarnaiton.* Calcutta: The Ramakrishna Mission Institute of Culture.

100. Toynbee, A. J. (1970). quoted from the *Forward* of Sri Ramakrishna and His Unique Message, cited in Swami Lokeswarnanda. (Ed.), *World Thinkers on Ramakrishna-Vivekananda (pp.10-11).* Calcutta: The Ramakrishna Mission.

101. Walsh R. N. et al. (1980). Paradigms in Collision. In Beyond Ego: Transpersonal Dimensions in Psychology, ed. R.N. Walsh and F. Vaughan. Los Angeles: Tarcher.

102. Williams, G. (1956). quoted from Harvard and Hinduism, *Prabuddha Bharata*, January, cited in Swami Lokeswarnanda. (Ed.), *World Thinkers on Ramakrishna-Vivekananda (p.12).* Calcutta: The Ramakrishna Mission.

103. Yajnik, J. A. (1972). *The Philosophy of Sri Svaminarayana.* Ahmedabad: L. D. Institute of Indology.

104. Younghusband, F. (1988). Sri Ramakrishna: Apostle of Religious Harmony. In *Studies on Sri Ramakrishna. (pp.22-24)* Calcutta: The Ramakrishna Mission Institute of Culture.